THE LESS NOBLE SEX

RACE, GENDER, AND SCIENCE
Anne Fausto-Sterling, General Editor

THE LESS NOBLE SEX

Scientific, Religious, and Philosophical
Conceptions of Woman's Nature

NANCY TUANA

INDIANA UNIVERSITY PRESS

Bloomington and Indianapolis

Library of Congress Cataloging-in-Publication Data
Tuana, Nancy.
    The less noble sex: scientific, religious, and philosophical conceptions of woman's nature / Nancy Tuana.
    p. cm. — (Race, gender, and science)
    Includes bibliographical references (p.) and index.
    ISBN 0-253-36098-6 (alk. paper). — ISBN 0-253-20830-0 (pbk. : alk. paper)
    1. Feminist theory. 2. Woman (Philosophy)—History. 3. Sexism in science—History. I. Title. II. Series.
HQ1190.T82 1993
305.42′01—dc20   92-47411

1 2 3 4 5 97 96 95 94 93

*This book is dedicated to
my mother,
Rosalind Doris Milani Tuana,
and my father,
Alexander Peter Fiorentina Tuana.*

Their love opened worlds to me.

CONTENTS

Preface

Aristotle proclaimed woman to be a misbegotten man. Insisting that the true form of all beings is the male, he concluded that when an organism develops fully, without impediment, it always becomes the male of the species. The female results from some defect, some imperfection in the developmental process. Believing male biological superiority to be a scientific fact, Aristotle documented empirical proof of woman's inferiority and constructed a systematic theory of development to explain it.

This book traces a centuries-old tradition within Western intellectual thought that views woman as inferior to man. Aristotle's conception of the misbegotten man held sway in science, philosophy, and theology at least until the nineteenth century.[1] Woman was not thought to have traits and characteristics unique to the female of the species; rather, she was depicted as an underdeveloped male, different not in kind but in degree from man. Woman's difference was defined in terms of lack: she was less rational, less moral, less evolved.

Along with documenting the pervasive presence of woman as misbegotten man within the Western intellectual tradition, this book considers a second theme—the interrelations of scientific, philosophical, and theological conceptions of woman's nature. To uncover the source of Aristotle's belief in the superiority of the male form, we must turn from science to cosmology, to Hesiod's *Theogony*, the primary creation epic of classical Greece.[2] According to Hesiod, the first generations of humans were male. Only later, and as a punishment to man, was the first woman, Pandora, created. Plato's philosophy similarly involved the belief that humans were originally created as men, and those men who did not live a good life were reincarnated as women.

Woman thus became a secondary being, less perfect than and created after man. Religious and philosophical conceptions of woman's nature both influenced and were affected by scientific theories of woman's nature. This book illustrates and documents these interrelations.

Philosophers, historians, and sociologists generally accept the view that science is a social institution, and as such is influenced by the cultural, political, and economic conditions under which it is practiced. Feminists have expanded upon this view by positing that science is "gendered," that sexist biases permeate the entire structure of science.[3] Helen Longino and Ruth Doell, for example, have argued that scientists' questions, interpretation of data, experimental design, and theory construction often reveal their assumption of "the inferiority of women, the legitimacy of their subordination, or the legitimacy of sex-based prescriptions of social roles and behaviors."[4]

This text provides evidence for the view that the practice of science has been infused with sexist beliefs. Lynn Hankinson Nelson states that "science is *permeated* with metaphysics and metaphysics is *part* of science."[5] The focus here is on the ways in which scientists' metaphysical inheritance from religious and philosophical systems influenced their empirical investigations on woman's nature. But the influence is not unidirectional. Scientific theories convey metaphysical commitments that affect social and political attitudes and policy. As Donna Haraway points out, "the biosocial sciences have not simply been sexist mirrors of our own social world. They have also been tools in the reproduction of that world, both in supplying legitimating ideologies and in enhancing material power."[6] This text also investigates the ways in which scientific conceptions of woman's nature have reinforced and perpetuated religious and philosophical attitudes.

However, the gender system in science goes even deeper, affecting the very conceptions of science. As Evelyn Fox Keller explained in her *Reflections on Gender and Science,* "the most immediate issue for a feminist perspective on the natural sciences is the deeply rooted popular mythology that casts objectivity, reason, and mind as male, and subjectivity, feeling, and nature as female. In this division of emotional and intellectual labor, women have been the guarantors and protectors of the personal, the emotional, the particular, whereas science—the province par excellence of the impersonal, the rational, and the general—has been the preserve of men.[7] By documenting the historical foundations of the association of certain traits—in particular, reason, objectivity, and morality—as characteristics that are more fully developed in men than in women, this book's analysis lends support to claims that the gender system affects our very conceptions of science.

I document the impact of metaphysical conceptions of woman's nature on science in order to clarify the ways in which certain values shape the development of scientific theories. I am not, however, claiming that science containing such values is thereby bad science. Bad science is not so simply because it is influenced by assumptions concerning woman's nature. My position is rather that values are an integral part of knowing, and cannot be purged from science.[8] Given this, I agree with Sandra Harding that a coherent notion of objectivity, what she calls "strong objectivity," must "include systematic examination of such powerful background beliefs."[9] My goal in examining the history of sexist biases within science is to begin this process of revealing the values underlying certain scientific programs. This process, I believe, provides the foundation for encouraging good science, which, in the words of Nelson, "must incorporate the taking of responsibility for the directions and use of knowledge developed and certified in scientific communities, and self-conscious and critical attention to the values incorporated in scientific theorizing."[10]

This book is organized thematically rather than chronologically, looking at five major beliefs about woman's nature generally accepted by Western philosophers, theologians, and scientists from the classical period to the nineteenth century.[11] These are that:

- woman is less perfect than man
- woman possesses inferior rational capacities
- woman has a defective moral sense

- man is the primary creative force
- woman is in need of control.

Section one examines the claim that woman is less perfect than man, the premise from which all other beliefs about woman evolve. The creation myths of religion and the hierarchical ordering of existence in the science of biology comprise the two primary sources in Western intellectual thought for the belief in woman's lack of perfection.

The second section of the book is devoted to specific imperfections attributed to woman through the centuries by philosophers, theologians, and scientists. I first attend to the metaphysical belief that woman is less divine than man, tracing the ways in which this conviction contributed to the view that woman's rational capacities are inferior. I then examine theories concerning woman's moral capacities, and end the section with an investigation of the perception that woman is more prone to mental illness than man.

Both sections one and two document a recurring theme in scientific, religious, and philosophical conceptions of woman's nature: that woman is less developed, less moral, less capable of rational thought, and less divine than man *because of* her role in reproduction. One would then expect that in the realm of procreation, woman would be seen as man's equal, if not his superior. However, section three chronicles a systematic deprecation of the female creative force in both religious cosmogonies and scientific theories of reproduction; these beliefs present the male creative force as more potent than that of the female.

I end the book with an overview of the impact of such beliefs. Theorists interpreted woman's inferior moral and rational capacities as precluding her ability to govern herself or society wisely; the conclusion was that a woman must always be under a man's control. Scientists and philosophers employed theories of woman's nature to limit her sphere to the private realm, where woman's desires and passions could be properly controlled by her husband and directed toward family welfare. Woman's exclusion from the public realm of government was justified as the inevitable result of biology.

This book reveals a set of beliefs about the nature of woman that have informed, and in turn have been reinforced by, science, religion, and philosophy from the classical period to the nineteenth century. The conception of woman as a misbegotten man is fundamental to the Western worldview. The belief that woman is less than man—less perfect, less evolved, less divine, less rational, less moral, less healthy—is more than simple bias, easily amenable to revision. It is part of our inherited metaphysics.

For us today, it is crucial to recognize this cluster of beliefs about woman's nature and perceive how they permeate not only our science and philosophy, but also our social, political, and cultural institutions. Although in this book I chose not to continue my analysis into the twentieth century, such beliefs are still part of Western thought. We have only to look at feminist critiques of contemporary science, religion, and philosophy to see the persistence of these views.[12] Centuries of theories and practices have defined and delimited what it is to be female.

We are told that women are emotional and not analytic, mothers and not rulers, intuitive and not rational, passive and not active. Only by becoming aware of the full natures of these theories and their related practices can women and men begin to examine them critically and be open to alternative conceptions.

My approach conceals as well as reveals. In surveying such a wide sweep of time, I lose certain particulars. For example, I cannot devote an entire chapter to the evolution of one concept, or offer a systematic rendition of any individual's philosophical system, scientific theory, or theological perspective. My texts are representative, not exhaustive. In choosing to emphasize continuities, I have minimized differences. Also, I have omitted those voices that are not part of the mainstream of tradition, especially those who, although a minority, had the courage to attack the tradition itself. Nor could I detail the ways in which metaphysical conceptions of woman's nature influenced and were affected by the various social, economic, and cultural institutions and practices of different cultures or time periods. Thus, the text provides a viewpoint that will be enhanced by combining it with others addressing these additional perspectives.[13]

No one text can weave together the manifold variety of elements that have influenced Western conceptions of woman's nature. Still, my discussion provides the reader with a general perspective from which to understand some of the most pervasive (and pernicious) themes. Our worldview, the basic assumptions we make about the nature of the world, are reflected in as well as constructed out of our religious, philosophical, and scientific frameworks. An awareness of the conceptions of woman's nature that have been both justified and perpetuated by these disciplines gives insight into the foundations of Western attitudes. This awareness also clarifies the sources of many societal practices concerning women.

Although subtitled "Conceptions of Woman's Nature," this is a book about men. It tells of male desire as well as male fear. I have culled the voices of men in order to understand the oppression and silencing of women. It is my sincere wish that those reading this text will use it as a key to unraveling our present beliefs about woman's character and abilities, and thereby reject all contemporary remnants of the conception of woman as misbegotten. Until we understand the ways in which this prejudice is woven into the very fabric of our thinking, our self-imaging, our lived experience, we run the risk of repeating it.

Acknowledgments

In the course of writing this book I have been assisted by many people. My initial research was supported by a postdoctoral fellowship from the American Association of University Women. During that year I was granted access to the collections of various libraries, including the National Libraries, George Washington University Library, Georgetown University Library, the Smithsonian Collections, and the Catholic University of America Library.

I am indebted to Anne Fausto-Sterling for her insightful editorial comments. My thanks and appreciation to all my friends and colleagues who offered advice and support during the long process of writing this book, with special thanks to Carol Adams, Paula England, Harvey Graff, Harriet Gross, Linda Lopez McAlister, and Karen Prager.

I

Between Man and Animal

The difference between a man and a woman, of this we may be perfectly confident, is quite as pronounced, quite as important as between a man and ape; our grounds for refusing to include women in our species would be quite as valid as for refusing to consider the chimpanzee our brother. Next to a naked woman stand a man of the same age and naked too; now examine them attentively, and you will be at no pains to discern the palpable and marked difference which (sex aside) exists in the composition of these two beings; you will be obliged to conclude that woman is simply man in an extraordinarily degraded form.

Marquis de Sade (1740–1814), *Juliette*

ONE

In the Beginning

Creation myths have always been central to human understanding. They delineate our role in a universe of mysteries. They embody a culture's beliefs about the nature of humankind and the purpose of existence. They account for the sources of life and define relationships between things, thus revealing many of our fundamental values.

The place of humankind in the scheme of creation is a basic focus of Western creation myths. They delineate not only the traits that differentiate humans from other animals, but also those that mark off humans from the gods. An image often used to explain humanity's status is that of a hierarchy of being based upon degrees of perfection.[1] In such a worldview all that exists is seen as a great ladder, composed of an immense number of steps. They range in hierarchical order from those things that barely exist, and thus have only a minuscule degree of perfection, to absolute perfection at the top of the scale—the gods or the good.

Let us examine the place of humans in this hierarchy of being. In the Western worldview, humans are set apart from other animals by their possession of reason and justice. Since these faculties are believed to be indicative of a higher degree of perfection, humankind stands above all other animals on this ladder of being. But it stands below the gods, for humans' faculty of reason and sense of justice are less perfect than those of the gods. Humankind is thus created "in the image of" the gods, but possesses less being. Humans are between god and animal in the hierarchy of being.

As we begin to examine Western creation myths we quickly discover that the explanation given above must be modified to account for the position of woman. Such myths generally depict the creation of woman as secondary to that of man both temporally and metaphysically. Not only is woman created after man, she is also seen as inferior to him in degree of perfection. In fact, woman is viewed as deficient in exactly those characteristics that form man's similarity to the gods— possession of the faculties of reason and justice. Woman is not denied humanity, for she is not devoid of reason or a sense of justice. Her faculties, though inferior to those of man, still situate her above other animals on the hierarchy of being. But woman's nature places her not between god and animal; she is between man and animal.[2]

PANDORA: MAN'S PUNISHMENT

An early Greek creation myth, Hesiod's *Theogony*, written between the second half of the eighth century and the first quarter of the seventh century BCE, gives

1. Lull's Ladder of Being offers an example of the scale of perfection. Ramon Lull, *De Nova Logica, De Correllativis, Necnon de Ascensu Descensu Intellectus.* Valencia, 1512.

an account of the creation of the world, of the gods, and of woman, and delineates the nature of woman's faculty of justice.

Although the *Theogony* does not offer an account of the creation of mankind, it tells of a time when human society was womanless, depicting man as existing prior to woman. Womankind is thus temporally secondary to man. Having described the genesis of the world and of the gods, Hesiod tells the story of Prometheus, the divine champion of man, and recounts the punishment of both Prometheus and mankind by the gods.

While preparing the ritual sacrifice for the gods, Prometheus devised a plan to deceive Zeus, the ruler of all. Prometheus took an ox, carved it, and divided the parts into two piles. In the first pile he placed meat, entrails, and fat within the hide, covering them over with the ox's stomach to render the pile unappealing. In the other pile he put only the bones of the ox, but covered them with fat, so that this pile would appear to be the more desirable of the two. When Zeus, seeing the two piles, accused Prometheus of being selfish and trying to keep the best for himself and man, Prometheus slyly replied that Zeus could have his pick. Zeus reached down, took the pile covered with fat, and carried it to Mount Olympus. Upon uncovering the bones, Zeus knew he had been deceived, and anger rushed through him. In retaliation, he took fire and kept it with him, declaring that mankind would no longer know its benefit. But Prometheus deceived Zeus yet again and, by hiding an ember within a hollowed fennel stalk, stole the fire from Zeus and returned it to man.

When Zeus saw the flash of fire among mortal men, his heart again filled with anger, and he devised terrible punishments for Prometheus and mankind. Because of his disobedience, Zeus chained Prometheus to a pillar where a long-winged eagle continually tore at his liver by day. To make sure there would be no end to Prometheus's pain, Zeus ordained that at night Prometheus's liver would grow whole again. Mankind he punished by contriving a special evil: Zeus created a being destined to live among men and cause them great suffering—woman.

> The famous lame smith took clay and, through Zeus's
> counsels, gave it the shape of a modest maiden.
> Athena, the gray-eyed goddess, clothed her and decked her
> out with a flashy garment and then with her hands
> she hung over her head a fine draping veil, a marvel to behold;
> Pallas Athena crowned her head with lovely wreaths
> of fresh flowers that had just bloomed in the green meadows.
> The famous lame smith placed on her head a crown of gold. . . .
> Once he had finished—not something good but a mixture of good
> and bad—he took the maiden before gods and men,
> and she delighted in the finery given her by gray-eyed Athena,
> daughter of a mighty father. Immortal gods and mortal men
> were amazed when they saw this tempting snare
> from which men cannot escape. From her comes the fair sex;
> yes, wicked womenfolk are her descendants.
> They live among mortal men as a nagging burden
> and are no good sharers of abject want, but only of wealth.

Men are like swarms of bees clinging to cave roofs
to feed drones that contribute only to malicious deeds.[3]

Thus, in response to Prometheus's twofold deception, Zeus created a deception for man. In fact, he employed the same trick that Prometheus had used with the ox. When creating woman, Zeus made her external appearance desirable in order to trick man into accepting the wickedness inside of her. Although woman has the appearance of a goddess, this external covering, like Prometheus's fat, merely disguises and masks reality—her thievish nature and her lies.[4] Woman's outward beauty is the bait for the trap that no man can resist. Once man embraces her, the deception is quickly uncovered, and woman is revealed for what she is—"a scourge for toiling man."[5]

The *Theogony* depicts woman's nature as inferior to that of man. Her existence is neither necessary nor desirable, but was merely the god's response to being deceived. Woman has the mind, not of a god or of a man, but of an inferior animal— "the mind of a bitch."[6] She is by nature thievish and deceitful. Clearly, woman is less capable than man of possessing the virtue of justice, the very faculty that distinguishes humans from other animals. "This is the law Zeus laid down for men, / but fish and wild beasts and winged birds / know not of justice and so eat one another. / Justice, the best thing there is, he gave to men."[7] Woman is thus less perfect than man. She is between man and animal in the hierarchy of being.[8]

PLATO'S *TIMAEUS:* FALLEN SOULS

Plato, writing in Athens in the fourth century BCE, offered an alternative creation myth in which he emphasized the importance of the faculty of reason, his *Timaeus*.[9] Having created the universe, the divine being made a mixture of the four elements from which he had formed the universe—earth, air, fire, and water.[10] He then added the soul of the universe to the mixture. "And having made it he divided the whole mixture into souls equal in number to the stars and assigned each soul to a star."[11] After dividing the mixture into souls, the god implanted each one in a body, and gave each man sensations and emotions, including love, fear, and anger. Each being was equal in perfection to all others, for this god would allow no one to suffer a disadvantage at his hands. In this way the race of man was created.

As in the *Theogony,* Plato posited an original world without woman. In their primordial state, all humans were male. Although all men were created equally perfect, each had to choose how to live his life and use his faculties. According to Plato, men's destinies were determined by how they dealt with their emotions and their sensations. "If they conquered these they would live righteously, and if they were conquered by them, unrighteously."[12] The soul of a man who retained control over his emotions and used his intellect to govern his sensations would, upon the death of his body, return to his appointed star, whereupon he would have a "blessed" existence. However, the man who failed to rein in his appetites would be reincarnated as a woman. "At the second birth he would pass into a woman, and if, when in that state of being, he did not desist from evil, he would continually be changed into some brute who resembled him in the evil nature which he had acquired."[13]

Plato's creation myth, like that of Hesiod, depicts woman as metaphysically inferior to man. She exists as a result of evil, the rule of passion. Those men who are unable to control their emotions, who are unable to overcome the desires of the body through the power of the soul, are reincarnated as women. Woman, then, is the result of man's weakness, his punishment for being tied to the world of sensation. Those individuals who continue, after their second birth, to be controlled by their passions will be further punished by being reincarnated as animals—an even lower state of being than woman.

Man is the primary creation, the true form of humanity. Woman is a degeneration of the original state of being. Woman represents a decline, a punishment, a further estrangement from the happiness of the heavens. She is less perfect than man because she is more tied to her passions. Yet she is more perfect than animals who possess even less control over their physical desires. Woman again falls between man and animal on the hierarchy of being.[14]

Plato implied that mind or reason is more perfect than sensation or emotion. Without denying the usefulness of these faculties, Plato makes it clear that they must be "conquered" by the intellect of man or he will lose perfection. Thus, soul is seen as more perfect than body, and that which is associated with soul—reason, intuition, aesthetic and moral faculties—are judged more perfect than those associated with body—sensation and emotions.[15] To live righteously, the faculties of the soul must be in complete control of the faculties of the body. However, women, since they were created from "those who were cowards or led unrighteous lives" in their first birth, will be less capable of such control.[16] As we shall see, these beliefs become prevalent themes of the Western worldview and have important implications for images of woman's nature and theories concerning the "proper" relationships between men and women.

EVE: BONE OF MY BONE

Genesis presents two accounts of the creation of humankind. In the first, Genesis 1:1–2.4a, the creation of humans is the divinity's final act.[17] After having created light, heaven, the earth, and the plants and creatures of the earth, God completed the creative act by bringing humans into being. "Then God said, 'Let us make man [*hā-'ādām*] in our image, after our likeness; and let them have dominion over the fish of the sea, and over the birds of the air, and over the cattle, and over all the earth, and over every creeping thing that creeps upon the earth.' So God created man in his own image, in the image of God he created him; male and female he created them" (Genesis 1:26–27).

In the second account, God created man immediately following the creation of the heavens and the earth. "In the day that the Lord God made the earth and the heavens, when no plant of the field was yet in the earth and no herb of the field had yet sprung up—for the Lord God had not caused it to rain upon the earth, and there was no man to till the ground; but a mist went up from the earth and watered the whole face of the ground—then the Lord God formed man of dust from the ground, and breathed into his nostrils the breath of life; and man became a living being" (Genesis 2:4–7).

Having created man, God planted a garden in Eden for man to till and keep. "Then the Lord God said, 'It is not good that the man should be alone; I will make him a helper fit for him,' " (Genesis 2:18). God created all forms of animal and bird, but found none of them a fit helper for man.

> So the Lord God caused a deep sleep to fall upon the man, and while he slept took one of his ribs and closed up its place with flesh; and the rib which the Lord God had taken from the man he made into a woman and brought her to the man. Then the man said,
> "This at last is bone of my bones
>   and flesh of my flesh;
> she shall be called Woman ['issa],
>   because she was taken out of Man ['is]."
>   (Genesis 2:21–23)

There are three important differences between these two accounts. First, in the initial account, woman and man are created at the same moment. Neither has temporal priority, while in the second version, man is created first and has clear temporal priority. Second, in the first version, woman and man are created in the same way. Although we are not told how God formed them, we can assume that the method of their creation was the same, since they were created simultaneously. However, in the second version, the creation of woman is quite different from that of man; he is created from dust and the breath of life, whereas she is created from man's rib. Third, according to the first account, woman and man are created in the image of God. "Let us make man [hā-'ādām] in our image, after our likeness" (Genesis 1:26). "Hā-'ādām" is a collective noun in Hebrew, referring not to an individual but to humankind as a whole. All of humankind is thus created in the image of God. But in the second account, no clear statement is made of woman or man being created in God's image.

The biblical creation myth contained in Genesis is far more open to interpretation than are the myths of Hesiod and Plato. The latter two accounts clearly represent woman's nature as metaphysically inferior to man's. But the Genesis account allows for three different readings: woman and man as equals, woman as superior to man, and man as superior to woman.

By emphasizing the first creation story, one can argue convincingly that woman and man were created as equals. They were created at the same moment, and both were given the same blessing and the same responsibilities: to be fruitful and multiply, and to exercise dominion over the earth and its creatures. The obvious conclusion is that woman and man possess equal perfection.

Interestingly, the second account of creation is open to all three readings. Its view of woman's nature turns upon the significance given to the material of her creation and her role as "helper." Arguments for any one of the three interpretations can be advanced by emphasizing the nature of her creation and the material out of which she was formed. If one focuses upon woman's role as helper, an argument can be made either for the equal perfection of woman and man or for the metaphysical superiority of man.

Looking first at the material of woman's creation, an argument for her metaphysical superiority can be derived from the second creation account by emphasizing the fact that woman was created from a man's rib, while man was created from dust. The basic tenet of this interpretation is the claim that being created out of a human rib means that woman was created out of more perfect material than was man. Since God formed man from dust, man's body is at a higher degree of development than dust and is thus a more perfect material. If one postulates that the degree of perfection of a being corresponds to the degree of perfection of the material out of which it is created, it follows that woman, formed from a more perfect substance, has more perfection than man. Hence the metaphysical superiority of woman.

But as we will see in the next section, many theologians reversed this argument. A focus on the material of woman's creation can lead to the opposite conclusion—namely, woman's metaphysical inferiority—if one accepts the belief that the degree of perfection of man's rib is inferior to that of the dust of the earth.

An argument for man's superiority can be bolstered by emphasizing woman's role. By defining "helper" as a person whose primary function is to serve the needs of another, one can conclude that man is the primary creation. This interpretation is based on the premise that man's being and purpose are independent of woman, whereas woman's being and purpose are dependent upon man. By adding to this conclusion the premise that dependence is a mark of imperfection, man's creation can be argued to be superior to that of woman. This point can also be applied to woman's creation out of man's rib: it can be argued that her existence is dependent upon his, she is a part of man, and thus is less perfect.

An alternative analysis advanced by Mieke Bal focuses on the nature of creation in the rib story in support of the conclusion that woman and man were created as equals.[18] Bal argues that there is linguistic evidence for seeing the being initially formed by Jahweh from dust as both sexless and unfinished. Jahweh, deciding that his work was not finished, caused a deep sleep to come upon the being and brought his creation to a higher level of perfection by separating the sexless earth being into two sexually differentiated beings—woman and man. In this interpretation, woman and man are thus created at the same time and in the same way, and should be seen as equals. Bal goes on to argue that the first creation story does not contradict the second version; rather, the second "provides a specified narration of what events are included in the idea that 'God created them male and female.' "[19]

This argument for the equality of woman and man can also be strengthened by offering an alternate account of the significance of woman's role as helper. Prior to creating woman, God "formed every beast of the field and every bird of the air . . . but for the man there was not found a helper fit for him" (Genesis 2:19–20). Realizing that none of these creatures was suitable for man, God created woman. One could argue that the reason these creatures were unsuitable was because they were inferior to man; to find a helper fit for man, God had to create a being equal to man in all ways. To do so, God formed woman out of man's body so that she would be "bone of his bone, flesh of his flesh," that is, she would possess the same being. This interpretation would contravene the claim that woman's existence is dependent upon man, but his is independent of her. As Bal explains, "The man is, then, not the parent from whom the woman is born . . . but if we stick to these inappropriate family metaphors, rather her brother."[20] Woman would thus be man's equal.

It should be emphasized that this interpretation is based upon a very different notion of the nature of a helper. In the previous account, a helper is by definition subordinate, and the view of woman as inferior to man arises directly from the connotations attached to the helper role. The second interpretation allows for a helper of equal being. By stressing the notion of a helper who is *fit for man,* an argument is made for the equal perfection of woman.

Despite the apparent plausibility of any of the above, by far the most prevalent interpretation of the Genesis creation story in the Christian tradition is that of man as metaphysically superior to woman. This was generally supported by the early church fathers and continued to be the dominant interpretation until the Protestant Reformation. The interpretation of the metaphysical equality of woman and man gained popularity during the Reformation, when both Martin Luther and John Calvin attacked the traditional church view that woman's initial creation was inferior to that of man.[21]

EARLY CHRISTIAN VIEWS.

The writings of Philo, a first-century Jewish philosopher, were very influential in the development of early Christian church doctrines. Philo embraced the Platonic doctrine that sense-perception must be under the control of reason, arguing that sense-perception is an inferior faculty that would give rise to disorders of the soul if it were not ruled by the faculty of reason. "Most profitless is it that Mind should listen to Sense-perception, and not Sense-perception to Mind: for it is always right that the superior should rule and the inferior be ruled; and Mind is superior to Sense-perception."[22] Also like Plato, Philo associated woman with sense-perception. "In us mind corresponds to man, the senses to woman."[23]

Philo's interpretation of the Genesis creation myth reflects the bias that woman is by nature man's inferior. Limiting himself to the rib version of the story, Philo focused on the fact that woman and man are created out of different matter. In response to the question of why God created woman out of man's rib, Philo said that this was "because woman is not equal in honour with man." In other words, Philo presupposed that creation out of a rib is inferior to creation from the dust of the earth.[24] Philo omitted any reference to the alternate interpretation in which the rib, being a transformation of dust by the hands of God, was a substance more perfect than the unformed stuff of the earth. Nor did he offer much support for his own perspective. He merely emphasized the rib's connection to the body in order to associate woman with the senses. Since Philo offered little evidence in support of his claim that woman's creation from man's rib is proof of her metaphysical inferiority, he appears to have assumed that his premise was so obvious that no argument was needed.

The one piece of evidence Philo offered to support his interpretation turns on the temporal priority of man's creation in the second version of the Genesis myth. Philo claimed that the order of creation reflects metaphysical priorities. "First He made mind, the man, for mind is most venerable in a human being, then bodily sense, the woman, then after them in the third place pleasure."[25] Philo omitted the fact that according to the second creation story, after creating man, God created "every beast of the field and every bird of the air," and then created woman. Given the logic of his analysis we would be forced to place woman *below* animals on the hierarchy of being.

Philo's association of woman with sensation and the passions became a standard tenet of Christian theology. Augustine (354–430) and Thomas Aquinas (1225–1274), perhaps the two most important medieval Christian theologians, perpetuated this connection in their writings. They continued to support the Platonic tenet that emotions and passions are inferior faculties, stressing that the superior faculty of reason must be in control of the sensations or humans would sin. Both Augustine and Aquinas argued that, because of the nature of her creation, woman is more tied to the senses than man. The obvious conclusion is woman's metaphysical inferiority.

Like Philo, both Augustine and Aquinas referred primarily to the second creation story. Although they agreed with Philo's conclusions, neither discussed the material of woman's creation. Instead, both focused on woman's role as a helper. Noting that woman was created to be a help to man, Aquinas attempted to determine the exact nature of this "help." He believed that this question could be best answered by reflecting on another, namely, "When God created a helper for man, why did he create a woman rather than a man?" Aquinas's reasoning here is quite circular. He believed that this question was relevant because it was his contention that another man would have proven a more effective helper in almost everything.[26] Notice that this judgment is based on the presupposition of man's superiority to woman. Thus, Aquinas did not infer woman's inferiority *from* Genesis; rather, his interpretation was framed *by* it.

Insisting that a man would have been a better helper than a woman in most ways, Aquinas believed that understanding why God created a woman rather than a man would clarify woman's role and nature. He held that there is one help a woman can provide that cannot be offered by a man—reproduction. "It was necessary for woman to be made, as the Scripture says, as a *helper* to man; not indeed, as a helpmate in other works, as some say, since man can be more efficiently helped by another man in other works; but as a helper in the work of generation."[27] Thus, woman's primary role, or help, is to bear children. Both Augustine and Aquinas concluded from this that woman is more tied to the senses than man. They saw woman's role in reproduction as causing her to be more swayed by emotions and passions. Like Philo, they held that God had to create woman separately from man in order to ensure the perfection of man's faculty of reason. "Therefore, there was greater reason for the distinction of these two forces in man; so that the female should be produced separately from the male."[28] Man was created first and given the faculty of reason. Woman's creation was second both temporally and metaphysically. .

Both Augustine and Aquinas viewed woman's generative powers as limiting her perfection, believing that they impede her rational abilities. Woman's divinely ordained purpose results in her having a weak temperament, such that "whatever she holds to, she holds to it weakly" and thus is more likely than man to sin.[29] Augustine concluded from this that God created woman to be "in sex subjected to the masculine sex, in the same way as the appetite which leads to action is subjected to the skill, mentally derived, of acting rightly."[30]

Eve, as she was envisioned by medieval Christian theologians, is a complex figure. She is unlike Pandora in that God did not create her to be a punishment to man. Still, her inferiority was not the result of an accident or coincidence. She is like Pandora in that her inferiority was divinely intended.

The themes raised by both Augustine and Aquinas are representative of the early Christian viewpoint. Because of the nature of woman's creation, she is more influenced than man by the body and the passions. Her connection to the senses is God's intent, for it enables her to accomplish her purpose—generation. In order to allow man to live a life of reason, God had to free him from the concerns of generation, for generation ties one to the body and prohibits a life of reason. Perpetuation of the human race thus became the function of woman. And woman's role in generation perpetuates her metaphysical inferiority, for it keeps her tied to the passions and precludes her becoming more perfect by living a life of reason. Woman is thus in a no-win situation: her nature condemns her to an inferior existence, for to attain perfection she must deny her divinely ordained nature. Woman is by God's decree inferior to man.

PROTESTANT REFORMATION.

Martin Luther (1483–1546) was one of the first influential Christian theologians to support the thesis that God initially created woman and man as equals. It is significant that he emphasized the first creation story in order to reject arguments for woman's original inferiority. Luther asserted that Genesis 1:26–27, in which God created both male and female in his own image, is uncontestable proof that woman was created as man's equal. "Moses puts the two sexes together and says that God created male and female in order to indicate that Eve, too, was made by God as a partaker of the divine image and of the divine similitude, likewise of the rule over everything."[31]

Although Luther's interpretation of the Genesis myth appears to contain a very positive image of woman's nature, there is a sharp tension in his writings, for Luther accepted the traditional view that woman was by nature different from man. In fact, he was one of the first theologians to advance an "equal but different" thesis. However, his discussion of the differences between woman's and man's natures often involved the claim that man's characteristics are superior to those of woman, thereby weakening his claim of equality. This thesis of "equal but different" gained acceptance after the sixteenth century and, as we will see, the tension found in Luther's writings carried over as well.

Luther emphasized the first creation story in order to make it clear that woman was not excluded from the "glory of the future life." Apparently, Luther thought that the conclusion that woman is so excluded would be a natural inference. What is revealing is that, rather than indicting the centuries of theologians who preached that woman was inferior, Luther claimed that the inference is to be expected because "woman appears to be a somewhat different being from the man, having different members and *a much weaker nature.*"[32] In other words, Luther feared that the characteristics that distinguish woman from man would lead people to doubt her suitability for salvation. But this would follow only if one believed that woman's characteristics were inferior to those of man. Luther's perception of woman's "difference" thus belies his claim of equality.

The inconsistency of Luther's position is apparent throughout his discussion of Genesis. He insisted that Eve was "similar to Adam so far as the image of God in concerned, that is in justice, wisdom and happiness," but in the next breath said "she was nevertheless a woman."[33] Lest the reader misunderstand his point, Luther offered an analogy: "For as the sun is more excellent than the moon (although the moon, too, is a very excellent body), so the woman, although she was a most beautiful work of God, nevertheless was not the equal of the male in glory and prestige."[34] Yet in a later passage, Luther insisted that if Eve had not listened to the serpent and sinned, "she would have been the equal of Adam in all respects."[35] Luther explained that before the fall, "Eve was not like the woman of today; her state was far better and more excellent, and she was in no respect inferior to Adam, whether you count the qualities of the body or those of the mind."[36] Luther wanted to deny Aquinas's view that woman is inferior to man by insisting that, despite her differences, she is man's equal. However, he could not escape the prejudice that the very fact of woman's differences makes her less perfect than man.

We see then that even Luther, despite his attempt to deny woman's inferiority, placed woman between man and animal in degree of perfection. His protests to the contrary, Luther viewed woman as less perfect than man even before the fall. "Satan's cleverness is perceived also in this, that he attacks the weak part of human nature, Eve the woman, not Adam the man. Although both were created equally righteous, nevertheless Adam had some advantage over Eve. Just as in all the rest of nature the strength of the male surpasses that of the other sex, so also in the perfect nature the male somewhat excelled the female."[37]

Luther's general position was that woman, although created the equal of man, lost that equality by disobeying God's command to refrain from eating from the tree of knowledge. Luther thus viewed the post-fall Eve and all womankind after her as less perfect than mankind. "For the punishment, that she is now subjected to the man, was imposed on her after sin and because of sin, just as the other hardships and dangers were: travail, pain, and countless other vexations."[38] Since woman is man's equal only in a very limited sense prior to the fall, the loss of perfection resulting from her sin of disobedience serves only to reinforce Luther's view that woman falls between man and animal with respect to being.[39]

John Calvin (1509–1564) shared Luther's desire to offer a more positive image of woman's nature than that of Augustine or Aquinas. His primary purpose in doing so, however, was to elevate the institution of marriage. Because of this concern, Calvin concentrated on the second story in which woman is created out of man's rib, believing that the common origin of woman and man would serve to make their union more sacred. "But if the two sexes had proceeded from different sources, there would have been occasion either of mutual contempt, or envy, or contentions."[40] God created woman from the rib of man "in order that he might embrace, with greater benevolence, a part of himself."[41] Despite this emphasis on origin from a common source, Calvin, like Luther, did not perceive woman as man's equal. He claimed, for example, that woman was in God's image only in the "second degree."[42] He also argued that even before the fall woman would have been subject to her husband.[43] Man's temporal primacy in the rib version of creation appears to have influenced Calvin to support his metaphysical primacy as well.

Although both Luther and Calvin attempted to modify the view, central to traditional Christian theology, that woman was created as man's inferior, their theories were affected by the very bias they were trying to deny.

ALCHEMY: PARACELSUS.

Scientists also employed the rib version of the Genesis creation story to document man's metaphysical superiority. The alchemist Theophrastus Bombastus von Hohenheim (1493?–1541), also known as Paracelsus, is a case in point.

The alchemical tradition in Europe began in the twelfth century, when Arabic alchemical texts were translated into Latin. The study of alchemy blossomed for two centuries, but began to lose credibility in intellectual circles in the fourteenth and fifteenth centuries because of numerous texts that purported to offer simple recipes for creating gold out of base metals. A resurgence in interest during the sixteenth century continued until the rise of chemistry in the seventeenth century. During this period, more theorists focused on a serious study of the science of alchemy. Among them were John Dee, Robert Fludd, and Michael Maier, as well as Paracelsus.

Alchemy, a science of transformations, was the precursor of modern chemistry. Like chemistry, it offered procedures for decomposing and recomposing substances. But unlike chemistry, it offered procedures for transforming substances into higher states of perfection and for transmuting one metal into another. The primary goal of alchemy was to render perfect what nature had left imperfect. Alchemists believed it was possible to accelerate the natural processes of perfection through complex chemical processes, bringing substances to their true form in a fraction of the time normally required. To alchemists gold was the perfect form of metal, for they saw it as the only metal that possessed a completely harmonious equilibrium of all elements. Alchemists believed that it was possible to transmute base metals such as lead into their perfect form—that is, turn them into gold.

Alchemy was also unlike chemistry in that alchemical theory was based on the premise that the spirit of humans and the substances of the universe were connected. Alchemists believed that one could transform a substance into a higher state of being—turn lead into gold—only if one also brought one's own spirit to a state of higher purity. Transmutation could occur only in conjunction with the spiritual perfection of the alchemist. The true goal of alchemy was not material riches, but spiritual perfection.

Alchemists believed that the elements of the universe and the processes of all things were mirrored in man.[44] Man was called the "microcosm," and in him was the image of the macrocosm—the universe and all its processes. "Man is called the lesser world (*mundus minor*), because in him is the figure of the heavens, of the earth, of the sun and moon, a visible figure upon earth and [at the same time] invisible, wherefore he is named the lesser world."[45]

This view of man as the microcosm of the universe was prevalent from the classical period to the Middle Ages. According to Plato's account of man's creation in the *Timaeus,* god formed man from a mixture of the four primary elements and the soul of the universe. Man thus contains within him the substance of the universe and, in possessing its soul, is in its image. Philo similarly claimed that "man in respect of his mind, is allied to the divine Reason, having come into being as a copy or fragment or ray of that blessed nature, but in the structure of his body he is allied to all the world, for he is compounded of the same things, earth, water, air, and fire."[46] Aquinas, in explaining why the first man was made of the slime of the universe, echoed this view: "the body of man is said to have been formed from the slime of the earth; because earth and water mingled are called slime, and for this reason man is called *a little world,* because all creatures of the world are in a way to be found in him."[47]

This image of man as a "little world" was central to the alchemical practice. Alchemists were able to bring substances to perfection because they contained within themselves direct knowledge of the universal processes.[48] This relationship also explained the belief that alchemists could perfect external substances only if they perfected their own souls. Alchemists argued that since the external world and the internal world of man are intimately connected, it would not be possible to perfect one without at the same time perfecting the other.[49]

Paracelsus was a Christian, and his alchemical worldview was strongly influenced by Christian beliefs. Like Calvin, he turned to the second version of the Genesis creation story, emphasizing the materials out of which man and woman were created. Man was formed by God out of the dust of the world, for God mixed water and dust to make clay, and out of the clay formed man. God then breathed into man and brought him into being.

Paracelsus noted that God created the world, the stars and planets, and all the animals and plants from his spoken word, by fiat and not out of any preexisting substance. Man, however, was the first created thing to be formed out of the stuff of the universe. "Everything but man was made out of nothing. Only man is created from what had been so created."[50] Paracelsus held that man, formed out of dust and water, contains the primary elements. And because God breathed

2. The image of man as microcosm of the macrocosm. Robert Fludd, *Utriusque Cosmi Maioris Scilicet Minoris Metaphysica, Physica Atque Technica Historia.* Oppenheim: J. T. De Bry, 1617.

into him, he contains in miniature the soul of the universe. "Hence man is a microcosm, or a little world, because he is an extract from all the stars and planets of the whole firmament, from the earth and the elements; and so he is their quintessence."[51] Man is the mirror and image of all.

Woman's creation differs significantly from that of man. She was formed not from the primary elements and the breath of God, but rather from man's rib. Following the basic logic of his position that humans are a microcosm of the stuff out of which they are created, Paracelsus concluded that woman is a microcosm, not of the universe, but of man. "Man is the Little World, but woman . . . is the Littlest World, and hence she is different from man. She has a different anatomy, a different theory, different effects and causes, different divisions and cares. . . . For the world is and was the first creature, man the second, and woman the third. Thus the cosmos is the greatest world, the world of man the next greatest, and that of woman the smallest and the least."[52] Man contains within him the image of the universe; woman contains only the image of the image of the universe. Borrowing Calvin's words, woman is in the image of the universe only in the second degree. Paracelsus concluded that man's being is more perfect than woman's because it most directly mirrors the universe. Woman, unlike animals, is a microcosm, but in a manner less perfect than man.

Paracelsus's alchemical theory offers a striking example of the way science can be informed by a creation myth. Although Paracelsus is relatively unique in that most scientists do not explicitly refer to such myths in the development of their theories, religious cosmologies do have an important influence upon the development of scientific theories. The metaphysical beliefs that are a part of a strongly accepted religious worldview are the background against which a science is generated and practiced. If scientists have grown up in a culture in which woman's inferiority is a fundamental belief, it is to be expected that their science will be influenced by, and will in turn reinforce, that belief. As we look next at biological theories of woman's nature, we will indeed find that the premise of woman's inherent imperfection has been a fundamental axiom of the biological sciences for centuries.

TWO

The Misbegotten Man

From the classical period well into the sixteenth century, the dominant Christian image of woman was a being less perfect than man. Christianity portrayed woman as possessing a less developed faculty of reason than man, and as far more influenced by the dictates of her passions and emotions. Theologians often implicated woman's role in generation as the source of her imperfection.

Science contains a parallel tradition of condemning woman to subordinate status. Scientists, like all theorists, work within the worldview of their times. The theories they develop, and the facts they accept, must be coherent with this system of beliefs. Religious tenets, comprising a significant part of this worldview, are deeply embedded in scientific accounts. Given the persistence of the image of woman as less perfect than man within Christianity, it is reasonable to expect this view to have a strong influence upon Western scientific theories. And this is indeed what we find. A clear indication of this influence is that the "fact" of woman's inferiority was often an assumption of scientists rather than a hypothesis open to investigation. Scientists did, however, devote considerable energy to developing a biological explanation and justification for the prejudice of woman's inferiority. This chapter will examine the scientific theories advanced to explain the assumption that woman, although more perfect than other animals, was inferior to man.

ARISTOTLE: WOMAN AS A NATURAL MONSTROSITY

Aristotle (384–322 BCE) provided the first systematic scientific explanation of woman's imperfection. In the *Generation of Animals* and the *History of Animals,* Aristotle offered a biological explanation of the idea of woman as an inferior man. Clearly, he was influenced by the bias found in the cosmologies of Hesiod and Plato—that the original or proper form of humankind is male. This tenet was a given fact for Aristotle, not a thesis subject to question. Yet he found it necessary to develop a detailed and seemingly rational scientific justification for this belief.

Aristotle based his biology on the premise that heat is the fundamental principle in the perfection of animals. Heat "concocts" matter, enabling it to develop. The more heat an animal generates, the more developed it will be. "That which has by nature a smaller portion of heat is weaker."[1] The amount of heat an animal can generate thus determines its degree of perfection.

The belief that woman is colder than man and therefore less perfect is central to Aristotle's biology. He employed it to account for numerous alleged physiological and psychological differences between woman and man, and to justify the perception of these differences as "defects." Because woman has less heat, she is smaller and weaker than man. "The male is larger and longer-lived than the female . . . the female is less muscular and less compactly jointed."[2] Woman's heat deficiency results in her brain being smaller and less developed; in turn, her inferior brain size is the cause of many other defects. Woman is "more jealous, more querulous, more apt to scold and to strike. She is, furthermore, more prone to despondency and less hopeful than the man, more void of shame, more false of speech, more deceptive, and of more retentive memory."[3]

Aristotle based his proof of woman's defect in heat upon a comparison of menstrual fluid and the male ejaculate, which he labeled "semen." He believed that semen is derived from blood, although it is white, insisting that its color was the result of heat. A substance is transformed by being concocted, he said, and heat is required for such concoction. On the basis of this, Aristotle concluded that the whiteness of male semen had to be the result of an infusion of heat that concentrated the potency of the blood and changed its appearance.

According to Aristotle, menstrual discharge is "analogous in females to the semen in males."[4] His justification for this belief was that "semen begins to appear in males and to be emitted at the same time of life that the menstrual flow begins in females" and that "in the decline of life the generative power fails in the one sex and the menstrual discharge in the other."[5] Since the menstrual flow, like the ability to emit semen, commences at puberty and ceases with old age, Aristotle correctly concluded that it must be associated with reproduction. Because the menstrual flow is abundant and resembles blood, Aristotle concluded that woman is unable to "cook" her semen to the point of purity—"proof" of her relative coldness. "It is necessary that the weaker animal also should have a residue greater in quantity and less concocted."[6]

The cause of woman's innate defect in heat, Aristotle explained, is that an embryo becomes female "when the first principle does not bear sway and cannot concoct the nourishment through lack of heat nor bring it into its proper form."[7] But this is not an explanation of the cause of woman's defect; it is rather an assertion of it. The statement reveals two important biases. First, Aristotle embraces the tenet that the "proper form" of a human is male.[8] In this respect, a woman is not fully human. This is a clear case of the impact of cosmological beliefs on science, for Aristotle offered no proof or explanation for his claim. The second bias, stemming from the first, is that a female embryo is caused by a deviation from nature. Holding that nature always aims to create the most perfectly formed being—a male, given the previous bias—Aristotle concluded that a female must be the result of either some lack of generative heat or some adversity. Hence, woman is a misbegotten man.

Because woman is not the "proper form" of a human, Aristotle labeled her a "monstrosity." Having defined a monstrosity as a "departure from type," Aristotle noted that the "first departure [from type] indeed is that the offspring should become female instead of male."[9] Since the male is the most perfect form of any animal, the male of any species will be higher on the scale of being than the female of that species.[10]

The evidence Aristotle offered in support of this explanation demonstrates the extent to which his biases affected his science. According to him, "observed facts confirm what we have said. For more females are produced by the young and by those verging on old age than by those in the prime of life; in the former the heat is not yet perfect, in the latter it is failing. And those of a moister and more feminine state of body are more wont to beget females, and a liquid semen causes this more than a thicker; now all these characteristics come of a deficiency in natural heat."[11] The claim that those individuals not in prime condition would be more likely to give birth to females follows logically from Aristotle's theory: such individuals are least able to provide the heat necessary for concoction of a fetus into its "proper form." However, a simple empirical study recording the gender of offspring born to younger and older women, and comparing this data to similar records of births to women "in their prime," would have disproven this hypothesis, since there is no correlation between the age of the pregnant woman and the sex of her offspring. Furthermore, the circularity of Aristotle's position is obvious in his claim that a "feminine" state of body results from a defect in natural heat.

Another contention that would not have stood careful testing was that the greater heat of the male fetus results in its developing more quickly than the female. Aristotle claimed that the male fetus first moves in the womb about the fortieth day, while the female does not move until the ninetieth day.[12] This is a reasonable inference from his theory, but one that could have been disproven by carefully recording the date of quickening and later recording the gender of the newborn.

Such studies would have been similar to the types of observations Aristotle conducted in other areas of his scientific investigations, for he was not an armchair biologist. Michael Boylan, in *Method and Practice in Aristotle's Biology*, demonstrates that Aristotle adopted the method of critical empiricism, a careful blend of observation and theory. Boylan argues that many of Aristotle's studies, particularly those of insects and marine animals, were based upon careful observations. Aristotle did rely additionally upon reports of others for data; for example, he often cites the accounts of beekeepers. But this would have been in keeping with his method. In such cases, Boylan notes that "Aristotle was on good ground to employ an eye trained through many years of observation as an empirical source by which he could generate and verify his theories."[13]

Still, there are times when Aristotle deviated from his method of critical empiricism, times when he relied upon *a priori* predilections and biases rather than careful observations. The two examples above are claims that Aristotle did not empirically verify; neither are they based on reliable testimony, as in the case of the reports of beekeepers. Since Aristotle could have conducted empirical studies, and given that none of them required sophisticated technology, the fact that he chose not to do so in violation of his own method shows the extent to which his belief in the superiority of the male form affected his science.

Furthermore, there are a number of points at which Aristotle's arguments are strained. He insisted that woman is a mutation resulting from some defect in heat. "The female is, as it were, a mutilated male."[14] Yet he noted that males are more often born defective than females. It would seem logical here to conclude that such higher rates of mutations in males are due to a defect in heat, thus arguing against the premise of male physiological superiority. Aristotle, however, turned the preponderance of birth defects in males into a mark of perfection! He insisted that male defects are caused not by a lack of heat, but rather by man's superiority in this regard. Twisting his own logic, Aristotle argued that because of man's greater natural heat, the male fetus "moves about more than the female, and on account of moving is more liable to injury."[15]

We see the power of Aristotle's biases once again as he attempted to account for woman's earlier entrance into puberty. Aristotle claimed that accelerated development was a mark of superior heat, the reason that male fetuses quicken earlier than females. But by making an unsupported distinction between prenatal and postnatal development, Aristotle pointed to the time of the onset of puberty as an additional proof of woman's imperfection. "For females are weaker and colder in nature, and we must look upon the female character as being a sort of natural deficiency. Accordingly while it is within the mother it develops slowly because of its coldness (for development is concoction, and it is heat that concocts, and what is hotter is easily concocted); but after birth it quickly arrives at maturity and old age on account of its weakness, for all inferior things come sooner to their perfection, and as this is true of works of art so it is of what is formed by nature."[16]

Aristotle reinforced his theory by arguing that woman's defect in heat is necessary for reproduction. Only an individual who was unable to concoct matter fully would be capable of nourishing a fetus. The male, capable of concocting all of his matter, would have no residue with which to feed a growing fetus. Woman's role in generation is thus tied to her imperfection. Aristotle concluded that although woman is a mutilated male, hers is a mutilation necessary for the perpetuation of the race.[17] Woman is less perfect than man, but her imperfection is a "natural" one.

Aristotle's biology, the first fully developed and systematic system of the science, remained influential well into the seventeenth century and carried with it the idea of woman as a misbegotten man.

THE ARISTOTELIAN TRADITION: FROM GALEN TO PARÉ

Galen (130?–?200), the influential Greek physician and theorist, accepted Aristotle's biological system as the foundation for his own theory, although he emended sections of it. Galen adopted without question Aristotle's basic position that a defect in heat causes woman's inferiority. "The female is less perfect than the male for one, principal reason—because she is colder."[18] However, he argued that Aristotle overlooked one of the most obvious indications of woman's imperfection—her genitals. "Aristotle was right in thinking the female less perfect than the male; he certainly did not, however, follow out his argument to its conclusion, but, as it seems to me, left out the main head of it, so to speak."[19]

Galen insisted that upon dissection of the genitals of the two sexes, one would realize that all the parts that man has, woman has too. Woman's genitals, however, are contained within the body, whereas man's are outside the body. "Consider first whichever ones you please, turn outward the woman's, turn inward, so to speak, and fold double the man's, and you will find them the same in both in every respect."[20]

Accepting the Aristotelian thesis that woman is like man but lower in the hierarchy of being, Galen conceived of her genitals as an inferior, interior copy of man's.[21] Woman's genitals, Galen explained, "were formed within her when she was still a fetus, but could not because of the defect in the heat emerge and project on the outside."[22] The internal location of woman's genitals is thus the "proof" that Aristotle overlooked. Once Galen had equated male and female genitals, he insisted that the internal location of woman's genitals could be explained only by an arrested development. Man's greater supply of innate heat causes his genitals to turn inside out and protrude form his body, but woman's heat is insufficient for this final stage of development.

In Galen's account, fully concocted genitals, the "true" form of genitals, are the penis and testicles. Woman remains, so to speak, half-baked. For centuries, anatomical drawings of woman's internal genitalia bore an uncanny resemblance to man's external genitalia, just as Galen described.

The death of Galen marks the end of progress in biological learning in the West for over eight centuries. With the decline of the Roman Empire and the subsequent decline in Latin culture, classical learning and theories all but disappeared in most of Europe. Except for a few fragments preserved by compilers, the biological and medical works of the Greeks and Romans were practically unknown during this period. These classics continued to be studied in the early Middle Ages by Arab scholars, but it was not until the tenth and eleventh centuries that a revival of learning and study of classics began in the Western world. This revival went hand in hand with a Christianizing of these classical texts.

One of the most influential of the attempts to reconcile Aristotelian biological theory with Christian theology was that of Aquinas. In his writings, we see clearly the impact of scientific conceptions of woman's nature upon religious thought. Religion not only influences science, it is influenced by it. Aristotle's biology reflected religious belief in the male as the true form, and itself reinforced Aquinas's theological tenet of woman's subordination to man.

Emphasizing the second version of the Genesis creation story, Aquinas insisted that there was a divine plan in the creation of woman separate from man. By giving woman the function of generation, God freed man to direct his life to "a vital operation nobler than generation."[23] Aquinas accepted Aristotle's theory that the generative function of females—their ability to nourish a fetus until birth—was a result of a defect in heat. We hear a clear echo of Aristotelian theory in Aquinas's view of the biological cause of woman's imperfection. "As regards the individual nature, woman is defective and misbegotten, for the active force in the male seed tends to the production of a perfect likeness in the masculine sex; while the production of woman comes from defect in the active force or from some material indisposition or even from some external influence."[24]

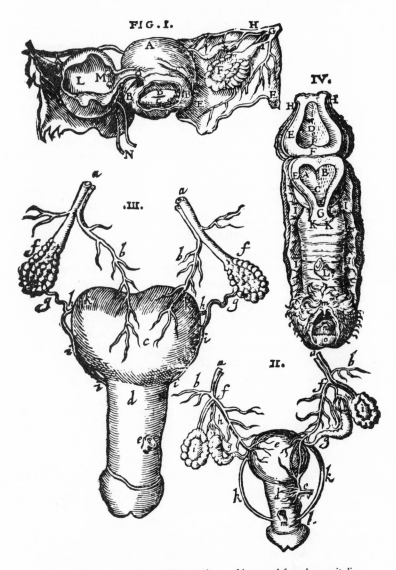

3. Paré offers a number of illustrations of internal female genitalia. Notice the phallic nature of these representations. Ambroise Paré, *Oeuvres complètes d'Ambroise Paré*. Paris: J. B. Bailliere, 1840–1841.

Aquinas attempted to modify Aristotle's view in light of the Christian belief that God would not intentionally create anything less perfect than it ought to be. Since God would create only the most perfect of all possible worlds, Aquinas had to justify the "perfection" of woman's smaller supply of heat. While accepting the premise that woman's creation was both temporally and metaphysically secondary, Aquinas insisted that it was God's intention to create her in this way and for a good reason—generation. "As regards human nature in general, woman is not misbegotten, but is included in nature's intention as directed to the work of generation."[25]

This subtle modification of Aristotle's theory is important because it enabled Aquinas to claim that, while woman has less being than man, she was not created defectively by God. This is crucial to the Christian framework. God, believed to be both benevolent and all-powerful, would not refrain from bringing beings to their true form. By holding that woman is a misbegotten male, "as being a product outside the purpose of nature considered in the individual case: *but not against the purpose of universal nature,*" Aquinas justified woman's inferiority without compromising his belief in the nature of God.[26]

Aristotle's view of woman as a misbegotten man remained, with relatively minor variations, the generally accepted position well into the Renaissance, and portions of his theory were influential until the late nineteenth century. Aristotle's association of heat with perfection, and his claim that man was more capable of generating heat than woman, had more impact upon early modern biological theory, as well as upon popular views, than any other parts of his system. As late as 1889, for example, the biologists Patrick Geddes and John Arthur Thomson claimed that the combs and wattles of male birds are caused by the fact that male "temperatures are known in some cases to be decidedly higher than those of the females."[27]

Legal and religious views concerning abortion are an excellent example of the persistence of this portion of the Aristotelian worldview. The premise that the superior heat of the male causes the male fetus to grow faster than the female was a basis of abortion regulations until the middle of the nineteenth century. It was generally accepted that the soul did not enter the fetus until it had reached a certain point of development, and that upon the infusion of the soul the fetus would quicken, or move. Abortion was considered legal and religiously acceptable until quickening. According to Gratian, the twelfth-century father of Christian canonical law, "he is not guilty of homicide who brings about abortion before the soul is infused into the body."[28] The male was believed to be developed enough to receive a soul within forty days, while a female fetus was thought to require from forty-five to eighty days to reach the level of development necessary for quickening. Ambroise Paré, a sixteenth-century biologist, stated that ". . . in male children, by reason of the more strong and forming heat which is engraffed in them, [the entrance of the soul] is about the fortieth day, and in females about the forty-fifth day."[29] Based on this belief, if a pregnant woman were carrying a male fetus she could not abort after the fortieth day from conception, whereas if her fetus were female she had from five days to five weeks of additional time, depending upon whose theory one accepted, during which she could acceptably abort the fetus.[30]

Such abortion laws, of course, presupposed a procedure for determining the sex of a fetus. Here again Aristotle's theory provided the framework. Since a female fetus was due to a defect in heat, physicians believed they could predict the sex of a fetus based on the health of the pregnant woman. If the woman was pale or sickly, this was a sign that she was carrying a female fetus. A healthy, radiant pregnancy was the sign of a male fetus.

Galen's elaboration upon Aristotle remained a popular position well into the eighteenth century. Paré accepted Galen's interpretation of the internal location of woman's genitals as proof of her inferior supply of heat. "What man hath apparent without, that women have hid within, both by the singular providence of Nature, as also by the defect of heat in women, which could not drive and thrust forth those parts as in men."[31] As late as the 1930s, Sigmund Freud would claim that "portions of the male sexual apparatus also appear in women's bodies, though in an atrophied state."[32]

Renaissance theorists also were influenced by the revision of the Aristotelian position begun by thinkers like Aquinas. While agreeing that the female has less perfection than the male, Aquinas insisted that woman is not defective when viewed in terms of the human race as a whole. Biological theories began to shift from the hierarchical model, which depicted woman as like man but inferior, to a model of complementary difference in which woman was seen as man's opposite and as perfect in her own way. Like Luther, scientists began to develop a notion of different but equal, but as we will see, woman fares no better with the scientists than she did with Luther. The very characteristics that made up woman's difference were often perceived as less perfect than those of man. Nor was the revision universal; many scientists continued to support an unmodified Aristotelian position of woman's inferiority. The nineteenth-century medical theorist Thomas Laycock, for example, in *An Essay on Hysteria,* cited approvingly the work of the physiologists Johann Friedrich Meckel, Henri de Blainville, and Isidore Geoffroy Saint-Hilaire, whom he characterized as viewing woman as "an imperfectly developed male; the primary formative nidus not being sufficiently powerful to carry the individuals through all the requisite phases of development."[33]

FROM THE BIOLOGY OF MAN TO THE BIOLOGY OF THE WORLD: ALCHEMY

The view of woman as a misbegotten or inferior man is central to the metaphysics of the alchemical tradition. While not dealing specifically with the biology of humans, alchemy could be said to deal with the biology of the world, for alchemists believed that all things, including stones and metals, were alive.

Alchemy was strongly influenced by Aristotelian science, and alchemical practice was grounded upon Aristotle's theory of elements. The basic components of existence were earth, air, fire, and water, and all things in the universe were

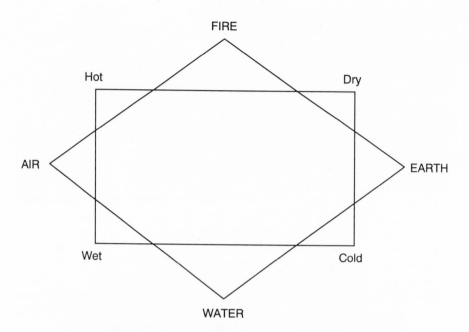

4. The square of elements depicting both physical and sensible qualities. Each physical form is believed to arise out of the combination of two sensible qualities. Water, for example, is the result of the combination of wet and cold.

believed to be composed of one or more of these elements. Furthermore, each element possessed particular qualities: earth was dry and cold, air was hot and moist, fire was hot and dry, and water was cold and moist. It was believed that all qualities of an object could be accounted for by the particular combination of elements found within it.

The alchemical theory of transmutation is based on this theory of elements. Since the qualities of any object are a function of the particular combination of its elemental substances, it would be possible, at least in principle, to transmute one object into another by modifying its elemental structure. For example, one obvious difference between lead and gold is the yellow color of gold. Based on the theory of elements, a high degree of fire in an object makes it yellow in color. Alchemists thus concluded that an increase in the amount of fire in the lead would turn it into a yellow substance—gold.

Gold was a desired end product of alchemical transmutations because it was believed to contain the perfect balance of the four elements. According to the metaphysics of alchemy, change was a sign of imperfection; a substance that was variable was in an imperfect state and had yet to reach its true form. Alchemists believed that gold was unlike all other metals in that it was incorruptible and immutable, indicating that it was the perfect form of metal. Since the alchemical process was designed to transform a substance into its perfect form, successfully transmuting another metal into gold was proof of success.

Given that the alchemical tradition was based upon Aristotelian science, it is reasonable to expect alchemists to have been influenced by the Aristotelian image of the female as an inferior stage of development. In order to document this attitude, it is necessary to detail the steps of the alchemical process.

One must start with the fundamental substance, *prima materia*. Because alchemists believed that their science must be kept secret from the uninitiated, it is quite difficult to identify their primary material. They did, however, describe certain aspects of its nature. It consisted of a combination of the four elements and an active principle, the soul of the substance. However, the elements of the primary matter were in a volatile and mobile state. Transmutation would be successful only if the alchemist obtained the pure forms of these four elements. Thus, the elements of the primary matter had to be separated and purified prior to being reunited to form a perfect substance.[34]

Alchemists believed that heat would free the soul of the primary matter, thus enabling separation and later purification of the elements of the substance. To bring about separation, alchemists employed two principles, Sol and Luna. Sol was seen as a male principle; Luna was depicted as a female principle. Sol was the male element embodied in sulphur in its purified form; Luna was the female element embodied in the purified form of mercury. Sol was a fixed principle, containing the properties of heat and dryness; Luna was a volatile principle that was cold and moist. These two principles were referred to by numerous other names, one of the most common being the two dragons. "He which is undermost without wings, he is fixed or the male; that which is uppermost is the volatile, or the female, black and obscure, which goes about to get the domination for many months. The first is called Sulphur or heat and dryness; and the latter Argent-vive, or cold and moisture; these are the Sun and the Moon of the Mercurial source."[35]

We can see here the influence of the Aristotelian view of the female as inferior. Although the female principle was viewed as necessary, it was not viewed as equal to the male principle. In the alchemical view, mutability and change are signs of imperfection. Gold, the perfect metal whose elements are in harmony, is seen as enduring and unchanging. The fact that Luna was seen as volatile and Sol as fixed indicates that alchemists saw Sol as more perfect than Luna. This interpretation is supported by the properties possessed by Sol and Luna. Influenced by the Aristotelian view, alchemists correlated heat and perfection. The more heat an object possesses, the more perfect it is. This belief is reflected in the practice of adding heat to a substance in order to raise its level of perfection. Since Sol possesses heat and Luna cold, it follows that alchemists viewed Luna as an inferior principle.

This valuation of the male principle over the female also applies to the soul of the alchemist, which is also being perfected during the alchemical process. "The soul of man consists chiefly of two portions, *Rua'h* and *Nephesh*—inferior and superior. The superior is masculine and eternal, the inferior feminine and mortal."[36] Since the alchemical transmutation of base metal into gold was believed to occur only in conjunction with a similar transmutation of the alchemist's soul from a base form to a perfect form, the valuation of the male soul over the female soul becomes a part of both processes of perfection. "The two forces or poles of human nature (the Sulphur and Quicksilver of the inward alchemical work) lie on the same level, there is nevertheless a difference in rank, similar to that of the right and left hands, so that the masculine pole can be said to be placed above the feminine. And indeed Sulphur, as the masculine pole, plays the role toward Quicksilver, the feminine pole, which is similar to that of the spirit in its action on the whole soul."[37] According to this alchemical view, all active knowledge belongs to the masculine side of the soul, and all passive knowledge belongs to its feminine side. Thus, thought-dominated consciousness is ascribed to the masculine pole, while all involuntary powers and capacities are seen as an expression of the feminine pole.

The perceived superiority of the male principle over the female is also reflected in the stages of the transmutation process. The primary matter is divided by being dissolved in Sol and Luna, the part of the transmutation process in which Sol and Luna are "married." This chemical marriage produces the hermaphrodite, for it unites the female and male principles in one substance.

The chemical marriage has three stages. In the first, the mixture of Sol and Luna causes the phlegmatic humidity of the mercury (Luna) to be dried up, and the remaining substance becomes black. This is referred to as the Nigredo stage, in which the substance dies and the soul of the primary matter is released.

Once that soul is released, the alchemist must purify the elements of the dead substance for reunification with the soul. In the second stage of the chemical marriage, the masculine principle, Sol, imparts the heat of nature to Luna, thereby transmuting it into a purer metal. This is the Albedo stage, in which the substance has a white color and is referred to as the white rose or the white queen. The Albedo stage is associated with the moon, for it is cold and moist and shines feebly compared to the next stage.

To achieve the third and final stage in the transmutation process, heat must be raised to its highest intensity. By adding heat to the Albedo, the final impurities are removed from the substance, as well as from the soul of the alchemist, and the substance is raised to its highest state of being—the red king. When one reaches this stage, the Rubedo, one has achieved the philosophers' stone. One has unlocked the mysteries of the universe and in doing so has received true wisdom.

The perceived superiority of the male principle over the female is thus reflected in the stages of the transmutation process. Like Aristotle, the alchemist sees the male as the true form of being. The perfect form, which is the goal of the alchemical process, is a male form. Gold, the perfect form of metals, is "a perfect masculine body without any superfluidity or diminution."[38] The final stage of the alchemical process, the red king, in which the alchemist achieved perfect form, is a masculine stage. The female stage, the cold and moist white queen, is a state of lower perfection. With the infusion of intense heat, alchemists believed

5. The second stage of the alchemical process of perfection, the white queen. Trismegistus Hermes, *Divine Pymander*. London: J. S. for T. Brewster, 1657.

6. The third and final stage of the alchemical process of perfection, the red king. Trismegistus Hermes, *Divine Pymander.* London: J. S. for T. Brewster, 1657.

that the male would gain victory over the female, a victory that would result in the female being perfected, that is, becoming male.

> Then is the fair White Woman
> Married to the Ruddy Man
> Understandinge thereof if you would get,
> When our *White Stone* shall suffer heate,
> And rest in fire as red as Blood,
> Then is the Marriage perfect and good;
> And you may truly know that time,
> How the seminall seed Masculine
> Has wrought and won the Victory
> Upon the menstruals worthily,
> And well converted them to his kind.[39]

It is important to remember that the same process that perfects the base metal also perfects the soul of the alchemist; the imperfect female portion of the alchemist's soul is also being converted. Given this, a woman practicing alchemy could at best achieve the philosophers' stone only by becoming "like a man," at least in terms of her soul. At worst she would be viewed as capable, because of the imperfections of her female body and soul, of participating in only the earlier stages of the alchemical processes.[40]

The victory over the female is a central metaphor in alchemical literature. Michael Maier, a seventeenth-century alchemist, wrote a text, *Atalanta Fleeing,* based on this alchemical metaphor. The frontispiece of Maier's book of emblems depicts the story of Atalanta.

In Greek mythology, Atalanta was the swiftest of all runners. When her father insisted that she marry, Atalanta, who did not wish to do so, agreed to marry only he who could conquer her in a race. She insisted that anyone who raced with her and lost be put to death. Hippomenes, wishing to marry Atalanta but knowing that she could not be outrun, designed a ruse to win the race. He brought with him three of the golden apples from the garden of the Hesperides. While they were running, Hippomenes threw the apples in Atalanta's path, knowing she would stop to pick them up. This enabled him to win the race.

For Maier, the story of Atalanta symbolized the alchemical process. He employed the image of Atalanta fleeing to remind the alchemist that the transmutation process is a dangerous one that can be accomplished only if one can conquer the volatile female principle. "Hippomenes represents the strength of the Sulphur, / She [Atalanta] the strength of the volatile Mercury; / In the race the woman is conquered by the man."[41]

What we see in Maier's text is that the alchemical process is successful when the female is transformed into the male. The chemical marriage brings together the female and the male principles, creating the hermaphrodite. But the process is complete only when the hermaphrodite becomes male. "For by the heat the sexual organs are driven out of the body, and as a woman is much colder than a man, they stay hidden in the body of a woman. . . . The warmth, which increases in force and movement at the same rate as the growth, makes the hidden organs

7. Maier's depiction of Hippomenes's victory over Atalanta. Michael Maier,
Atalanta Fugiens: Emblemata nova de secretis naturae chymica. Omenheimii:
John Theodori de Bry, 1618. Frontispiece.

EMBLEMA XXXIII. *De secretis Naturæ.*

Hermaphroditus mortuo similis, in tenebris ja-
cens, igne indiget.

EPIGRAMMA XXXIII.

Ille biceps gemini sexus, en funeris instar
    Apparet, postquam est humiditatis inops:
Nocte tenebrosâ si conditur, indiget igne,
    Hunc illi præstes, & modò vita redit.
Omnis in igne latet lapidis vis, omnis in auro
    Sulfuris, argento Mercurii vigor est.

N

8. The hermaphrodite—the merging of female and male. Michael Maier, *Atalanta Fugiens: Emblemata nova de secretis naturae chymica.* Omen-heimii: John Theodori de Bry, 1618. Emblem XXXIII.

appear and become visible. In the same way, a woman is made into a man in the Philosophical Work, namely by adding warmth to the Hermaphrodite, by which the female nature is converted into a powerful male nature, in which nothing weak is inherent."[42]

Maier's alchemical theory is an application of the Galenic version of Aristotelian biology to the world. The interior location of a woman's genitals is proof of her imperfect nature. Because of a defect in heat during the formation process, woman is unable to develop into true human form. Just so with the alchemical process. The white queen is a lower stage of development. Lacking the heat of the male, she has not yet reached her final form. Only through the addition of heat will "the hidden organs appear and become visible," and "a woman is made into a man."

This image is repeated in Emblem XXI, which represents the entire alchemical process. The motto of this emblem reads: "Make a circle out of a man and a woman, out of this a square, / out of this a triangle, / make a circle and you will have the Philosophers' Stone."[43] The man and woman represent the sulphur and mercury from which the philosophers' stone originates. From them the alchemist should make a circle—that is, marry the two elements so that they are a unity. This is the hermaphrodite. From this unity one creates a square—that is, from the mixture of sulphur and mercury the alchemist is able to separate the four elements: earth, air, fire, and water. The next step is to bring these elements to their purified form. The process for doing so includes the three stages of Nigredo, Albedo, and Rubedo, symbolized by the triangle. From these stages arises the circle, the reunification of the elements and the primary principle into their perfect form—the red king, gold, the philosophers' stone. Maier states that the process of transforming the triangle into a circle, of bringing the elements into their perfect form, is an action by which "woman changes into a man."[44]

Alchemists thus incorporate the Aristotelian view of woman as an inferior male in their biology of the world. The male is the final stage of all things. The female, though a necessary stage in the evolution to perfection, must be conquered in that evolution.

EVOLUTION AND SEXUAL DIFFERENTIATION

This image of evolution to perfection, or at least to higher and more complex states of being, was also a component of Charles Darwin's (1809–1882) theory of evolution and of the views of later exponents of his theory. The theory of evolution required important revisions in the complex of beliefs surrounding the view that there was a hierarchy or scale of created things. However, the belief in a chain or ladder of being remained intact. As we will see, woman's position on this ladder of being was also unchanged.

The doctrine of a scale of perfection, which flourished in Western thought in the Middle Ages and was widespread in the literature of the seventeenth and eighteenth centuries, contained tenets incompatible with a belief in evolution. In the Middle Ages, the view of a ladder of perfection was wedded to Christian

EMBLEMA XXI. *De secretis Naturæ.*

Fac ex mare & fœmina circulum, inde quadran-gulum, hinc triangulum, fac circulum & ha-bebis lap. Philosophorum.

EPIGRAMMA XXI.

Fœmina masque unus fiant tibi circulus, ex quo
  Surgat, habens æquum forma quadrata latus.
Hinc Trigonum ducas, omni qui parte rotundam
  In sphæram redeat: Tum Lapis ortus erit.
Si res tanta tuæ non mox venit obvia menti,
  Dogma Geometræ si capis, omne scies.

9. Maier's representation of the alchemical process. Michael Maier, *Atalanta Fugiens: Emblemata nova de secretis naturae chymica.* Omenheimii: John Theodori de Bry, 1618. Emblem XXI.

beliefs concerning the nature of creation, the most important of these being that the entire chain of being was created by God and was therefore immutable. From this premise it followed that the order of perfection was unalterably imposed upon the universe at the moment of creation. Change and evolution were thus not possible.

Darwin's theory of evolution contained a modified image of a scale of perfection. In order to incorporate the doctrine of a hierarchy of being into an evolutionary framework, two important revisions had to be accepted: the mutability of form and vast quantities of time. The view of creation as instantaneous and fixed had to be replaced with the belief that nature is continuously being made. Darwin postulated that humans and other complex organisms had evolved over long periods of time from less complex forms of life. Life could no longer be seen as created in its entirety by divine fiat, but had to be viewed as constantly emerging and achieving complexity. The scale of nature was thus not fixed, but was in the process of becoming as a result of the evolution of life forms.

Some of the tenets of the pre-Darwinian theory of a scale of nature carried over into the evolutionary framework. The Darwinian notion of complexity was understood to mean degree of perfection, so that the more complex an organism, the more perfect. Darwin and post-Darwinians began to talk of "higher" and "lower" species in ways that involved clear value judgments concerning their perfection.

Another carry-over from the original doctrine of the scale of nature was the belief in continuity—that there would be no gaps in the ladder of perfection. "The whole chasm in Nature, from a Plant to a Man, is filled up with diverse Kinds of Creatures, rising one over another by such a gentle and easy Ascent, that the little Transitions and Deviations from one Species to another, are almost insensible."[45] Since there could be no gap between apes and humans, the continuity hypothesis required that many degrees of perfection could be found within the human species. As supposedly "primitive" cultures were being discovered, the perceived gulf between these societies and those of Europe was accepted by evolutionists as evidence that "primitive" peoples stood on a scale above the apes but below "civilized" humans. Georges Pouchet, the nineteenth-century French anthropologist, wrote that "examples are not wanting of races placed so low, that they have quite naturally appeared to resemble the ape tribe. These people, much nearer than ourselves to a state of nature, deserve on that account every attention on the part of the anthropologist."[46] Having firmly inscribed racism onto the evolutionary scale, the framework was thus set for determining the locations of women on this scale of perfection.

Darwin's discussion of woman's nature occurs in the work *The Descent of Man, and Selection in Relation to Sex*. The major theme of this text is the phenomenon of sexual selection, which he had defined in *On the Origin of Species*.

> This form of selection depends, not on a struggle for existence in relation to other organic beings or to external conditions, but on a struggle between the individuals of one sex, generally the males, for possession of the other sex. The result is not death to the unsuccessful competitor, but few or no offspring. Sexual selection is, therefore,

less rigorous than natural selection. Generally, the most vigorous males, those which are best fitted for their places in nature, will leave most progeny. But in many cases, victory depends not so much on general vigour, as on having special weapons, confined to the male sex.[47]

Sexual selection, unlike natural selection, occurs only between members of the same species. It "depends on the advantage which certain individuals have over others of the same sex and species solely in respect of reproduction."[48]

Darwin thus postulated a second mechanism of evolution in addition to natural selection. He claimed that some structures and instincts develop as a result of their ability to attract the opposite sex. Included among these were male courage and pugnacity, the weapons of offense and defense that enable males to fight with and drive away rivals, and male ornaments such as plumage, voice, and odors that serve to allure and excite females. Darwin argued that such structures could not be the result of natural selection "since unarmed, unornamented, or unattractive males would succeed equally well in the battle for life and in leaving numerous progeny but for the presence of better endowed males."[49]

There is one additional component of sexual selection—female choice. The males will fight with other males for advantage, but males' ornaments develop because females are more attracted to the males of striking appearance. "The females are most excited by, or prefer pairing with, the more ornamented males, or those which are the best songsters, or play the best antics; but it is obviously probable that they would at the same time prefer the more vigorous and lively males."[50]

Darwin's theory of evolution contained the thesis that sexual differentiation increased as animals evolved. According to his theory, organisms reproduced asexually in the lowest divisions of the animal kingdom. As organisms became more complex, sexual reproduction was slowly established, initially accomplished by the conjunction of identical organisms. The gradual differentiation of organisms resulted in two separate and distinct sexes that became increasingly specialized in form and function. Thus, the more differences that existed between the sexes, the more evolved they were.

Darwin's thesis of sexual selection had important consequences for theories of woman's nature. Since Darwin believed that it is generally males who contend for and are selected by females, he concluded that only males would evolve as a result of sexual selection. The female, whose role is to choose but who does not compete, does not evolve and thus "retains a closer resemblance to the young of her own species." The chosen male is selected because he is judged to be superior to other males. The successful males then "transmit their superiority to their male offspring"—evolution via sexual selection.[51]

Throughout Darwin's discussion, we find a connection between male superiority and the greater male variability resulting from sexual selection. Darwin's theory involves the thesis that evolution results in greater complexity of the organism: the more highly evolved an organism is, the more complex it will be. Like pre-evolutionary views concerning the scale of being, an organism's degree of perfection is seen as analogous to its state of evolution. A logical consequence of

Darwin's view of greater male variation is the premise of the greater perfection of the male.

When we examine the physical and psychological differences between woman and man that Darwin claimed to result from sexual selection, we find that in each case the male traits are those generally associated with higher degrees of perfection. "Man on an average is considerably taller, heavier, and stronger than woman, with squarer shoulders and more plainly pronounced muscles. . . . Man is more courageous, pugnacious, and energetic than woman, and has a more inventive genius."[52] Female traits are clearly associated with less evolved states. "The female . . . in the formation of her skull is said to be intermediate between the child and the man."[53] "It is generally admitted that with women the powers of intuition, of rapid perception, and perhaps of imitation, are more strongly marked than in man; but some, at least, of these faculties are characteristic of the lower races, and therefore of a past and lower state of civilization."[54] Here the sexism of Darwin's theory intermingles with its racism. Darwin perceived the races of "man" to be hierarchically arranged from lowest or most primitive to most perfect—not surprisingly the civilized European races. Within each race, woman was seen as at a lower stage of perfection than the man of that race. This allowed for some women, namely upper-class, white, European women, to be seen as more highly evolved than some men, such as black, African men, within the general tenet that woman is less evolved than man.

In addition to sexual selection, Darwin argued that the greater variability and complexity of males were also made possible by their role in procreation. Darwin echoed the Aristotelian tradition in insisting that the female must expend much of her energy in nourishing fetuses, claiming that this expenditure of energy precludes female variation. The male, needing only a small amount of energy to form his seed and having no role in fetal development, has a reserve of energy available for his own development.[55] "The female has to expend much organic matter in the formation of her ova, whereas the male expends much force in fierce contests with his rivals, in wandering about in search of the female, in exerting his voice, pouring out odoriferous secretions, and etc."[56]

Darwin's theory of evolution thus perpetuates the view of woman as less perfect than man. There is, however, a change in metaphor that becomes important in post-Darwinian views. Rather than placing woman between man and animal, theorists begin to talk of woman as falling between man and child. As Darwin put it, woman is "intermediate between the child and the man."[57] Although perhaps more positive an image than that of being like an animal, the view of woman as child carries with it the view of woman as an incomplete or undeveloped human. This change in metaphor went hand in hand with a similar change concerning races labeled "primitive." Women and men from primitive races were depicted as children in comparison to the evolved adults of the civilized races. This image justified a kind of race and gender paternalism in which all women and some races of men needed the guidance and control of "superior" males.

Three of Darwin's themes in *The Descent of Man* remain central to post-Darwinian discussions of woman's nature. These are the claims that the more evolved a species, the more the sexes will be differentiated; that females resemble the young of their species; and that because females must expend so much energy on fetal development, they have little energy for developmental variations. Revised and elaborated upon, these three themes become the focus of nineteenth-century views of woman's nature.

CIVILIZATION AND SEX ROLE DIFFERENTIATION

A common tenet of Victorian science was that female and male role differentiation was the product of a long evolutionary process. Darwin had postulated a process toward greater biological variation and differentiation. By associating sexual differentiation with such variation, scientists concluded that the degree of such differentiation correlated with the degree of evolutionary advance. Scientists were quick to apply this argument to humans, the obvious conclusion being that the differences between woman and man were widening with evolutionary progress.

This conclusion became the foundation of the popular attack upon the nineteenth-century women's rights movement. Since role differentiation was believed to be the result of evolution, critics argued that any attempt to minimize this differentiation would go against biology and result in the devolution of the human race. In *The Saturday Review,* for example, an anonymous author argued that

> . . . if our better halves alter the conditions which have raised us from the condition of orang-outangs, a relapse into savagery is quite possible . . . the advance of our race has been marked by an increasing diversity between men and women, which makes one, not the contradiction, but the complement of the other. The lower we go among savage tribes, the less of this diversity there would seem to be; so that it appears to be a direct retrogression to assimilate the work of the highly-developed woman to that of her mate; and if perfection is to be the aim of our efforts, it will be best advanced by further divergence of male and female characteristics. . . . The agitation for women's so-called emancipation should be strenuously resisted.[58]

Various "proofs" of greater differentiation between the sexes in the more "civilized" races became abundant in scientific and popular literature. A number of scientists who studied brain size began to compare the brains of females and males across a variety of cultures. They constructed "proofs" that although female brains were always smaller than male brains, the ratio of this differentiation was larger in what they considered to be the more civilized races.[59] The general conclusion was that women's brains were, in structure and size, intermediate between those of children and men. In a variation of Aristotle's image of a misbegotten man, the female came to be seen as the basic race type from which the male was a higher development. This position is clearly illustrated in a paper read by James McGrigor Allan to London anthropologists.

> . . . the female skull approaches in many respects that of the infant, and still more that of the lower races; with this is connected the remarkable circumstance, that the difference between the sexes, as regards cranial cavity, increases with the develop-

ment of race, so that the male European excels much more the female than the negro the negress. . . . Women preserves in the information of the head, the earlier stage from which the race or tribe has been developed, or into which it has relapsed; hence is partly explained the fact, that inequality of the sexes increases with the progress of civilization.[60]

Post-Darwinian theorists postulated an evolutionary pattern concerning sexual differentiation in which the least evolved species exhibited female superiority and the most evolved exhibited male superiority. Equality of the sexes was relegated to a stage between those two. This tenet was articulated in *Popular Science Monthly* by Gaetan Delauney, who claimed that "the two sexes, at first unequal in consequence of the superiority of the female over the male characterizing the lowest species, became equal among species a little more elevated in the animal scale, and become unequal again in consequence of the pre-eminence of male over female, which is observed in all the higher species."[61]

Various theories were proposed suggesting that human evolution went through these stages. Johann Jakob Bachofen, Henry Maine, Friedrich Engels, and Robert Briffault postulated a period of matriarchy at the earliest stages of human evolution.[62] In this stage the female was viewed as superior to the male. However, in successive stages of evolution, the sexes would pass then through a period of female/male equality until they reached the highest stage of evolution—patriarchy. To support this hypothesis, theorists cited numerous examples of non-European cultures in which the women were supposedly more vigorous and more intelligent than the men, and others in which women and men generally shared roles. The implicit assumption, of course, was that non-European races were at a lower level of evolutionary development. Since the European races were viewed as the most evolutionarily advanced, much scientific energy was devoted to documenting the superiority of the male in these races.

There is a complex interweaving of racism and sexism in such theories, which allowed nineteenth-century scientists to conclude that European women were superior to the males of non-European races because those males were at a lower stage of evolution, while continuing to hold that European women were inferior to European men. Some scientists protested against the latter characterization (but not the former) by arguing that European woman was civilized man's complement, not his inferior. But, as we will see, this turns out to be a distinction without a difference.

Scientists stressed the social implications of the hypothesis that male superiority was a natural consequence of evolution, and their warnings became a regular subject of popular literature. It was argued that any attempt to bring about the equality of the sexes would at best fail, and at worst result in the devolution of the race. In this view, sex differences were a part of human biology. Allan, for example, argued that "thousands of years have amply demonstrated the mental supremacy of man, and any attempt to revolutionize the education and *status* of woman on the assumption of an imaginary sexual equality, would be at variance with the normal order of things, and as Dr. Broca says, induce 'a perturbance in the evolution of races.' "[63]

It is important to notice that the "normal order of things" presupposes a relative devolution of females as a result of the evolution of the species. As the species evolves, man becomes more varied and more specialized. In the words of the U.S. psychologist G. Stanley Hall, "the male is the agent of variation and progress, and transmits variations best, so that perhaps the male cell and sex itself originated in order to produce variation."[64] Woman, however, as the result of species evolution becomes increasingly less specialized in comparison to man. "She is by nature more typical and a better representative of the race and less prone to specialization."[65] On this theory, evolutionary advance enables man to choose from a variety of roles, while limiting woman to reproductive and child-raising roles.

BETWEEN MAN AND CHILD: RECAPITULATION

In the nineteenth century, yet another theory was added to the variety of explanations of woman's inferiority. With the acceptance of evolutionary theory, the biological sciences turned their attention to reconstructing the stages of evolutionary development. Fossils offered only partial evidence, so biologists had to consider other sources of data.

One popular result was recapitulation. According to this theory, the stages of individual embryonic growth parallel the life history of its species; it was believed that one could trace ancestral adult stages in the embryonic stages of descendants. The embryonic stages of fetuses were thus seen as physical remnants of previous ancestors. For example, the gill slits of the human fetus in the very early stages of development were evidence of an ancestral adult fish, and the temporary tail that occurs at a later stage of fetal development paralleled a reptilian or mammalian ancestor. The German Darwinian Ernst Haeckel, one of the central proponents of recapitulation, explained this process in terms of a biogenetic law in which man

> . . . rises upwards from a simple cellular state, and as it progresses in its differentiating and perfecting, it passes through the same series of transformations which its animal progenitors have passed through, during immense spaces of time, inconceivable ages ago . . . certain very early and low states in the development of man, and other vertebrate animals in general, correspond completely in many points of structure with conditions which last for life in the lower fishes. The next phase which follows on this presents us with a change of the fish-like being into a kind of amphibious animal. At a later period the mammal, with its special characteristics, develops out of the amphibian . . . [66]

In brief, ontogeny recapitulates phylogeny.

Recapitulation provided a powerful mechanism for explaining racial, as well as sexual, inferiority.[67] The theory maintained that adults of inferior classes of humans would retain the childlike traits of superior classes of humans. According to an anonymous contributor to the *Anthropological Review,*

> The leading characters of the various races of mankind are simply the representatives of particular stages in the development of the highest Caucasian type. The Negro

exhibits permanently the imperfect brow, projecting lower jaw, and slender bent limbs of a Caucasian child some considerable time before the period of its birth. The aboriginal American represents the same child nearer birth. The Mongolian, the same child newly born.[68]

Similarly, demonstrating that adult women had traits that men possessed only when they were children would prove that women were at a more primitive stage of human development. Such a view of women is a clear premise of the following passage by Gustave Le Bon (1841–1931), the founder of social psychology:

> In the most intelligent races, such as the Parisians, there is a notable proportion of the female population whose skulls are closer in volume to those of gorillas than to the skulls of the most developed males . . . the lesser size of the female skull, principally in the superior races, is accompanied by a corresponding intellectual inferiority. . . . This inferiority is too evident to be debated for a moment, and one can hardly even dispute the degree of this inferiority. All the psychologists who have studied the intelligence of women . . . recognize that they represent the most inferior forms of human evolution and are much closer to children and savages than to civilized adult males.[69]

Notice that the view of woman as between man and child is actually the centuries-old image of woman as between man and animal in a thinly veiled disguise.

THE MARKS OF INFERIORITY: EDWARD DRINKER COPE.

The use of recapitulation theory to account for woman's inferiority is well illustrated in the work of Edward Drinker Cope (1840–1897), one of the first American evolutionary theoreticians. Cope believed that recapitulation was central to evolution, and he was devoted to explicating the mechanism of this process. His theory focused on developmental growth rates.

Cope proposed that there is a correlation between speed of growth and degree of complexity, such that higher degrees of complexity are acquired through the joint mechanisms of what he labeled "acceleration" and "retardation." He characterized acceleration as the process in which adult stages of ancestors are crowded back into the juvenile stages of an organism, so that there is an increase in the rate of assumption of successive characteristics. Retardation was the slowing down of individual development. Cope concluded that "high development in intellectual things is accomplished by rapidity in traversing the preliminary stages of inferiority common to all, while low development signifies sluggishness in that progress, and a corresponding retention of inferiority."[70] The perfection of a being is related not only to the rate of development through such stages (acceleration), but also to the absolute length of the growth period (retardation). "Of two beings whose characters are assumed at the same rate of succession, that with the quickest or shortest growth is necessarily inferior."[71]

It is easy to predict the consequences of applying this view to the development of woman. From Aristotle to the present, it has been commonly accepted that woman reaches maturity long before man. Although the underlying theory varied, this fact was used as evidence of woman's physiological and psychological inferiority. Cope's work is no exception. Claiming that woman's period of individual development is shorter than man's, he concluded that she is "necessarily inferior." Cope argued that the traits woman held in common with man were "very similar in essential nature to those which men exhibit at an early stage of development," and explained that the cause of this "may be in some way related to the fact that physical maturity occurs earlier in women."[72] In other words, woman's early maturation is actually an arrest of development that results in the retention of infantile or primitive qualities that males "grow out of," and prohibits the development of more advanced characteristics. "Probably, most men can recollect some early period of their lives when the emotional nature predominated . . . this is the "woman stage" of character: in a large number of cases it is early passed; in some it lasts longer; while in a very few men it persists through life."[73]

For Aristotle, a defect in heat resulted in an inability to concoct, causing woman's imperfection. For Cope, woman's developmental arrest underlies her inferiority. For both theorists, her role in reproduction accounts for this "flaw," and for both the consequences are the same—woman is an undeveloped man.[74]

To support his theory, Cope cataloged traits of man and woman in order to prove that woman retained more infantile characteristics. He accepted the premises that the most civilized races are the most highly evolved and that sex differences are more pronounced in the most evolved races. Cope selected the Indo-European race for his comparison of sex differences because he believed it to be the superior race and therefore that in which the differences would be greatest. The following list was the result of this study:

WOMEN	MEN
shoulders sloped	shoulders square
waist more constricted	waist less constricted
hips wider	hips narrower
legs shorter	legs longer
muscles smaller	muscles larger
less hair on body, that of head longer	more hair on body, that of head shorter
no beard	beard
skin smoother	skin rougher
superciliary ridges low	superciliary ridges more prominent
eyes often larger	eyes often smaller.[75]

On the basis of this list, Cope concluded that man retains only two infantile characteristics, narrow hips and short hair, while woman retains five: shorter legs, smaller muscles, absence of beard, low superciliary ridges, and larger eyes. Cope believed he had demonstrated successfully that "civilized" woman represents a more primitive stage of evolution than does "civilized" man.

This conclusion was repeated over and over in the literature. "The female sex is the more persistently true to the ancestral type, i.e. closer to our savage forbears."[76] "Woman's body and soul is phyletically older and more primitive, while man is more modern, variable, and less conservative."[77] "From the earliest ages philosophers have contended that woman is but an undeveloped man; Darwin's theory of sexual selection presupposes a superiority and an entail in the male line; for Spencer, the development of woman is early arrested by procreative functions. In short, Darwin's man is as it were an evolved woman, the Spencer's woman an arrested man."[78] Woman is no longer a misbegotten man. She has become an unevolved man.

The Problem of Evidence: Craniology and Recapitulation.

A glance at Cope's listing of infantile traits of woman and man suggests that his classification was problematic. There were no clear criteria for categorizing traits as more or less infantile, the result being that the initial assumption of female inferiority often determined such classification. This pattern can be documented in the nineteenth-century study of craniology.

Craniologists were part of the science of physical anthropology that emerged in the mid-nineteenth century. Influenced by the reports of missionaries, ethnologists, and other students of the diversities among races, physical anthropologists began a "science of man," attempting to classify the races by means of physical structures, such as skeletal structure, brain size and configuration, and skin color.[79] Physical anthropologists assumed a hierarchy of perfection among the races, and set out to identify the physical characteristics associated with each racial type that would demonstrate their location on this ladder of being.

The science of physical anthropology was quickly applied to the "problem of the sexes." If woman was indeed less perfect than man, this inferiority would be mapped onto her body. Although scientists, as we have seen with Cope, identified numerous physiological differences between the sexes—skeletal differences, menstruation, and so on—cranial measurements were among the most popular markers of sexual difference, since craniologists accepted that skull size and shape would reveal the nature of an individual's mind. They did not, however, agree upon the classification of traits that would show inferior or superior development. The classification indices of three craniologists, Hermann Schaaffhausen, Alexander Ecker, and John Cleland, offer excellent examples of the way in which selection of the characteristics employed to prove female inferiority actually *presupposed* it.

Earlier attempts had been made to document female inferiority by pointing to woman's smaller brain size. But by the middle of the nineteenth century, problems had arisen with this criterion that were too severe for many theorists to ignore.[80] As a result, craniologists began to look for alternate indices by which to determine a group's stage of evolution. Schaaffhausen offered such an alternative, insisting that aspects of the shape of an individual's skull would show her or his stage of evolution. Schaaffhausen claimed that there were five characteristics of female skulls that proved that woman's development is imperfect in comparison to man's: "the projection of the parietal protuberances, the lesser elevation of the frontal bone, the shorter and narrower cranial base . . . the more elliptical

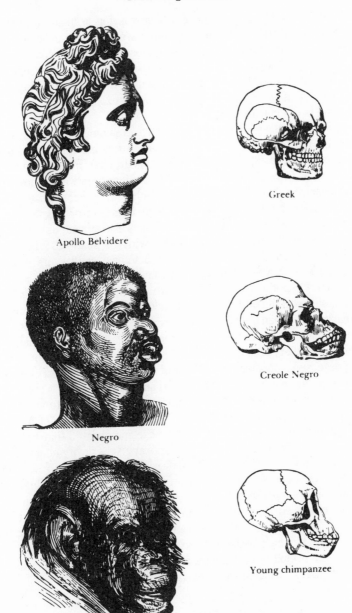

Apollo Belvidere

Greek

Negro

Creole Negro

Young chimpanzee

Young chimpanzee

10. Scale of evolution by skull angle. The Creole Negro jaw is falsely extended to evince the alleged low evolutionary status of blacks. J. C. Nott and G. R. Gliddon, *Types of Mankind.* Philadelphia: Lippincott, Grambo, and Co., 1854.

dental arch and the inclination to prognathism [having a small facial angle]."[81] Schaaffhausen argued that these characteristics were reliable indicators of more primitive skulls *because* they were traits possessed both by women and non-European races. In other words, Schaaffhausen presupposed the inferiority of women and non-European men in order to obtain a list of characteristics by which to classify skull types as primitive! A more obvious example of unconscious, circular reasoning is difficult to find.

Following Schaaffhausen's lead, Ecker conducted a comparison study of female and male skulls, but discovered that Schaaffhausen was incorrect in arguing that females had a small facial angle (that is, were prognathous). Instead, he found that woman had a larger facial angle than man did (that is, woman was orthognathous). Rather than conclude that woman was more evolved than Schaaffhausen's study had indicated, Ecker claimed that woman's high degree of orthognathism was a mark of evolutionary inferiority, arguing that it was also a trait possessed by children. "On comparing the female cranial profile with the infantile, it is undeniable that they nearly approach each other . . . the female skull in its proportions stands intermediate between the male and infantile skull."[82]

Ecker's general hypothesis, consistent with the theory of recapitulation, was that female skulls were infantile in form. In addition to orthognathism, Ecker offered six marks of woman's infantile form evinced by the shape of her skull. In comparison to male skulls, Ecker claimed that female skulls were smaller, had a flatter cranial roof, were less developed in terms of the processes for muscle attachment, possessed a smaller ratio of size of facial bones to size of cranium, had a lower cranium, and had more cranial roof than cranial base.

Cleland's revision of Ecker's indices demonstrates the extent to which racism, as well as sexism, permeated this debate. Noting that the skulls of Australians, blacks, and Kaffirs possessed high foreheads, Cleland insisted that Ecker's positing of cranial height as an indicator of evolutionary superiority could not be accurate. He rejected Ecker's criteria and replaced them with yet another measure, the angle between the baseline of the skull and the vertebral column. This criterion supported the belief that woman possessed an infantile form of skull, but also classified all non-European races as less developed than the European races.[83] The cases of Schaaffhausen, Ecker, and Cleland clearly demonstrate the manner in which sexist and racist biases are inscribed on science, for in these cases the prejudice of woman's and non-European male's inferiority dictated the fundamental principles of theorizing.

REPRODUCTION AND ENERGY

The third theme of Darwin's theory of evolution that greatly influenced later views of woman's nature was his work on reproduction and development. It was Darwin's contention that females expend so much energy on fetal development that they have far less energy than males for developmental variations. The relationship between reproductive roles and female development became a central theme of the social Darwinist Herbert Spencer (1820–1903).

Spencer argued that sex differences could be accounted for by the "somewhat earlier arrest of individual evolution in women than in men, necessitated by the reservation of vital power to meet the cost of reproduction."[84] The premise underlying this perspective is that each organism possesses a limited amount of energy. Energy expended for brain development, for example, is not available for other types of development. Since fetal development and lactation were viewed as requiring large amounts of energy, Spencer concluded that woman would have less available energy than man for intellectual and psychic growth.

Furthermore, Spencer insisted that the need for excess energy to support fetal development required a shorter maturation period for woman than for man. Since woman could not use all of her energy for her own development, she would reach adolescence earlier. Accepting the retardation hypothesis of recapitulation theory, Spencer concluded that this delay in maturity enabled man to reach a higher level of complexity: man was more evolved than woman. "Among the superior organisms, and especially those leading active lives, there is a marked tendency for completion of structure to go along with arrest in growth."[85] In other words, the longer it takes for an organism to reach complete maturity, the more highly evolved it is. Thus, Spencer concluded that the demands of woman's reproductive system precluded her full individual evolution.

Despite the fact that more than twenty centuries and numerous changes in biological theory separate Spencer and Aristotle, the commonality of their conclusions concerning woman's nature is startling. Both assumed that developmental energy is limited, and that woman expends much more energy in reproduction than man. Both insisted that man uses his "excess" of energy to become more perfect. Woman, needing to reserve this energy for fetal development, reaches her complete form more quickly, and her development stops at a lower stage. Aristotle stressed an inability to concoct resulting from a defect in heat, while Spencer pointed to an early arrest of individual evolution. Although the mechanism varies for the two, the conclusion is the same—woman is an unevolved man. She is between man and animal.

As we have seen, the image of woman as less perfect than man is as prevalent in scientific theories as in creation myths. Interestingly, the theme of creation from different "stuff," a component of many creation myths, did not have much influence in biology until the late nineteenth century when the Scottish biologist Patrick Geddes (1854–1932) adopted and elaborated upon August Weismann's germ-plasm theory. The acceptance of this theory resulted in a shift from viewing woman as an incompletely developed man to that of a creation made of different basic materials.

In his *Continuity of the Germ Plasm,* August Weismann (1834–1914), a German cytologist, postulated that the nature of each individual organism may be traced back to a sperm and egg cell. He developed a theory founded upon the idea that heredity involves the transmission from one generation to another of a substance with a definite chemical and molecular constitution. "If we wished to attack the problem of heredity at its roots we should first of all have to try to understand the process of life itself as a series of physio-chemical sequences."[86] Weismann saw the role of sexual reproduction as the source of individual variation, a theme that played only a minor role in Darwin's thinking. "The hereditary substance of the child is formed half from the paternal, half from the maternal hereditary substance."[87] Weismann argued that the combination of these two substances is the cause of hereditary individual characteristics, and that these individual differences in turn form the material out of which natural selection produces new species.

Geddes's interpretation of Weismann's germ-plasm theory is a biological explanation of sex differences founded on a basic difference in the material of creation. Denying Darwin's claim that sexual selection accounted for sex differences, Geddes argued instead that they were the result of basic differences in the cell metabolisms of women and men. He claimed that at the level of the cell, maleness is characterized by the disposition to dissipate energy, or a "katabolic" habit of body, femaleness by the disposition to conserve energy, or an "anabolic" habit of body. Based on this thesis, Geddes postulated that sex differences were a function of the general energy state of an organism at the time of fertilization.[88]

Geddes also insisted that cell metabolism had a disposition to dissipate energy when it was produced under unfavorable conditions—extreme heat or a preponderance of wasted energy. A disposition to conserve energy would then be the result of a metabolism produced under conditions of abundance of energy. Geddes claimed that "adverse circumstances, especially of nutrition, but also including age and the like, tend to the production of males, the reverse conditions favoring females."[89] Male sperm were katabolic and female ova were anabolic. Geddes argued that all differences between the sexes could ultimately be traced back to such metabolic characteristics. This is an interesting twist on the Aristotelian position. Not only is the sex of an organism the result of basic differences in the stuff of its creation, but less than optimum reproductive conditions result in the production of males—the reverse of the Aristotelian view.

As discussed earlier, Aristotle found numerous empirical "proofs" of his belief that female births were the result of some adversity in reproductive conditions. It would be a mistake, however, to think that theoretical biases resulted in manufactured empirical proofs only during science's infancy. Despite the growing sophistication of the scientific method during the centuries that separated Aristotle and Geddes, the latter employed the same type of manufactured proof. "Statistics seem to show, that after an epidemic or a war the male births are in a greater majority than is usually the case. Dusing also points out that females with small placenta and little menstruation bear more boys, and contends that the number of males varies with the harvests and prices. In towns, and in prosperous families, there seem to be more females, while males are more numerous in the country and among the poor."[90]

Like Aristotle, Geddes saw menstruation as proof of his theory. Notice, however, how menstruation receives a radically different interpretation given Geddes's premise of female anabolism. "If the female sex be indeed preponderatingly anabolic, we should expect this to show itself in distinctive functions. Menstruation is one of these, and is interpretable as a means of getting rid of the anabolic surplus, in absence of its consumption by the development of offspring."[91]

Based on his theory that sex differences result from the metabolic dispositions of cells, Geddes argued that the view of woman as an inferior man was erroneous and had to be rejected. He stressed that each sex was different from the other, and both were perfect in their own respects. "To dispute whether males or females are the higher, is like disputing the relative superiority of animals and plants. Each is higher in its own way, and the two are complementary."[92] This was surely an infelicitous analogy since animals were seen as having a higher degree of complexity than plants and thus, on the scale of being, a higher degree of perfection. But it appears to have been more than a mere slip of the pen, for we can find such a bias throughout Geddes's theory.

Despite his insistence that speculation on the superiority of one sex over the other was an error, Geddes did not practice what he preached. In discussing the insect kingdom, Geddes noted that the existence of females is one of passivity and parasitism, while males are active and free. "The insect order of bee parasites (Strepsiptera) is remarkable for the completely passive and even larval character of the blind parasitic females, while the adult males are free, winged, and short-lived."[93] Caught up in this comparison, he noted that "throughout the class of insects there are numerous illustrations of the *excellence of the males over the females,* alike in muscular power and sensory acuteness."[94] Just after this discussion he claimed that "a review of the animal kingdom, or a perusal of Darwin's pages, will amply confirm the conclusion that on an average the females incline to passivity, the males to activity."[95] The reader has every reason to think that Geddes also applied his inference from male activity to greater male excellence in the animal kingdom.

This inconsistency can, at least in part, be accounted for by the fact that the character traits Geddes attributed to the male constitution were those that Western culture was generally regarded as most desirable. For example, Geddes insisted that "males are more active, energetic, eager, passionate, and variable; the females more passive, conservative, sluggish, and stable."[96] One cannot help but picture woman in terms of Geddes's description of the female Strepsiptera—passive, larval, blind, and parasitic. Similarly, consider the value judgements in Geddes description of males in the following quote: "males are stronger, handsomer, or more emotional, simply because they are males, i.e., of more active physiological habit than their mates."[97]

Geddes's theory initially appears to be a radical alternative to the Aristotelian premise of a defect in heat in woman that results in her earlier arrest in development. Instead, Geddes actually posits basic differences in the generative material of females and males. Still, his conclusions concerning woman's nature differ little from those of Aristotle. Woman's characteristics are necessitated by her role in reproduction. Man is active, woman passive. Man is strong, woman weak. Man is intelligent, woman altruistic. Man is more variable, more handsome, more independent, more courageous—in sum, more excellent.[98]

For over two millennia, science's view of woman remained fundamentally unchanged—woman is between man and animal. The parallels between the images of woman found in Western creation myths and Aristotelian biology to nineteenth-century evolutionary theory are not coincidental. A culture's creation myths provide the basic metaphysic upon which other theories will be grounded. The fact that Aristotle inherited a worldview in which woman's basic inferiority was an unquestioned tenet had an influence upon the development of his science. It is to be expected that scientists working within a metaphysic that privileges the male and views the female as inferior will incorporate that bias in the practice of science.[99] Although the terms had changed from "inferior" to "different" or "complementary" by the time of Darwin, difference was still perceived through the lens of a hierarchical system. The ways in which man differed from woman was a sign of his higher evolution, that is, his greater perfection.

II

The Weaker Vessel

Give honour unto the wife, as unto the weaker vessel, and as being heirs together of the grace of life.

William Tyndale (1526), *Epistle to the Ephesians*

THREE

Not in God's Image

Western ethical and legal theories, strongly influenced by Christianity, refer most commonly to the soul or the mind to demonstrate human superiority over all other animals. Some theorists, claiming that *only* humans possess a soul, view this as proof that humans alone are "in God's image."

The idea of woman as a misbegotten or unevolved man typically incorporated the belief that these "higher" faculties of soul and mind would be less developed in woman. In other words, woman was a fainter image of God. Having examined the religious and scientific theories offered as justification and explanation of the imperfection of the vessel itself, let us look at those who contemplated the contents of the vessel and found them wanting.

CLASSICAL IMAGES OF THE SOUL

COSMOGONY AND SOUL: PLATO.

Plato viewed the passions as the cause of the imperfection that is woman. In the Platonic account, man is the primary creation. Although the gods originally created all beings as equally perfect, not all remained so, for some were unable to control their passions. Uncontrolled passions make a person "rebellious against the divine element within," which in turn results in a rebirth into a lower state of being, with a less perfect soul.[1] "As human nature was of two kinds, the superior race . . . would hereafter be called man."[2] The inferior race is woman.

Plato deviated from many Western thinkers in denying that the bodily differences between woman and man, even the reproductive differences, are the cause of woman's inferiority. "But if it appears that they differ only in just this respect that the female bears and the male begets, we shall say that no proof has yet been produced that the woman differs from the man for our purposes."[3] Nevertheless, Plato did view woman as inferior to man, and he attributed this inferiority to the nature of woman's soul.

Plato depicted the soul as "divine, immortal, intelligible, uniform, indissoluble, and ever self-consistent and invariable," while seeing the body as "mortal, multiform, unintelligible, dissoluble, and never self-consistent."[4] For Plato, the soul is the source of true knowledge, of eternal truths. But one is capable of such "divine thoughts" only if the senses and the passions are under the mind's control.

Gender differences enter Plato's philosophy concerning the nature of the soul—that is, the extent to which an individual's soul is capable of knowing eternal truths, and its ability to rule the appetites. Woman, the inferior race, born from men who were unable to govern their appetites, will possess an inferior soul. This inferiority will be manifest in woman's abilities. Explaining that a naturally gifted man is one who learns easily, who with slight instruction can discover much for himself in the matter studied, and for whom the bodily faculties adequately serve the mind, Plato insisted that there is nothing "practiced by mankind in which the masculine sex does not surpass the female on all these points."[5] Woman's soul limits her natural gifts.

Plato pointed to women when he wanted to illustrate the negative consequences of allowing the passions to control one's actions. In one example, Plato recounts the trial of Socrates, who, convicted of corrupting the minds of the young and threatened with a death sentence, explains that to appeal to the jury with a flood of tears or to bring in infant children to excite sympathy is to act "no better than women."[6] In another, Plato prohibited men who desire to be rulers of the polis from imitating or theatrically portraying the parts of women, madmen, or male slaves, for all three groups display the passions. Only by imitating the good man will such men emulate appropriate action.[7] As a final example, Plato argued that the most just punishment for a soldier who is a coward on the battlefield would be that he be turned into a woman because of his "unmanly spirit."[8]

Those readers familiar with Plato's *Republic* and the secondary literature on Plato may find this depiction of his view of woman difficult to reconcile with his inclusion of women in the ruling class of his ideal city (the guardians), and with those scholars who have labeled Plato "the first feminist."[9] This tension can be resolved by understanding that, without discounting the importance of gender differences in the nature of the soul, Plato viewed class differences as more relevant. He advocated a philosophy of natural classes in which different groups of humans would possess different natures.

Depicting the soul as divided into three parts—the rational element, the spirit, and the appetite—Plato posited three classes of people whose natures parallel the soul's divisions. The guardian class consists of those whose powers of reason are most perfect. The soldiers are those representing spirit—that is, those individuals who possess courage and who love contention. The third class, the artisans and the producers, represents the appetite. Plato's hierarchy also includes a fourth class of individuals, slaves, but Plato thought slaves represented none of the elements of the soul, and so depicted them as barely human. Plato's ideal for both the individual and society at large is to have the rational element, assisted by spirit, govern the appetite.

We cannot talk about Plato's view of woman without also discussing his views concerning classes of individuals.[10] Plato did not deviate from the cosmology of the *Timaeus*, in which the souls of women are inferior; he complicated it with his presumption of natural classes. Given these natural classes, the souls of some women—guardian women—would be superior to the souls of some men—those of inferior classes. But within each class, woman would be less perfect than man. Even the most perfect women, the guardian women, possess souls inferior to those of guardian men. The women and men of the guardian class "have the same nature in respect to the guardianship of the state, save in so far as the one is weaker, and the other stronger."[11] Guardian women "must take their part with the men in war and the other duties of civic guardianship," but "in these very duties lighter tasks must be assigned to the women then to the men because of their weakness as a class."[12] This weakness is the result of woman's inferior soul.

BIOLOGY AND SOUL: ARISTOTLE.

As the cosmology of Plato became the science of Aristotle, a biological explanation was offered for the imperfection of woman's soul. For Aristotle, soul is "better than body." It has a higher degree of being and is more "noble and divine."[13]

Aristotle divided the faculties of the soul into five parts. Listed in order of perfection from least to greatest, they are: the nutritive, the sensitive, the appetitive, the motive, and the intellectual. Although he believed that all living beings have souls, Aristotle did not think that every being possesses all of these faculties. Plants possess only the nutritive faculty, while animals also have the sensitive and appetitive faculties. The higher animals also have the motive faculty, but only humans possess all five faculties, including the intellectual. Aristotle ranked these faculties of the soul in terms of their "honor and dishonor," so that organisms possessing only the lesser faculties are lower on the scale of perfection. Not surprisingly, an animal's degree of heat determines which faculties she or he possesses. Aristotle explained, for example, that man's brain is the largest "because the heat in man's heart is purest," and concludes that man's "intellect shows how well he is tempered, for man is the wisest of animals."[14]

Degree of heat thus becomes the biological mechanism by which Aristotle explained woman's inferiority. He argued that due to woman's defect in heat, her soul is less perfect than that of man. In woman the highest faculty, the intellectual, is at best imperfectly developed, and is thus "without authority." She, like Pandora and the fallen souls of Plato, is controlled by her desires and passions.

Aristotle claimed that brain suture configurations prove that woman has a smaller brain than man in proportion to her size. According to his "observations," woman's sutures are circular in form, while man has three sutures that meet at a point. This view corresponds to his theory that man is hotter than woman, since the sutures cool the brain by providing it with ventilation. "Man, again, has more sutures in his skull than any other animal, and the male more than the female. The explanation is again to be found in the greater size of the brain, which demands free ventilation, proportionate to its bulk."[15] This is an additional example of Aristotle's deviation from critical empiricism, since the sutures of female and male skulls are actually identical.

Aristotle reinforced his belief in the superiority of male souls when he argued that only man partakes in the divine by passing on soul to future generations. Woman provides only the nutritive and generative soul in conception, while man supplies the higher faculties of the soul—the sensitive, motive, and intellectual faculties. Woman's contribution to generation is less noble than man's, which "is better and more divine in its nature than the material on which it works."[16] It is the male semen that makes the soul human; the female merely nurtures the soul placed in her by the male. Aristotle thus gave two reasons for viewing man as a more perfect image of the divine: he has a more perfect soul, and he partakes in the divine by reproducing himself.

CHRISTIAN IMAGES OF THE SOUL

During the Middle Ages, there was no uniform Christian position on the nature of woman's soul. Theologians based their theories on a number of foundations, including the Genesis myth in which woman was created from the rib of man; the belief that Eve was centrally responsible for the fall; the Aristotelian view of woman as misbegotten and consequently more affected by her appetites; and the Platonic view that the passions and desires must be under the control of reason if one is to achieve perfection. Depending upon their interpretations, theologians held one of three positions concerning woman's soul: that woman does not possess a soul and is not in the image of God; that woman is in the image of God only when she becomes "like a man"; and that woman has a soul but one inferior to that of man, and is thus a fainter image of God.

NOT IN THE IMAGE OF GOD: GRATIAN.

Gratian, a twelfth-century Benedictine monk often considered the father of canon law, was the primary proponent of the position that woman lacked a soul and was not in God's image. In the *Decretum,* a systematization of canon law that became the primary text for the teaching of this subject for centuries, Gratian attempted to establish the preeminence and primacy of man, and the secondary position of woman, by stressing the second version of the Genesis creation myth. "It is not without significance that woman was not formed from the same earth as Adam, but rather was created from a rib of this Adam. . . . So at the beginning [of the creation] it was not two who were created, man and woman, nor two men nor two women, but first the man and after him the woman out of him."[17] On the basis of the temporal primacy of man's creation, Gratian concluded that only man is in God's image. "This is the likeness of God in man [the male], that he is created as the only being, from whom the others have come, and that he possesses, as it were, the dominion of God as His representative, since he bears in himself the image of the one God. *So woman is not created in the image of God: that is what [scripture] says.*"[18]

Gratian claimed that the Pauline law dictating the veiling of woman is necessitated by her lack of soul. "Man certainly must not cover his head, because he is image and reflection of God, but woman must cover her head because she is neither reflection nor the image of God."[19] Gratian further argued that woman's veiling is a sign of her sin, since it was a woman who was seduced by the serpent and thus caused the fall. "Women must cover their heads because they are not the image of God. They must do this as a sign of their subjection to authority and because sin came into the world through them. . . . Because of original sin they must show themselves submissive."[20]

Gratian went so far as to suggest that even the designations "woman" and "man" reflect this difference in perfection. He claimed that *vir* (man) is derived from *virtus animi,* meaning moral strength and perfection, while *mulier* (woman) derives from *mollities mentis,* meaning weakness and softness of character.[21] Woman is thus the weaker sex who was not created in the image of God.

BECOMING MAN: PHILO.

The Gospel of Thomas, an apocryphal gospel compiled about 200 CE, depicts woman as achieving salvation only if she becomes male. This gospel includes a conversation between Simon Peter and Jesus, who had come to preach to the apostles. Seeing that he was accompanied by Mary, Simon Peter said to Jesus, "Let Mary go out from among us, because women are not worthy of the Life." Jesus replied, "See, I shall lead her, so that I will make her male, that she too may become a living spirit, resembling you males. For every woman who makes herself male will enter the Kingdom of Heaven."[22]

The *Gospel of Thomas* presents a hierarchy of salvation. For a man to achieve salvation, he must become a "living spirit," that is, like Adam prior to the fall. But a woman must first become like a man. This hierarchy, from female to male to living spirit, mirrors the initial creation from the rib. Woman arose out of the male, who was the living spirit formed from dust and God's breath. In order for woman to achieve salvation, she must return to her origin. She must become like a man.[23]

This hierarchy of salvation influenced the writings of many church fathers. An illustration is Philo, who held that "the female is incomplete and in subjection and belongs to the category of the passive rather than the active."[24] This image of woman seems to preclude her salvation; Philo argued that salvation was possible only through reason, for only reason enabled one to transcend the corrupting influences of the senses and the bodily passions, and thereby attain salvation.[25] "And woman is more accustomed to be deceived than man. For his judgment, like his body, is masculine and is capable of dissolving or destroying the designs of deception; but the judgment of woman is more feminine, and because of softness she easily gives way and is taken in by plausible falsehoods which resemble the truth."[26]

Given his theological views, Philo could have opted for Simon Peter's position. He could have argued that woman is not in God's image and is tied to the material world, and thus cannot be saved. But in fact, Philo adopted a position similar to that of Jesus as recorded by Thomas—woman must become like man. Woman's salvation requires "giving up of the female gender by changing into the male, since the female gender is material, passive, corporeal and sense-perceptible, while the male is active, rational, incorporeal and more akin to mind and thought."[27]

Just as Mary required Jesus's grace to become like a man, Philo explained that every woman requires the grace of God. "When God begins to consort with the soul, He makes what before was a woman into a virgin again, for He takes away the degenerate and emasculate passions which unmanned it and plants instead the native growth of unpolluted virtues. Thus He will not talk with Sarah till she has ceased from all that is after the manner of women (Gen. xviii.11), and is ranked once more as a pure virgin."[28] Only by becoming male can woman partake in "the rational which belongs to mind and reason [which] is of the masculine gender."[29]

Those offering theories like Philo's present woman with a paradox. For a woman, to act according to her nature as well as her prescribed social role precluded her salvation. But to reach salvation, a woman had to deny her nature and become what she was not—like man.

FAINTER IMAGES: AUGUSTINE.

The third position, that woman was created with a soul but one inferior to that of man, is illustrated in the writings of Augustine. Augustine, like Gratian, took seriously the words of Paul about the veiling of women. "Why, then, is the man on that account not bound to cover his head, because he is the image and glory of God, while the woman is bound to do so, because she is the glory of the man."[30]

But unlike Gratian, Augustine emphasized the first creation story in Genesis: "God created man: in the image of God created He him; male and female created He them: and He blessed them."[31] Committed to reconciling Paul's words with this depiction of human creation, Augustine included woman within God's image by concluding that human nature, "which is complete only in both sexes," is made in the image of God.

Although Augustine included woman within God's image, she is included only when she is "together with her own husband . . . so that the whole substance may be one image."[32] However, taken apart from man, "when she is referred separately to her quality of *help-meet*, which regards the woman herself alone, then she is not the image of God."[33] Woman is in God's image only through the marriage bond.[34]

Augustine depicted man's participation in the image of God as superior to that of woman. "But as regards the man alone, he is the image of God as fully and completely as when the woman too is joined with him in one."[35] Man's own being is in God's image; woman's divinity depends upon her connection to man. Woman is in God's image only in a secondary sense.

Like Philo, Augustine cited woman's inferior rational abilities to explain why she is not in God's image in her own being. Accepting the premise that humans are in the image of God through their rational minds, Augustine admitted that both males and females have minds; thus, both are made in God's image. But the nature of women's bodies inhibits the functioning of their minds. "In the sex of their body they [women] do not signify this [mind]; therefore they are bidden to be veiled."[36]

While noting no defect in woman's mind, Augustine denounced her body as precluding full development of her rational powers. "But because too great a progression towards inferior things is dangerous to that rational cognition that is conversant with things corporeal and temporal; this ought to have power on its head, which the covering indicates, by which it is signified that it ought to be restrained."[37] Woman requires "power on her head," that is, the rule of her husband, who provides the authority she lacks. The veil prescribed by Paul, then, is a reminder of woman's need for authority. Only under the guidance of her husband can a woman overcome the sex of her body and thereby be part of the image of God.

FROM SOULS TO MINDS: WITCH-HUNTS.

A theme underlying Christian discussions of the divinity of woman is the nature of her rational faculties. Philo, like Plato, believed that woman is, by nature, more influenced by the passions than by reason. Aristotle accounted for this characteristic by arguing that woman's ability to generate heat is insufficient for the full development of rational faculties. Augustine also tied the *imago dei* to the rational faculty, insisting that the nature of woman's body inhibits contemplation and results in the imperfection of her faculty of reason. Indeed, for all Christian thinkers, the belief in the inferiority of woman's rational capacities was reinforced by the circumstances of the fall. Theologians frequently argued that the serpent appealed to Eve's passions in order to deceive her into eating the forbidden fruit; Adam would not have been so deceived.

In the sixteenth century, emphasis began to shift from the quality of woman's soul to the quality of her rational faculties. One example of this transition can be found in the theological views of witchcraft. From the late fifteenth through the seventeenth centuries, thousands of people were tried for witchcraft in Germany, Italy, France, and England, with women making up over 85 percent of those executed. Their crimes ranged from copulation with the devil and cannibalism of newborn infants, to performing abortions and assisting in difficult births.[38]

One of the most influential treatises on witchcraft was the *Malleus Maleficarum* (*The Witches' Hammer*), written by the Dominican monks Jacob Sprenger and Heinrich Kramer in 1484.[39] Sprenger and Kramer provide a detailed explanation of the "fact" that the majority of witches were women. Interestingly, they made no mention of the quality of woman's soul to account for this, but instead turn to the nature of her intellectual faculties. One such explanation is based upon the gullibility of women. "They are more credulous; and since the chief aim of the devil is to corrupt faith, therefore he rather attacks them . . . women are naturally more impressionable, and more ready to receive the influence of a disembodied spirit."[40]

Sprenger and Kramer traced this gullibility back to rational capacities, in regard to which women "seem to be of a different nature from men."[41] To support their view, they cited authorities who maintained that woman's intellectual abilities are as undeveloped as those of a child, and are insufficient for the comprehension of philosophical or spiritual matters. This native defect results in woman's faith being weaker and thereby more easily rejected. Since denial of the Christian faith is "the root of witchcraft," it comes as no surprise to Sprenger and Kramer that the majority of witches are women.

A second defect contributes to woman's greater susceptibility to witchcraft— her inordinate passions. "And indeed, just as through the first defect in their intelligence they are more prone to abjure the faith; so through their second defect of inordinate affections and passions they search for, brood over, and inflict various vengeances, either by witchcraft, or by some other means."[42] These two defects, of course, go hand in hand. Passions require the rule of reason; without such rule, an individual will be overwhelmed by emotions and desires. Woman's typically inferior intellectual capacities are too weak for her to successfully control her passions.

Although belief in witches gradually died out in the seventeenth century, theorists of the eighteenth and nineteenth centuries frequently repeated the view of woman's nature inherent in Sprenger and Kramer's account. Philosophy defined reason as male and passion as female. Science found woman's nature to be more strongly affiliated with the emotional than the intellectual faculties. The conclusion was that woman was lacking in rational faculties.

WITHOUT GOOD REASON

DEFINING REASON AS MALE: DESCARTES.

Philo defined reason as male and passion as female, and instructed his followers to cast out that which was female within them. To identify reason with maleness does not mean that woman is incapable of being rational; it does, however, entail that in order to be rational, a woman must transcend the feminine. This model of reason presents a dilemma. To develop her rational abilities, a woman must deny those characteristics seen as making up her nature, and become instead "like a man." Over a millennium later, René Descartes (1596–1650) would offer a conception of reason almost identical to that of Philo, one that would dominate Western philosophical and scientific definitions of rationality for centuries.[43]

In *Rules for the Direction of the Mind,* Descartes offered a method designed to provide certain knowledge of the nature of the universe. One can acquire such knowledge, he argued, by breaking down complex beliefs and experiences into their basic constitutive elements until one reaches what is simple and self-evident. Once these "simple natures" are uncovered, they must be carefully scrutinized in order to understand how they combine to make up complex objects. "The whole of human knowledge," he concluded, "consists in a distinct perception of the way in which those simple natures combine in order to build up other objects."[44] According to Descartes, this method is applicable to all realms of knowledge. "We must not fancy that one kind of knowledge is more obscure than another, since all knowledge is of the same nature throughout, and consists solely in combining what is self-evident."[45]

Descartes's rules are, in a sense, instructions for properly regulating and operating our minds. "Certain and simple rules such that, if a man observes them accurately, he shall never assume what is false as true, and will never spend his mental efforts to no purpose, but will always gradually increase his knowledge and so arrive at a true understanding of all that does not surpass his powers."[46]

It was Descartes's conviction that as long as investigators limited their reason to that which could be known clearly and followed their rational powers exclusively, they would obtain incontrovertible knowledge.

There are two very important assumptions here. The first is that the logic of reason mirrors the structure of reality. The second is that clear and distinct ideas are a source of truth about the world. If either of these presuppositions is incorrect, then knowledge is not certain.

To guarantee or ground both of these beliefs, Descartes attempted to prove the existence of a divine being, God, who so structured both the mind and the world. Descartes's philosophy shows clear influence of the Christian tenet that man was made in God's image; he envisioned man as being "like God" in the sense of possessing ability to achieve, through reason, a "god's-eye view." Descartes thus defined knowledge as objective, that is, independent of human concerns or values. To ensure this absolute objectivity of reason, Descartes distinguished between reason, which can be a source of certainty, on the one hand, and the "fluctuating testimony of the senses" and the "blundering constructions of imagination," on the other.[47] The senses and the imagination are excluded from the realm of reason because these faculties are subjective and thus, according to Descartes, only impede the quest for objectivity.

A crucial component of Descartes's conception of rationality is his radical separation of mind and matter. Noting the variability of the senses and fluctuating bodily needs, Descartes concluded that certainty can be assured only if its source is mental, with no connection to the body. He described his technique for transcending the body during his quest for certainty in the *Meditations*. "I shall now close my eyes, I shall stop my ears, I shall call away all my senses, I shall efface even from my thoughts all the images of corporeal things, or at least (for that is hardly possible) I shall esteem them as vain and false; and thus holding converse only with myself and considering my own nature, I shall try little by little to reach a better knowledge of and a more familiar acquaintanceship with myself."[48]

For Descartes, the body is an impediment to knowledge. One begins the Cartesian journey to truth not through the body, but by learning to overcome it. To be rational, one must be detached from the needs, desires, and particularities of the body. In Descartes's account, only those activities that successfully do so are sources of true knowledge: science, mathematics, and philosophy.

The Cartesian ideal not only separates mind and matter, it polarizes reason and emotion. The mind is an indivisible mental substance—a thing that thinks. By limiting the mind to cognitions, Descartes excluded emotions from the realm of the mental. He believed that the passions of the soul—love, desire, despair, pride, anger, and joy—"are caused, maintained, and fortified by some movement of the spirits, *'animal spirits' that arise from the body*."[49] "The little filaments of our nerves are so distributed in all its parts, that on the occasion of the diverse movements which are there excited by sensible objects, they open in diverse ways the pores of the brain, which causes the animal spirits contained in these cavities to enter in diverse ways in to the muscles, by which means they can move the members in all the different ways in which they are capable of being moved."[50]

Thus, the body is rejected as a source of knowledge and emotion is excluded from the realm of the rational, to be seen instead as a source of error. To gain truth, individuals must purify their thoughts of all distortions—expectations, emotional attachments, and biases. One must reject all prejudice, scrutinize all beliefs no matter how obvious, and overcome the distractions of the body.

Descartes equated rationality with reason, seeing the latter as a restricted activity that applies only in the sciences and philosophy—areas Descartes believed could be completely divorced from the particularities of the body. He rejected the notion of a practical reason that would enable an individual to function within the world of daily concerns. He did not even see such activity as an inferior sort of rationality, but instead entirely excluded it from the rational realm. Descartes did not condemn the senses as worthless, in fact admitting that they are reliable guides to our well-being. But he remained adamant about excluding senses and passions from the realm of rationality, arguing that they should not be seen as sources of truth. He explained that nature

. . . truly teaches me to flee from things which cause the sensation of pain, and seek after the things which communicate to me the sentiment of pleasure and so forth; but I do not see that beyond this it teaches me that from those diverse sense-perceptions we should ever form any conclusion regarding things outside of us, without having [carefully and maturely] mentally examined them beforehand. For it seems to me that it is mind alone, and not mind and body in conjunction, that is requisite to a knowledge of the truth in regard to such things.[51]

Descartes believed that rationality is difficult to attain, and advocated careful discipline for anyone who wishes to achieve it. While admitting that the training would be arduous, he insisted that all people are capable of rationality: "even those who have the feeblest souls can acquire a very absolute dominion over all their passions if sufficient industry is applied in training and guiding them."[52] His rules were designed as guidelines for a course of training that would enable one to silence the demands and interests of the body, to separate oneself from the human perspective and achieve a Cartesian "god-like" viewpoint.

Descartes did not perceive this new image of rationality as in any way excluding women; in fact, he insisted that all people equally possess the light of reason. "The power of forming a good judgment and of distinguishing the true from the false, which is properly speaking what is called Good sense or Reason, is by nature equal in all men."[53] In other words, each of us is capable of objectivity, as long as we are capable of avoiding all subjective influences—our inclinations, our point of view, and our bodily needs. In fact, Descartes's belief that all people possess the "natural light of reason" led him to argue that his method was possible for anyone, even a woman, to follow.[54] Just like a man, a woman is capable, through training and careful attention to learning, of ignoring her emotions, her appetites, and everything else relating to the body. It would thus appear that

Descartes's "man" of reason is gender-neutral. If we look beyond the surface, however, we find that the rational person is male.

To achieve a life of reason, one must be able to transcend bodily desires and focus on only universal issues, completely ignoring anything that is particular and personal. The needs of the body must be suppressed by the mind; the emotions must be dominated by the will. This conception of the rational person is in complete opposition to all characteristics historically conceived as female and associated with woman—the body, emotion, and passivity. For centuries prior to Descartes and for centuries after, woman was seen as inescapably bound to the concerns of the body by her role in reproduction—her pregnancies, her lactations, and her menses. Given this conception of woman's nature, even if one accepts Descartes's view that woman has the same mental capacities as man, one will still conclude that the suppression of the body is a far more arduous task for a woman, and thus one in which she is less likely to succeed. Nineteenth-century science offered substantial evidence of the impediments of woman's body, and argued that the quest for a life of the mind was ill-advised for a woman, for it would be her ruin.

Woman's social role also handicaps her. The vast majority of Western philosophers, theologians, and scientists writing both before and after Descartes have accepted the Aristotelian view of the natural role of "civilized" woman as that of wife and mother. That is, the natural destiny of woman will prevent her from living a life of the mind. The arduous training and dedication of Descartes's rational man will be obstructed by the daily chores and responsibilities of nurturing children and running a household. The leisure necessary for the pursuit of reason is not available to a wife and mother. This point was well made by Princess Elizabeth of Bohemia, who corresponded with Descartes about his method. "The life I am constrained to lead does not allow me enough free time to acquire a habit of meditation in accordance with your rules. Sometimes the interests of my household, which I must not neglect, sometimes conversations and civilities I cannot eschew, so thoroughly deject this weak mind with annoyances or boredom that it remains, for a long time afterward, useless for anything else."[55]

Furthermore, Descartes's claim that the rational person must attend to only the universal and avoid the particular is inconsistent with the social image of woman as mother. In the realm of the family, woman is seen as sensitive to the particular needs of each child, offering to each the type of warmth and protection appropriate to her or his personality. This perception of maternal care, with its necessary ties to the particular, the personal, and the emotional, stands in opposition to Descartes's image of the rational person.

The "uncivilized" woman, the woman who is a slave or a serf or a laborer, or from a "savage" race, is even more handicapped by her social role, as well as by societal prejudices concerning her natural abilities. The grueling labors necessary for basic survival by women of these groups completely precludes the life of leisure Descartes prescribes. Princess Elizabeth found it difficult to find sufficient free time to acquire Descartes's habit of meditation; a poor woman would find it impossible. By factoring in class and race in this way, it becomes clear that Descartes's rational man is not only male, he is an upper-class, European male.

The man of reason is not gender neutral.[56] Should a woman wish to pursue the rational life, she would have to deny all that is seen as female—attachment to individuals, private interests, and maternal feelings. She would have to learn to be cool, dispassionate, impersonal, distant, and detached. She would have to deny the many voices of her upbringing and culture whose definition of her would preclude her success in the arduous training required for the life of reason, for all these traits are stereotypically masculine. Even the positive characteristics associated with woman, such as empathy, nurturance, and imagination, would have to be rejected, for they are relegated to the irrational in the Cartesian system.

Descartes's sharp opposition of mind and body, reason and emotion, masculinizes rationality. A woman who wishes to follow Descartes's method must reject her culturally prescribed roles; she must see the skills and thought processes associated with those roles as devoid of reason.[57] She must discipline a body whose dictates she has been taught to see as far more demanding than those of man's and must overcome the socially dictated view of herself as passive, weaker, and timid. She must renounce all those things that define her as female. She must become the *man* of reason.[58]

THE SCIENCE OF THE MIND

The Cartesian definition of rationality defined philosophical conceptions for centuries. Adopted and adapted by Francis Bacon in the seventeenth century, it provided a foundation for the Western scientific view of rationality. With rationality defined as male, it is not surprising that woman would be considered less rational than man, and equally unsurprising that nineteenth- and early twentieth-century science would provide numerous explanations for woman's intellectual deficiency.

A few scientists developed modern versions of Gratian's denial that woman possessed soul, arguing that woman was totally incapable of reason. But the majority of scientists took the more moderate position that woman was capable of reason, only less capable than man. While accepting a concept that required woman to become "like a man" in order to act rationally, these scientists enjoined women to refuse to do so. Unlike Philo, who urged women to make every effort to become male, modern scientists warned that any such attempt would be disastrous, both for the individual woman and ultimately for society.

THE MINDLESS WOMAN: WEININGER.

An influential text presenting the position that woman was incapable of reason is *Sex and Character,* written by the Austrian theorist Otto Weininger (1880–1903). This philosophical and scientific study received much attention, especially in Vienna after Weininger's suicide.

Weininger devoted *Sex and Character* to an analysis of femaleness and maleness. His goal was to develop a "science of character" in which the ideal "female mental type" and the "ideal male type" are clearly delineated. Such an analysis, he believed, was a necessary foundation for a scientific study of character. Weininger did admit that these universal types never occur as actual individuals, since every human being "oscillates between the maleness and femaleness of his constitution." But he argued that clearly defined notions of femaleness and maleness would provide the scientist dealing with character (the psychologist) the ability to determine the particular sexual makeup of each client and accordingly tailor her or his "treatment of the soul."[59]

Gratian argued that woman is soulless, Weininger that she is mindless. In an analysis reminiscent of Aristotle, Weininger explained that woman cannot comprehend general principles: she is so controlled by her sexual desires that she is incapable of any rational thought. He claimed that man is capable of controlling his sexuality, but a woman is "always sexual." "To put it bluntly, man possesses sexual organs; her sexual organs possess woman."[60] A woman is "completely occupied and content with sexual matters." A man, being able to go beyond the sexual, "is interested in much else, in war and sport, in social affairs and feasting, in philosophy and science, in business and politics, in religion and art."[61]

According to Weininger, woman's sexuality results in a general "absence of memory amongst women, who recall only those events connected with the sexual impulse and reproduction."[62] As a result, woman is incapable of a continuous memory. Since Weininger believed that memory is "a special character unconnected with the lower spheres of psychical life, and the exclusive property of human beings," his denial of woman's capacity for memory has significant consequences.[63] Without this capability, woman ends up closer to animals than to man.

Weininger argued that woman's general lack of memory precludes rational, or even conscious, action, and renders her indifferent to a sense of her own identity over time. Lacking consciousness of her own identity, woman is unable to perceive identity in general. In other words, she is unable to control her memory sufficiently to say that $A = A$, and is thus incapable of understanding the principle of identity ($A = A$), the foundation of logic. Weininger concluded that "woman is without logic."[64] Given that Weininger accepted the logical faculty as necessary for comprehension of truth, he thereby negated woman's ability to participate in the sciences, philosophy, and all other disciplines that search for truth.

At this point Weininger has gone well beyond his initial goal of describing an ideal type, the "absolute female." He now talks about actual women, and of what women as a group are capable and incapable. "The unconceptual nature of the thinking of a woman is simply the result of her less perfect consciousness, of her want of an ego . . . in her "mind" subjective and objective are not separated; there is no possibility of making judgments, and no possibility of reaching, or of desiring, truth. No woman is really interested in science: she may deceive herself and many good men, but bad psychologists, by thinking so."[65]

Weininger's final view of woman is shockingly negative. Woman possesses no individuality, personality, character, or will. Incapable of any relation to the absolute, to God, women have "no existence and no essence; they are not, they are nothing."[66] Weininger is thus able to account for what he believed to be the deepest fear of man—the fear of woman, who represents "unconsciousness, the alluring abyss of annihilation." "However, degraded a man may be, he is immeasurably above the most superior woman, so much so that comparison and classification of the two are impossible."[67]

THE MIND OF WOMAN: NATURAL SELECTION, ARRESTED DEVELOPMENT, AND GERM PLASM.

Despite exceptions like Weininger, the majority of nineteenth- and early twentieth-century scientists concluded that woman is capable of reason—though less capable than man. For centuries, Aristotle's explanation that a defect in heat impaired female brain development had been the accepted scientific explanation of woman's intellectual inferiority. By the nineteenth century three alternative explanations emerged: (1) natural selection, (2) arrested development, and (3) the nature of germ plasm.

"The chief distinction in the intellectual powers of the two sexes," according to Darwin, "is shown by man's attaining to a higher eminence, in whatever he takes up, than can woman—whether requiring deep thought, reason, or imagination, or merely the use of the senses and hands."[68] In a statement echoing those of philosophers from Plato to Hegel, Darwin offered as empirical "fact" his belief in man's intellectual superiority, and his claim extended to race and evolutionary scale. Although so-called "primitive" man's rational capacities were seen as far inferior to those of "civilized" man, they were nevertheless superior to those of "primitive" woman.

Darwin rejected any attempt to argue that any differences in the intellectual abilities of the sexes might be caused even in part by socialization, and denied that such differences could be erased or even minimized through education. Darwin insisted that if every possible effort were made to increase woman's intellect, man's intellect would still outstrip woman's, for biology would dictate that men "maintain themselves and their families; and this will tend to keep up or even increase their mental powers, and, as a consequence, the present inequality between the sexes."[69] Woman's natural role includes the bearing and care of children, while man's role is to support and protect the family. The latter, according to Darwin, requires more intelligence than the former. For Darwin, biology is destiny.

Interestingly, Darwin identified natural rather than sexual selection as the cause of the mental differences between the sexes. That is, man's intellectual prowess did not arise merely because it enhances his ability to attract a woman; it is a characteristic that improves the species' chances in the battle for life. "The greater intellectual vigour and power of invention in man is probably due to natural selection, combined with the inherited effects of habit, for the most able men will have succeeded best in defending and providing for themselves and for their wives and offspring."[70]

Darwin postulated a hierarchy of mental functions that results from the process of natural selection. Instinct is the least highly evolved, followed by emotion, intuition, imagination, and, finally, reason. He attributed to woman a more developed faculty of intuition than is found in man. "It is generally admitted that with women the powers of intuition, of rapid perception, and perhaps of imitation, are more strongly marked than in man."[71] But this can hardly be seen as a positive factor, since he put the intuitive faculty at a lower, less civilized state of evolution. The obvious conclusion is that woman is less evolved than man.

Herbert Spencer elaborated upon this account of woman's mental inferiority in his essay "Psychology of the Sexes." Supporting Darwin's view of woman as less evolved than man, Spencer, like Darwin, pointed to an "earlier arrest of individual evolution in women than in men," designed to conserve energy needed for reproduction, to account for woman's inferior intellectual abilities.[72] In Spencer's account, the mental manifestations of woman's earlier arrest of development were a "somewhat less general power or massiveness; and beyond this there is a perceptible falling short in those two faculties, intellectual and emotional, which are the latest products of human evolution."[73] Since abstract reasoning and the ability to comprehend general principles are the last characteristics to result from human evolution, woman, not surprisingly, is seen as deficient in just these areas. In harmony with philosophical accounts, Spencer pinpointed woman's deficiencies as a lack of "the power of abstract reasoning and that most abstract of the emotions, the sentiment of justice."[74] Because man's contribution to reproduction is limited to fertilization, his individual evolution continues "until the physiological cost of self-maintenance very nearly balances what nutrition supplies."[75] Not having woman's additional burden, man's evolution can include the development of the higher intellectual faculties.

There were scientists who admitted that woman possesses abilities superior to those of man in certain areas, but examined closely, these "superior" abilities turn out to be marks of woman's developmental inferiority. Edward Drinker Cope attributed to woman a greater facility in language, greater tact or finesse, and a greater love of children. Cope explained, however, that these traits are all indications of woman's "immaturity," that is, her earlier arrest in maturation.[76] Together with woman's emotional characteristics, they are the result of what Cope referred to as woman's greater impressibility of mind. "The gentler sex is characterized by a greater impressibility, often seen in the influence exercised by a stronger character, as well as by music, color, or spectacle generally; warmth of emotion, submission to its influence rather than that of logic; timidity and irregularity of action in the outer world. All these qualities belong to the male sex, as a general rule, at some period of life, though different individuals lose them at very various periods."[77] In other words, woman's traits are those that man outgrows.

The third explanation of woman's mental inferiority, the nature of germ plasm, is offered by Patrick Geddes, who believed that the majority of sex differences are innate and due to differences in female and male constitutions. Man, possessing a katabolic metabolism, has active physiological habits and lives in a manner that is variable and expends energy. Woman, possessing an anabolic metabolism, has constructive physiological habits that preserve energy. Geddes's explanation, like those of Darwin and Spencer, is grounded upon the very assumption that scientists and philosophers have made since the time of Aristotle—woman devotes more of her developmental energy to reproduction than does man.

Geddes supported the traditional view that "man thinks more, woman feels more."[78] Man's disposition to expend energy results in a wider range of experiences, which, according to Geddes, accounts for men having "bigger brains and more intelligence."[79] Women develop their capacities for social feelings through the nurturing of their offspring, and have "a larger and more habitual share of the altruistic emotions."[80] While man is capable of "greater cerebral variability and therefore more originality," woman has greater cerebral "stability and therefore more 'common sense.' " Man is capable of grasping general principles, while woman is interested in the particulars of a situation. Man is capable of greater mental concentration, "scientific insight," discovery of new facts and ideas, and "cerebral experiment with impressions." Woman's mental capacities are expressed in "greater patience, more open-mindedness, greater appreciation of subtle details, and consequently what we call more rapid intuition."[81] Once again, we see that woman's biological destiny is motherhood, and motherhood is incompatible with intellectual achievement.

THE CONTOURS OF A WOMAN'S BRAIN

In addition to developing explanations of evolutionary mechanisms to account for mental differences between the sexes, scientists expended an amazing amount of energy attempting to document differences in the size and structure of the brains of woman and man. Such documentation, a central goal of nineteenth-century craniology, involved the important presupposition that differences in mental abilities would be reflected in physiological differences in the brain. If woman's mental faculties were indeed different from those of man, there had to be differences in brain structure or size.

Although the study of sex differences in the brain and the recording of cranial differences flourished in the nineteenth century, it has a much longer history. Aristotle referred to suture differences of woman's and man's skulls to prove that man has a larger brain and more developed intellectual capacities, while Nicolas de Malebranche (1638–1715) pointed to the constitution of woman's "cerebral fiber" to account for her intellectual deficiencies. Finding that woman's cerebral fiber is soft and delicate in comparison to the solidity and consistency of man's fiber, de Malebranche concluded that women's minds are such that "everything that depends on taste is within their area of competence, but normally they are incapable of penetrating to truths that are slightly difficult to discover. Everything abstract is incomprehensible to them."[82]

The popularity of craniology in the nineteenth century can be explained at least in part by its political usefulness. It could, for example, be easily manipulated to demonstrate the inferiority of a racial group. In Europe and the United States it was a popular method of justifying slavery.[83] It was also used to combat the growing women's rights movement.

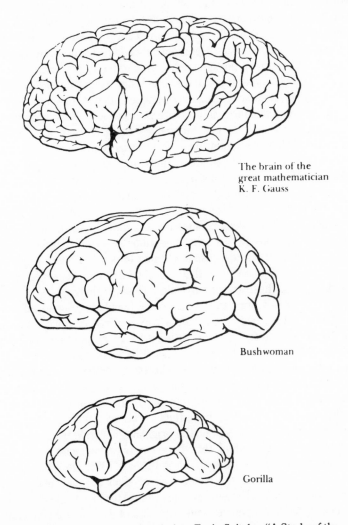

The brain of the
great mathematician
K. F. Gauss

Bushwoman

Gorilla

11. Brain size as a measure of evolution. E. A. Spitzka, "A Study of the
Brain of the Late Major J. W. Powell," *American Anthropology* 5 (1903):
585–643.

Women's brains are on the average smaller and lighter than men's. Absolute
brain size thus became the obvious starting point in the attempt to use craniology
to document woman's intellectual inferiority. Researchers often based their findings on cranial capacity, usually measuring the content size of skulls by filling
them with seed or shot and then recording the volume differences. Other researchers, however, removed and weighed the actual brains, and on the basis of
such observations, many scientists claimed a 12 to 14 percent difference in the
brain weights of women and men. Paul Broca (1824–1880), founder of the An-

thropological Society of Paris and one of Europe's most prestigious anthropologists, recorded a 14 percent difference between the brain weights of women and men; Robert Boyd (1858–1912), a U.S. physician and founder of the Negro Medical Association, calculated a 12 percent advantage in men; Hermann Vierordt (1853–1943), the German physiologist, computed a 14 percent difference.[84]

According to contemporary studies, the brain weight difference between the sexes is 8 percent, a clear discrepancy between current measurements and earlier records of sex differences in absolute brain weight.[85] To account for this divergence, we must look at the techniques used to take and interpret such measurements. When a scientist measures actual brain weight, a number of factors are relevant to later comparisons. Since the brain loses weight with age, the age of the individual at death must be part of the calculation. If female brains are, on the average, taken from older individuals than are male brains and one does not adjust for this difference, one will erroneously attribute to men a larger advantage in absolute brain weight. Similarly, one must know the cause of death and the duration of any disease, for acute infections result in significant brain weight reductions and chronic diseases can result in a 14 percent brain weight loss. Since women tend to die at a later age than men and are more likely to die of chronic illnesses than men, these factors are likely to skew findings.

Furthermore, how a brain is preserved and how long it is stored will affect its weight. Brains were usually preserved in formalin and carbolic acid. The former expands the brain at first, but then causes it to shrink, so that the longer a brain is kept in formalin, the smaller it becomes. It is a common scientific practice to check data that do not fit expectations. Therefore, embarrassing measurements, such as an unusually large female brain, would warrant remeasurement. Doing so, however, would show a smaller brain size than was initially recorded because of the shrinkage caused by the fixing fluids. The scientist's hunch of a "mismeasurement" would be confirmed, and the original calculation would be "corrected."

It would be a mistake to think that these complicating factors were unknown to craniologists. For example, Joseph Barnard Davis (1801–1881), a respected British craniologist, argued for the superiority of skull volume measurements over direct brain weight measurements because the latter are "subject to considerable fluctuations, dependent upon sex, age, the kind of disease with which the person has been affected, and the condition of the organ at the period of death." He noted that "chronic diseases tend to change the proportions between the weight of the brain and the fluids of the cranium."[86]

Since craniologists were aware of the complexities of brain weight calculations, we must conclude that their prejudices account for their skewed results.[87] Scientists expected to find significant differences between the brain weights of women and men, and measurements that confirmed this expectation appeared correct. They therefore had no reason to question the conditions of the testing or to correct for contaminating factors.

One might expect measurements of skull volumes to result in a smaller degree of difference between the brain weights of women and men, since such factors as age and cause of death will not affect the size of the skull. However, the scientists who measured skull volume often documented a sex difference in brain size significantly larger than current measurements. Broca, for example, based his conclusion of a 14 percent brain weight advantage in men solely upon skull volume measurements. Two major factors account for this discrepancy: the determination of the sex of the skull and the technique of measurement. Both of these factors permitted the scientists' biases free reign.

Many craniologists studied skulls discovered in archeological digs or acquired in other circumstances in which the sex of the individual was not known. In such cases they had to determine the sex of each skull from its size and shape. A recent study of such classifications indicated that female crania were incorrectly sexed in 50 percent of the cases![88] Since the scientists expected female skulls to be small, they classified relatively large female skulls as male.

Methods employed to determine skull volume were also inexact. The technique involved filling the skull cavity with a substance, usually shot or seed, that could be removed and weighed. Given the irregularity of the skull, the amount of shot or seed would vary according to how carefully it was packed within. Tapping and shaking the skull would assist the settling of the shot or seed as well as filling up open pockets. Consider this report from a scientist studying the technique of using mustard seed to determine skull capacity.

> . . . I poured in a quantity of seed enough to fill the cavity about half-full, and then gave it a vigorous shaking, so as to get the seed well into the frontal part of the skull; I then filled up the cavity with more seed, to the rim of the foramen magnum, and shook and tapped; the seed of course flowed away in all directions, and I proceeded to fill up, and shake and tap again. This process went on until I was satisfied that I could get practically no more seed into the skull, but one of the greatest difficulties in the operation was to decide when this point was reached: often, when the skull seemed quite full, a turn of the hand would cause the seed to slip away into some unsuspected empty nook.[89]

If a scientist expected a large volume, he or she might be more careful in the packing process than in a case in which a small volume was anticipated.

In addition to problems of measuring techniques, arbitrary explanations were frequently offered to discount findings in favor of women. Davis, for example, when measuring skull volume, deducted 15 percent from the total to account for membranes and fluids. However, in a decision reflecting both sexism and racism, upon recording weights higher than expected when measuring the skulls of Bushwomen, he conjectured that "in small brains the membranes will be proportionately heavier than in large ones."[90] Both the underlying theory and the experimental techniques were vague enough to permit a scientist to discount awkward findings.

Although the attempt to explain woman's mental inferiority on the basis of smaller brain size seemed promising at first, it was eventually shown to be flawed. Theorists began to point out that the absolute size of the brain could not be taken as the measure of intelligence, or animals with larger brains than humans would have to be judged superior in intellect.

> Only last year [1899], two public men in England, well known though not of first-class standing, gave it as their reason for voting against a certain citizen claim on behalf of

women that their brains are smaller than men's. Was that merely a popular prejudice, or was there some scientific basis in it? Of course it is not conceivable that they referred to merely absolute size. That would be too childish, for every boy could understand that naturally, as the smaller animal, woman would have the smaller brain, while it would be quite possible that all the same her brain endowment might in proportion be equal, or even ampler than man's.[91]

Some alternate measures were devised. A number of theorists suggested that the relative weight of the brain to the body was the true measure of intelligence. Using this measure, the influential German anatomist Friedrich Tiedemann (1781–1861) and others demonstrated that the female brain, while absolutely lighter than that of the male, was proportionately heavier relative to body weight.[92] But very few theorists concluded from this that the dominant view of woman's intellectual inferiority was erroneous. The majority protested that additional factors must be considered, and they argued for the greater accuracy of other measures. The fact that absolute brain size, in which man has the advantage, was employed as a relevant criterion of intellectual ability for over fifty years before it was abandoned, while the measure of brain weight to body size, which shows a brain weight advantage in woman, was rejected almost immediately as a relevant criterion, testifies to the strength of scientific bias concerning the inferiority of woman. Consider the case of Alexander Sutherland (1852–1902), who in his article "Woman's Brain" quickly rejected the validity of absolute brain size as a measure of intelligence upon noting woman's brain weight superiority:

> The most obvious and most usual [measure] is to compare the brain weight with the body weight. If this be done woman has proportionately a larger brain than man, for Boyd's figures show that she has .50 ounce of brain for every pound of weight in her body, while man has only .47 ounce. Here she has an advantage of 6 per cent. . . . Is the ignominious conclusion then to be swallowed and digested that, after all, instead of being inferior, woman is more richly endowed with brain than man? Morphology comes to the rescue by showing that, in proportion to its body weight, the smaller animal has always the larger brain. . . . Simple comparison of brain weight with body weight is, therefore, quite inadmissable. For which relief the male sex owes its thanks.[93]

Sutherland wears his prejudice on his sleeve!

Broca provides another excellent example of the power of prejudice to rule the interpretation of data. He rejected the inference of intellectual equality for woman and man based on measurements of brain weight in proportion to body weight. Despite findings of an advantage for woman on this measurement, Broca continued to insist that woman's smaller absolute brain size was, at least in part, proof of her intellectual inferiority. Broca did not deny that brain size correlated with body size. On the contrary, he used the factor of brain weight in proportion to body weight to argue against the conclusions of his opponent, the French scientist Louis Pierre Gratiolet (1815–1865), who attempted to prove that brain size had nothing to do with intelligence by pointing out that German brains were 100 grams larger than French brains. Despite his use of such a correlation in defense of national honor, Broca rejected its use as an explanation of sex differences, citing the obvious objection that woman is less intelligent than man—a clear case of begging the question. "We might ask if the small size of the female brain depends exclusively on the small size of her body. Tiedemann has proposed this explanation. But we must not forget that women are, on the average, a little less intelligent than men, a difference which we should not exaggerate but which is, nonetheless, real. We are therefore permitted to suppose that the relatively small size of the female brain depends in part upon her physical inferiority and in part upon her intellectual inferiority."[94]

Other measurements were numerous and imaginative, although not always well conceived. One criterion for evaluating such measures was that they be rejected as erroneous if they gave an advantage to woman in terms of intellectual ability. George Manouvrier proposed the comparison of the weight of the brain with that of the thigh bone.[95] J. Blakeman proposed taking stature into account, thereby comparing brain mass relative to body height.[96] Sutherland proposed a measure of the surface area of the brain, arguing that the number of neurons is proportionate to surface area.[97] Broca, Ludwig Buchner and Emil Huschke argued that the frontal lobes, viewed as the seat of the higher mental faculties, were less developed in woman than in man, while the occipital lobes, viewed as the seat of sentiment, were larger in woman.[98] Robert Dunn insisted that in character and complexity of structure, the convolutions of a woman's brain were infantile in quality.[99] One sample of this type of reasoning is illustrative:

> The development of the female brain is less as regards the front portion and greater as regards the top or crown portion in comparison to the male; so that if one looks at a woman's skull from above, its outline approximates to that of two cones with blunted ends joined together at their bases, whereas a man's skull presents from a similar point of view, an egg-like appearance, expanding in the middle and towards the back. It is also a matter of daily observation that, as a rule, the forehead and temples are lower in women than in men. . . . In other words, the woman possesses more crown and middle brain, the man more forehead and thinking brain. Now, according to many scientific experiments, the details of which would lead us too far from the subject, it may be assumed that the front sections of the brain are the seat of the intelligence and higher intellectual activities, that is, the powers of imagination, proportion, and determination, whilst the *locus operandi* of the emotions and feelings lies in the crown or hinder part.[100]

In addition to brain measurements, craniologists pointed to skull characteristics as proof of woman's inferior intellectual capacities. Woman's brain is less developed than man's, Schaaffhausen argued, because the sutures of woman's brain close earlier than do those of man.[101] Gratiolet maintained that the frontal sutures in the cranium of woman close earlier, an explanation he offered to account for the "fact" that woman's frontal lobes are less developed and her occipital lobes more developed than man's.[102] Anders Adolf Retzius (1796–1860), the Swedish anthropologist whose work greatly influenced the development of physical anthropology, believed that the facial angle of the skull corresponded to both skull capacity and the development of the parts of the brain. His conclusion was that, in regard to facial angle, "the female skull approaches in many respects that of the infant, and still more that of the lower races."[103]

The conclusions drawn from these apparent anatomical differences are identical to those asserted by the philosophers: woman's intellect is weaker than man's, she is limited to subjective or practical reason, and she is unable to understand general principles.[104] On the basis of a five-ounce difference in brain weight between the sexes, George Romanes (1848–1894), one of the most brilliant of the second generation of British Darwinists and author of *Mental Evolution in Man,* claimed that on anatomical grounds alone we "should be prepared to expect a marked inferiority of intellectual power" in woman.[105] This is most apparent "in a comparative absence of originality, and this more especially in the higher levels of intellectual work."[106] A woman's knowledge, at its best, is "less wide and deep and thorough than that of a man" for man has "a greater power of amassing knowledge."[107] Although woman's senses are more highly evolved than those of man, "with regard to judgment . . . the female mind stands considerably below the male. It is much more apt to take superficial views of circumstances calling for decision, and also to be guided by less impartiality."[108] In the words of J. McGrigor Allan, an anthropologist and popularizer of this image, if "all the male intellect in the world be suddenly paralysed or annihilated, there is not sufficient development of the abstract principles of justice, morality, truth, or causality and inventive power in the female sex, to hold the mechanism of society together for one week."[109]

The science of craniology provides a fascinating study of the extent to which scientists' presuppositions can influence their experimental design and observational interpretation. Nineteenth-century craniology helped reinforce and rationalize the image of man as more advanced on an evolutionary scale than woman, and thus her intellectual superior. Equally important, it served to ensure that woman's knowledge would in fact be different from that of man's by providing a justification for different educational programs for the two sexes.

BRAINS OR WOMBS: SEX AND EDUCATION

The growing feminist movement of the nineteenth century was viewed by many as a potentially serious threat to the social order. One of the central contentions of feminists was that inequalities in the abilities of woman and man resulted from differences in the socialization and education of the sexes. Some feminists denied the existence of essential sex differences between the minds of woman and man, and argued instead that if girls received the same education as boys, they would develop the same mental abilities. The response to such claims was predictable. According to George Harris, president of the Anthropological Society of Manchester:

> Any efforts to obliterate this difference, or to assimilate the nature of the two [sexes], by engaging either in pursuits proper only for the other, are but attempts to violate nature, and as such can never be successful, except to prove the folly and futility of all such exertions. Against undertakings of this kind the voice of nature, the

experience of all time, and in all nations, savage as well as civilized, raise their decided protest. Change their pursuits, their studies, their style of education, as you may, male and female, in all their characteristics, in their dispositions and their capacities, will still exhibit the same peculiarities throughout, marked and distinct as ever.[110]

In addition to scientific documentation of anatomical differences between brains, defenders of essential biological differences between the sexes drew upon the work of Hermann von Helmholtz (1821–1894) in thermodynamics, particularly his principle of conservation of energy. Spencer worked out the application of this principle to the human body.[111] According to him, each body forms a closed system, which contains only a finite amount of energy. Since the functioning of each organ requires expenditure of energy, any undue demand placed upon one organ inevitably depletes some other. The organs of the body were thus seen as competing for limited resources. The central battle, according to this theory, was between the brain and the reproductive organs—two of the most powerful organs of the human body. It was believed that the brain could be developed only at the expense of the reproductive organs and vice versa.

This theory was then applied to the traditional view that reproduction is central to woman's biological life, while rationality is central to man's being. Men were warned of the dangers of sexual indulgence, for channeling energy to the sexual organs would use up energy needed to develop their intellectual abilities. Men were urged to cultivate their brains in order to control the power of their sexual drives, and were warned of the dangers of debilitating their energy by unnecessarily "spending their seed." Women, on the other hand, were told that they must ensure the development of their reproductive organs, since procreation was their function and goal in life. Add to this the neo-Darwinian view that the female contributes far greater energy to reproduction than does the male, and the inescapable conclusion was that woman's developmental energy must be devoted to reproduction at the expense of her intellectual abilities.

Nineteenth-century scientific views concerning menstruation contributed to the credibility of this conclusion. It was believed that during menstruation, the vast majority of a woman's energy was taken up by her reproductive organs. Any attempt to channel energy for another purpose would cause an imbalance in her body, resulting in exhaustion, infection, or disorders of the reproductive organs, which in turn might cause pathological reactions in other parts of the body. Charles Meigs (1792–1869), a leader in nineteenth-century U.S. obstetrics, claimed that after five or six weeks of education, a woman who had previously been healthy would "lose the habit of menstruation" and suffer numerous ills—the result of depriving her body for the sake of her mind. A young woman who is busy at her studies "is too busy with the mind to attend to the body—the confinement, the study, the devotion of innervative power to thinking in one train of thought, prevents the healthful innervation of the muscles, the skin, the alimentary apparatus—the biliary organs give way, the kidneys fail to cast out the nitrogenous surplusage of the economy, and the whole mass of blood loses its fine and delicate crasis, and the endangium itself loses the power to keep up the constitution of the blood to its normal standard."[112]

These theorists insisted that all intellectual endeavors must be suspended during menstruation, yet another proof of the impossibility of the intellectual equality of woman and man. "In intellectual labour, man has surpassed, does now, and always will surpass woman, for the obvious reason that nature does not periodically interrupt his thought and application."[113] The opinion of much of the medical establishment was that menstruation caused a type of temporary mental instability if not insanity:

> Although the duration of the menstrual period differs greatly according to race, temperament, and health, it will be within the mark to state that women are unwell, from this cause, on the average two days in the month, or say one month in the year. At such times, women are unfit for any great mental or physical labour. They suffer under a languor and depression which disqualify them for thought or action, and render it extremely doubtful how far they can be considered responsible beings while the crisis lasts. Much of the inconsequent conduct of women, their petulance, caprice, and irritability, may be traced directly to this cause. It is not improbable that instances of feminine cruelty (which startle us as so inconsistent with the normal gentleness of the sex) are attributable to mental excitement caused by this periodical illness.[114]

The general conclusion was that education could never make woman the intellectual equal of man. Any attempt in this direction would go against the dictates of nature and would permanently damage woman's finer sensibilities as well as her reproductive abilities, resulting in sickly, irritable babies. This view is nowhere more clearly developed than in *Sex in Education, or a Fair Chance for the Girls,* a book written by Edward Clarke (1820–1877) during the height of the demand for coeducation and the admission of women to universities. Harvard University, where Clarke was a member of the medical faculty, was considering establishing Radcliffe as an annex. Based on an extensive review of scientific theories of woman's nature, including those of Darwin and Spencer, Clarke concluded that higher education would result in irreparable damage to women's constitutions and their childbearing capabilities. This text was very popular, going through seventeen editions in a few years, and served as the basis for many other attacks on higher education for women.

Interestingly enough, Clarke was willing to admit that the brains of woman and man did not differ anatomically in any significant respect, justifying the exclusion of woman from higher education solely on the basis of her sexual organs. "Woman, in the interest of the race, is dowered with a set of organs peculiar to herself, whose complexity, delicacy, sympathies, and force are among the marvels of creation. If properly nurtured and cared for, they are a source of strength and power to her. If neglected and mismanaged, they retaliate upon their possessor with weakness and disease, as well of the mind as of the body."[115]

According to Clarke, a girl's passage into puberty is much more costly and sudden than that of a boy, who not only expends less energy in puberty, but also experiences a gradual development into maturity. There is thus a period, the years between fourteen and twenty, when the majority of a woman's energy must be devoted to reproductive development. During this time, if sufficient energy is not available, a woman's reproductive organs will be permanently damaged. "Nature has reserved the catamenial week for the process of ovulation, and for the development and perfection of the reproductive system. Previously to the age of eighteen or twenty, opportunity must be periodically allowed for the accomplishment of this task. Both muscular and brain labor must be remitted enough to yield sufficient force for the work. If the reproductive machinery is not manufactured then, it will not be later. If it is imperfectly made then, it can only be patched up, not made perfect, afterwards."[116]

Clarke thus opposed advanced education for women on the grounds that it would occur just at the crucial age when a woman's energy must be devoted to reproductive development. Stealing energy from her reproductive organs to develop the brain would be to risk sterility and nervous breakdown. To illustrate the potential dangers of advanced education for women, Clarke offered a host of examples of women who, although successful in college, suffered various illnesses, including amenorrhea, menorrhagia, dysmenorrhea, hysteria, anemia, and chorea. He warned that the illnesses caused by advanced education were cumulative and would affect a woman long after her studies were completed.

One such example was the case of Miss E. On Clarke's reckoning, Miss E had a "right to a good brain," for her father was one of the America's leading scholars and her mother one of the most "accomplished American women." Her parents gave her literary training, but although Miss E's health seemed unimpaired by her studies, Clarke found that her well-being was illusory. At the age of twenty-one, her "catamenial function began to show signs of failure of power," and soon ceased altogether. She then began to suffer severe headaches, as well as "forbodings and despondent feelings." Unable to cure her, Clarke was "obliged to consign her to an asylum."[117] Influenced by Clarke's speculations, numerous studies were published at the turn of the century documenting the increase of insanity among educated women.[118]

The upshot of Clarke's position is that a woman receives an advanced education only at the expense of her womanhood.

A woman, whether married or unmarried, whether called to the offices of maternity or relieved from them, who has been defrauded by her education or otherwise of such an essential part of her development, is not so much of a woman, intellectually and morally as well as physically, in consequence of this defect. Her nervous system and brain, her instincts and character, are on a lower plane, and incapable of their harmonious and best development, if she is possessed, on reaching adult age, of only a portion of a breast and an ovary, or none at all.[119]

Clarke charged the practice of supporting advanced education for women with destroying U.S. society, attributing the falling U.S. birthrate to the degeneration of women's reproductive organs caused by education. He predicted that members of the poor, uneducated, and immigrant classes would soon outnumber the middle class, whose reproductive capacity he insisted would be unalterably diminished. Using warnings of race suicide and moral degeneration, Clarke therefore rejected equal educational opportunity for women as a "crime before God and humanity."[120]

Clarke thus mounted a defense of his book's theme: U.S. education does not give a fair chance to the girls. It does not allow for their full development as women. Enlightened systems of female education must, according to Clarke, take women's reproductive development into account, so that girls study fewer hours than do boys and have a monthly intermission in their course of study.

Views like those of Philo, that woman should strive to be like man, were overthrown by nineteenth-century scientists. They feared that any attempt by women to become equal to men would enervate the individual woman and, if taken to an extreme via higher education for women, would ultimately lead to the weakening of the race. These beliefs ensured that few women would be willing, or if willing, allowed, to attempt the life of the mind, defined by philosophy as masculine. As we will see, the belief that woman's strength lay in the realm of the instincts and the sentiments, rather than reason, resulted in an interesting twist to the question of the moral capacities of the sexes.

FOUR

The Less Noble Sex

Like reason, the moral faculty traditionally has been interpreted as one that distinguishes man from other animals and connects him to the divine. Many accounts link moral and rational abilities, with knowledge of the good obtained through reason. Given the view that woman's rational faculty is inferior to man's, the perception of woman as man's moral inferior is not surprising.

PASSION AND LUST:
CLASSICAL AND CHRISTIAN IMAGES

Woman was usually seen as morally inferior to man. Consider one of the first women, Pandora. Hesiod stated in his *Works and Days* that justice distinguishes humans from other animals, and Pandora was created with "the mind of a bitch and a thievish nature."[1] This lying tendency of woman makes her less capable of possessing the virtue of justice; she is more like an animal, concerned with the satisfaction of immediate wants and basing her actions on desire. "You trust a thief when you trust a woman."[2] Woman's weaker sense of justice makes her more likely to act immorally and thereby bring misery to man. "The price for the stolen fire will be a gift of evil / to charm the hearts of all men as they hug their own doom."[3] Pandora and the wicked womenfolk who are her descendants are more animal than human in regard to moral ability.

Or consider Eve, or at least the Eve of the second creation myth in Genesis, who was created from the rib of Adam rather than the dust of the universe, was approached by the serpent of evil, and was deceived by its lies. It was Eve, not Adam, who succumbed to the serpent's temptation. It was Eve whose weakness led to the fall of Adam and to the sickness, toil, and death that all humans must endure. As with Pandora, Eve's moral weakness was the cause of man's suffering.

Classical science accounted for woman's moral inferiority in terms of the humors of her body. Believing the female sex to be the result of a defect in heat, theorists argued that woman's humors would be moister than those of man, whose greater heat removed such moisture. And moisture was associated with the passions. Plato, for example, argued that its excess caused incontinence of pleasure. "The truth is that sexual intemperance is a disease of the soul due chiefly to the moisture and fluidity which is produced in one of the elements by the loose consistency of the bones."[4] This is a situation in which the soul is rendered foolish and disordered by the ill disposition of the body. Since woman is by nature moister than man, she is far more apt to be controlled by her passions. Woman's coldness thus accounts for her relative lack of moral ability.

Aristotle reinforced this image of woman, for his biology predicated woman's nature upon her defect in heat. Not only was woman misbegotten in body, according to Aristotle, but her lack of heat generated numerous psychological differences between the sexes. Woman "is more mischievous, less simple, more impulsive, and more attentive to the nurture of the young."[5] Woman "is more jealous, more querulous, more apt to scold and to strike. She is furthermore, more prone to despondency and less hopeful than the man, more void of shame, more false of speech, more deceptive."[6] Aristotle's biological theory of human nature rose out of the social prejudice that woman was a deviation from the true, male form. But his theory, in turn, reinforced the prejudice by positing a causal mechanism to account for this perceived inferiority. Just as the chorus of gods created Pandora with a lying and thievish nature, woman's lack of heat results in her deceptive, jealous nature. Woman's defective body renders her less moral than man.

Aristotle was very clear in identifying the distinguishing characteristic of human beings—knowledge of justice. "It is a characteristic of man that he alone has any sense of good and evil, of just and unjust."[7] But such perceptions of justice are possible only through reason, when emotions are under the control of the mind. "A living creature consists in the first place of soul and body, and of these two, the one is by nature the ruler and the other subject . . . it is clear that the rule of the soul over the body, and of the mind and the rational element over the passionate, is natural and expedient."[8] However, woman's physiology precludes the full exercise of reason, making her incapable of controlling her emotions, and devoid of a full understanding of justice.

Hesiod described woman as man's punishment, for man must spend his life balancing the good and bad in woman lest her bad qualities overwhelm her good ones. Both Plato and Aristotle agreed with Hesiod, arguing that the passions must be controlled by reason, but woman's inferior rational faculties are inadequate to control her own passions. Neither denied that woman has a sense of justice, but both held that her inability to master her passions renders her more likely to act unjustly.

That inability continues to be a major theme in Christian images of woman's moral capacities. For Philo, moral progress involves the transcendence of the senses and bodily passions through reason. Since woman's mind is "devoid of steadfastness and firm foundation," she is unable to set aside her desires and falls prey to passion. Not only is woman more likely than man to succumb to temptation, she is more prone to be mistaken and deceived about the truth. Given the weakness of her rational faculties, woman "easily gives way and is taken in by plausible falsehoods which resemble the truth."[9] Like Eve with the serpent, woman often unwittingly sins.

The Christian tradition retains a theme similar to that of the Pandora myth— woman is an evil unto man. This theme is directly tied to the belief that woman is unable to control her passions. In the Western tradition, lust has been the most powerful and dangerous passion. Behind this Christian view is a Pandora-like image—a woman controlled by her sexual desires, a sexual trap for man. This theme is explicit in the *Testament of Rubin*.

> Women are evil, my children: because they have no power or strength *to stand up* against a man, they use wiles and try to ensnare him by *their* charms; and *man*, whom *woman* cannot subdue by strength, she subdues by guile. For, indeed, the angel of God told me about them and taught me that women yield to the spirit of fornication more *easily* than man *does*, and they lay plots in *their* hearts against men: by the way they adorn themselves they first lead their minds astray, and by a look they instill poison, and then in the act *itself* they take them captive—for a woman cannot overcome a man by force. So shun fornication, my children, and command your wives and daughters not to adorn their heads and faces, for every woman that uses wiles of this kind has been reserved for eternal punishment.[10]

In creating Pandora, Zeus ordered Aphrodite to pour "stinging desire and limb-gnawing passion" on the maiden's head, giving woman a sexual drive that can "roast even a stalwart man and age him before his time."[11] The daughters of Eve, yielding to lust more easily than men, were seen as posing a temptation that man must avoid at all costs. In a passage from Proverbs often quoted in Christian literature, men are warned that "the lips of a loose woman drip honey, / and her speech is smoother than oil; / but in the end she is bitter as wormwood, / sharp as a two-edged sword. / Her feet go down to death; / her steps follow the path to Sheol" (Proverbs 5:3–5). Not only is woman less moral than man, she poses the greatest threat to man's morality.

This theme, that the wickedness of woman is the result of her inability to control her sexual passions, is central to the medieval view of witchcraft. In the *Malleus Maleficarum*, Sprenger and Kramer argued that "all witchcraft comes from carnal lust, which is in woman insatiable. . . . Wherefore for the sake of fulfilling their lusts they consort even with devils."[12] In other words, because of the strength of her passions, woman is willing to reject the Christian faith and ally with Satan in order to find sexual satisfaction. "Three general vices appear to have special dominion over wicked women, namely, infidelity, ambition, and lust . . . since of these three vices the last chiefly predominates, women being insatiable, etc., it follows that those among ambitious women are more deeply infected who are more hot to satisfy their filthy lusts; and such are adulteresses, fornicatresses, and the concubines of the Great [Satan]."[13]

The classical and Christian views of woman's nature delineated the moral defectiveness of woman. Woman was not without a sense of good and evil, but she was less able to control her passions and thus less likely to choose the good, especially if it were contrary to her desires. Woman's moral defect was tied to her inferior rational faculty; since her mental abilities were less developed than those of man, she was often unable to follow the guide of reason and instead acted according to her passions. It was believed that woman's sexual passions frequently led her from the path of good and, if not controlled, could cause man's downfall. These themes continued to be a central component of both philosophical and scientific conceptions of woman's moral abilities.

MODEST WOMEN AND JUST MEN:
EIGHTEENTH- AND NINETEENTH-CENTURY IMAGES

Eighteenth- and nineteenth-century philosophical and scientific investigations of woman's moral abilities reflected the influence of earlier Christian views. Although theorists often supported a view of complementarity rather than inferiority, they endorsed tenets almost identical to the earlier views: woman is incapable of understanding general principles; woman acts on the basis of desires and tastes; woman follows the guide of the senses rather than that of reason. Relabeling the very same qualities that were once used to prove woman's inferiority as "complementary traits" does little to change people's values. Furthermore, these same theorists continued to emphasize the sexual power of woman, her ability to control a man's actions through promise of sex. Although a philosopher might emphasize the ways in which a woman could use this power to aid men, the power of sexual attraction remained a double-edged sword, for it was made clear that it could hinder as easily as it could assist.

THE MARRIAGE OF REASON AND MORALITY.

Philosophical conceptions of morality in the eighteenth and nineteenth centuries were directly influenced by the Cartesian view of rationality, with its privileging of masculine characteristics. Many philosophers posited reason as the sole, or at least primary, source of moral action: Moral principles came to be viewed as universal, valid for all individuals and knowable by any rational agent.

The moral philosophy of Immanuel Kant (1724–1804) epitomizes this centering of moral action on reason. To be moral, by Kant's account, one must base her or his actions on the universal law of morality, what he called the categorical imperative: "I should never act except in such a way that I can also will that my maxim should become a universal law."[14] In his *Grounding for the Metaphysics of Morals,* Kant argued that an action must be performed from duty alone in order to have moral worth; an action resulting from inclination, even if it happens to accord with duty, is excluded from the moral realm. Giving the example of a person who is naturally sympathetic and who desires to help those in need, Kant maintained, "that in such a case an action of this kind, however dutiful and amiable it may be, has nevertheless no true moral worth."[15] Only the person whose action is divorced from her or his desires or inclinations is capable of acting from duty. It is not necessary that moral persons be without such feelings as sympathy, caring, or love, but they must be able to suspend their feelings in order to base their action on obedience to the categorical imperative. "Only the law itself can be an object of respect and hence can be a command."[16] Kantian moral persons must learn to distance themselves from their emotions and desires and act solely on the basis of reason.

This linking of moral action and reason has obvious consequences for woman. As long as woman is seen as lacking in the rational faculties, she will also be seen as similarly deficient in the moral realm. And this, indeed, was Kant's position.

In his discussion of the sexes in *Observations on the Feeling of the Beautiful and the Sublime*, Kant argued that the sexes possess complementary natures, seeing this complementarity as most obvious in the natures of woman's and man's faculties of understanding. Kant explained that "the fair sex has just as much understanding as the male, but it is a *beautiful understanding*, whereas ours [men's] should be a *deep understanding*, an expression that signifies identity with the sublime."[17] Civilized man has knowledge of general principles, of science and mathematics, and of the nature of the sublime. The subject of civilized woman's understanding is that which is pleasing, that which adorns.[18] Man's knowledge requires meditation, while woman's understanding is intuitive and requires neither education nor reflection. "The virtue of woman is a *beautiful virtue* . . . women will avoid the wicked not because it is unright, but because it is ugly; and virtuous actions mean to them such as are morally beautiful. Nothing of duty, nothing of compulsion, nothing of obligation."[19]

If woman indeed knows nothing of duty, compulsion, or obligation, then she also will know nothing of morality. Kant's direct linkage of reason and moral action, and his denial of woman's rational abilities, result in woman being viewed as amoral, incapable of comprehending moral imperatives.

Jean Jacques Rousseau (1712–1778), a contemporary of Kant, developed a similar view that morality requires a sense of justice based on duty. He rejected theories that based moral sense on instinct or intuition and insisted that it was derived solely from reason. And like Kant, Rousseau excluded woman from the moral realm.

Rousseau also believed that abstract principles are "not within the competence of women."[20] Like Kant's "beautiful understanding," Rousseau attributed to woman the ability to act on the basis of taste, but not the ability to ground her actions in duty or justice. "Consult the taste of women in physical things connected with the judgment of the senses, but consult the taste of men in moral things that depend more on the understanding."[21] Like the medieval theologians before them, Kant and Rousseau associated woman with the realm of the senses, man with that of reason.

The consequence of this exclusion of woman from the moral realm was to see woman as less perfect than man. Rousseau held that the ability to act morally was one of the advances achieved in man's passage from the original state of nature to what he called the civil state. According to Rousseau, this transition is a source of ennoblement, which results in man's transformation from a "stupid, limited animal" to an "intelligent being and a man." The change is produced "by substituting justice for instinct in his behavior," which gives man's actions "the morality they had previously lacked."[22] Since woman is not "substituting justice for instinct," one cannot help but conclude that she is more like a "stupid, limited animal" than an "intelligent being and a man." Woman's defect in reason is sign and symptom of her inferior development, not only morally, but also metaphysically.

THE INSPIRATION OF MAN.

Kant and Rousseau both viewed woman as a source of moral inspiration for man. Rousseau saw woman's power in the sexual desire she produces in man, while Kant believed love to be an additional pillar of this inspiration.

Rousseau's belief in woman's inability to act according to general principles led him to conclude that women must "never cease to be subjected either to a man or to the judgments of men and they are never permitted to put themselves above these judgments."[23] But Rousseau also argued that woman was more clever than man, "a compensation without which women would be not man's companion but his slave." Her cleverness enables her to "govern him while obeying him."[24]

We see in this account of woman's cleverness clear influence of previous views of woman's sexual power over men. Rousseau wrote that this cleverness consists of the "modesty and shame with which nature armed the weak in order to enslave the strong."[25] It is on the basis of man's sexual desire for woman that she is able to "enslave" him. Rousseau believed it to be a "law of nature" that woman is capable of exciting the sexual desires of man beyond his ability to satisfy them. "This causes the latter [man], whether he likes it or not, to depend on the former's [woman's] wish and constrains him to seek to please her in turn, so that she will consent to let him be the stronger."[26]

Rousseau viewed the sexual power of woman as a source of inspiration rather than a "snare more bitter than death." "If woman is made to please and to be subjugated, she ought to make herself agreeable to man instead of arousing him. Her own violence is in her charms. It is by these that she ought to constrain him to find his strength and make use of it. The surest art for animating that strength is to make it necessary by resistance."[27]

As we see, Rousseau's account is not without ambivalence concerning woman's power. Her charm can be an instrument of man's ennoblement, but it is also a potential source of danger. When woman's sexual desires are constrained by modesty and shame, she can inspire man to virtuous acts. But without such constraint, "men would be tyrannized by women. For, given the ease with which women arouse men's senses and reawaken in the depths of their hearts the remains of ardors which are almost extinguished, men would finally be their victims and would see themselves dragged to death without ever being able to defend themselves."[28] Rousseau's image here could have been directly inspired by the "loose" woman of Proverbs whose lips drip honey while her feet go down to death.

Given his recognition that this power of woman could be used for good or for evil, Rousseau was quite insistent that woman's education reinforce her modesty, so that her "charms" and "cleverness" would serve man rather than enslave him. He also believed such education would ensure the continuation of the family. Rousseau believed that a man loves and cares for his children only when the mother "gives him the confidence to call them his own."[29] In other words, a man must have no doubts about his paternity. Such confidence is possible, Rousseau explained, only if women pay "the most scrupulous attention to their conduct, their manners, and their bearing," for a wife must not only be faithful, she must be "judged to be faithful by her husband, by those near her, by everyone."[30] A woman must be "modest, attentive, reserved," and, in all her actions, give evidence of her fidelity.

Kant also emphasized woman's ability to control man. His attitude toward woman's potential for domination is quite similar to that of Rousseau, although Kant included love along with lust as mechanisms by which woman controls man: woman uses "men for her purposes by the love she inspires in them."[31] Additionally, Kant believed that, to some extent, men consent to this control. Using men's love, women are able to "dominate and enchain its [love's] vassals by their [men's] own inclinations . . . [women] use *charm*, which implies a desire on man's part to be dominated."[32]

The charms of woman, with which she "exercises her great power over the other sex," are twofold. Exterior charms are related to sexual attractiveness, and include "a well-proportioned figure, regular features, colors of eyes and face which contrast prettily, beauties pure and simple."[33] Interior charms are the basis upon which a man of noble understanding loves a woman; a woman possessing them "lets the glimmer of a beautiful understanding play forth through discreet glances, and as in her face she portrays a tender feeling and a benevolent heart . . . [or] she exhibits merriment and wit in laughing eyes, something of fine mischief, the playfulness of jest and sly coyness."[34]

Kant stressed the positive aspects of woman's ability to dominate man. This ability is a part of nature's purpose, for it assists in the preservation of the species and enables woman to cultivate and refine society. Woman uses her power over man to make a bond between father and child, without which Kant, like Rousseau, believed man would be unwilling to care for and support his children. Through woman's direction, man "finds himself imperceptibly fettered by a child through his own generosity."[35]

Woman's power is also used to inspire refinement in man and prepare him for a moral life. "Since nature also wanted to instill the more refined feelings that belong to culture—the feelings, namely, of sociability and decorum—it made woman man's ruler through her modesty and her eloquence in speech and expression. It made her precociously shrewd in claiming gentle and courteous treatment by the male, so that he . . . [is] led by it, if not to morality itself, at least to its clothing, the cultivated propriety that is the preparatory training for morality and its recommendation."[36] According to Kant, the principle object of the interaction between man and woman is that "the man should become more perfect as a man, and the woman as a wife; that is, that the motives of the sexual inclination work according to the hint of nature, still more to ennoble the one and to beautify the qualities of the other."[37] We see quite clearly that woman's role is derivative. Intercourse between the sexes will make a man a better man—more moral, more wise. But it will make a woman only a better help to a man—that is, a better wife.

Kant protested that the qualities that have been labeled "female weaknesses" are actually strengths, for they enable woman to gain control over man. But despite Kant's protests, a close examination of his theory reveals the same fears that were expressed by Rousseau and by the theologians who wrote centuries before them both—woman's unbridled sexual passions are a danger to man and to society.

Kant's biases became clear in his discussion of the dangers of "luxury." Kant claimed that in a period of luxury, the institution of marriage would be overthrown. Male adultery, he believed, was compatible with "monogamous" marriage, but adultery on the part of the wife would undermine it. Kant argued that luxury would result in women demanding gallantry on the part of men, which he interpreted as meaning that a woman would make "no secret of having lovers other than her husband."[38] In such a state, "the feminine character reveals itself; by man's leave, woman lays claim to freedom over against man and, at the same time, to the conquest of the whole male sex."[39]

Remove the veneer of the loving woman who inspires man, and we find the danger of control gone awry through the power of woman's insatiable lust. Woman is a source of inspiration for man, but she remains, even in her glory, a danger. Woman under control is a help to man; woman out of control is his destruction.

SCIENTIFIC IMAGES OF WOMAN'S MORALITY.

Eighteenth- and nineteenth-century science contained similar accounts of woman's moral abilities. Influenced by theories such as those of Kant and Rousseau, most scientists accepted the linkage of rationality and morality. In the context of numerous scientific "proofs" of woman's inferior rational capacities, the belief that woman possessed an inferior or, at best, different moral sense was a logical inference.

Scientific argument concerning woman's moral ability was strikingly similar to that of the philosophers. Given the energy woman must devote to reproduction, she is unable to develop her rational faculties as fully as man. In moral situations, woman acts on the basis of emotion and inclination, while man turns to reason for instruction. Charles Meigs explained that "as to the more strictly moral attributes and propensities of the female, what are the facts? Is not her heart, in general, the seat of tenderer and gentler emotions than those of her mate? Her susceptible soul is acutely alive to the human charities and trembling sympathies that spring spontaneously in the delicate innervations of her feminine constitution. She cannot unmoved look on scenes of woe."[40] Seeing another being in need or in pain causes the spontaneous response of sympathy and charity. The scientific view was that woman's role in raising and nurturing children results in a highly developed sense of empathy and altruism.

The moral sensitivities of woman were greatly esteemed in the eighteenth and nineteenth centuries. Lauded as a part of woman's evolutionary development and seen as central to the survival of the species, her heartfelt sympathies were the object of much praise. But although honored, woman's moral sense was nevertheless seen as inferior to that of man. Only man, with his developed rational sense, was capable of the conscious deliberation needed for full morality. The scientific consensus was that the earlier arrest of individual evolution in woman, necessary to meet the costs of reproduction, precluded her full moral development.

Herbert Spencer echoed this sentiment when he wrote that, due to this earlier cessation of individual evolution in woman, "there is a perceptible falling short in those two faculties, intellectual and emotional, which are the latest products of human evolution—the power of abstract reasoning and that most abstract of the emotions, the sentiment of justice."[41] And, like many of his fellow scientists, Spencer concluded that this undeveloped sense of justice prevents woman from participation in the public realm. "The love of the helpless, which in her maternal capacity woman displays in a more special form than man, inevitably affects all her thoughts and sentiments; and, this being joined in her with a less developed sentiment of abstract justice, she responds more readily when appeals to pity are made than when appeals are made to equity . . . and this difference between their ways of estimating consequences, affecting their judgments on social affairs as on domestic affairs, makes women err still more than men do in seeking what seems an immediate public good without thought of distant public evils."[42]

Careful attention to the literature also reveals a residual distrust of woman's sensitivities, a fear that her tastes might be undeveloped or misused. Notice, for example, how conflicted Meigs is about woman's modesty. "Women possess a peculiar trait—it is modesty—and is one of the most charming of their attributes; springing probably from their natural timidity and sense of dependence. All rude, boisterous, and immodest speech or action unsexes and disgraces her. This modesty is one of her strongest attractions; *and she sometimes, perhaps, affects to possess it for the purpose of riveting her chains on the conqueror man.*"[43] Given such concerns, many theorists supported the careful training of women's tastes and warned that women must also scrupulously avoid anything that might corrupt them.

THE EGO-LESS WOMAN:
EARLY TWENTIETH-CENTURY IMAGES

There was a movement among nineteenth-century supporters of women's rights to reject the tenet that woman's moral abilities were defective, and replace it with the view that woman was actually the moral superior of man. Interestingly enough, this superiority was based on an image of woman as more sexually reserved than man and thus less subject to the desires of the flesh. This view was championed by many feminists who believed that woman's identification as a sexual being was the major cause of her oppression.[44]

Numerous counterreactions followed such attempts to elevate woman's moral abilities. Perhaps the most extreme was that of Otto Weininger, who accepted both the position that moral acts must be based on absolute principles and the belief that woman is incapable of comprehending such principles. "The absolute female knows neither the logical nor the moral imperative, and the words law and duty, duty towards herself, are words which are least familiar to her."[45] While philosophers and scientists alike attempted to soften such a view by expounding on and praising woman's moral sensitivities arising from modesty and taste, Weininger took the far more extreme step of arguing that woman has no moral sense. "I am not arguing that woman is evil and anti-moral; I state that she can-not be really evil; *she is merely non-moral.*"[46] According to Weininger, woman ex-ists in a stage of evolution prior to the development of a moral sense. She is like a child, knowing neither good nor bad and thus is not responsible for her actions. Woman is an innocent, but Weininger cautioned against viewing such innocence as a privileged stage. "Women have been regarded as virtuous, simply because the problem of morality has not presented itself to them; they have been held to be even more moral than man; this is simply because they do not understand im-morality. The innocence of a child is not meritorious."[47]

Woman, far from being more moral than man, is at a pre-moral stage of de-velopment, and Weininger implicated her biological role in reproduction as the primary cause of that amorality. Woman's only concern is with the propagation of the race, so she values only that which will assist her in this goal. Her existence is so tied to the preservation of the species that she "possesses neither ego nor individuality, personality nor freedom, character nor will."[48] This ego-less woman is capable neither of morality nor rationality. Like a child, she is concerned only with that which satisfies her needs—one of which is her desire to reproduce.

Weininger's solution to the problem that is woman echoes that of the early fa-thers of the Christian church—she must become like man. "The woman question is as old as sex itself, and as young as mankind. And the answer to it? Man must free himself of sex, for in that way, and that way alone, can he free woman. In his purity, not, as she believes, in his impurity, lies her salvation. She must certainly be destroyed, as woman; but only to be raised again from the ashes—new, re-stored to youth—as a real human being."[49]

While many late nineteenth- and early twentieth-century feminists marched under the banner of woman's more refined moral sensibilities, contemporary philosophical and scientific theories belied their protests. What these feminists missed was that the tenet of woman's inferior moral sense for centuries had been grounded in what theorists perceived to be her biological and psychological role in the family. Theories concerning the nature of woman's sexual drives were de-rived from the same source. By denying that women experienced sexual desire, these feminists were, at best, undercutting one leg of the scientific and philo-sophical edifice. They failed to remove the primary foundation: woman as defined by her reproductive functions.

The failure of feminist accounts of woman's moral superiority was assured by the eventual impact of Sigmund Freud (1856–1939), who made a clear case for the inferiority of woman's moral development that was to be accepted for de-cades. Although his conclusions were similar to those of earlier theorists, his sci-ence of the mind located the cause of woman's moral deficiency in her psychological development rather than in her intellectual capacities.

Freud predicated the moral abilities of humans on the development of the su-perego, that part of the psyche that controls the libido and the instincts. Only through the development of the superego are humans capable of overcoming their personal needs and desires. The superego enables humans to transcend subjec-tivity and ground their actions in the objective realm of morality. Although his explanation is different, Freud is in concert with earlier theorists in holding that woman is less capable than man of acting on the basis of justice and duty. He argued that the development of the superego is a prerequisite for moral action, then claimed that woman's formation of a superego is incomplete.

According to Freudian theory, an important stage in a young male's development is the so-called Oedipus complex. Freud explained that as a boy develops his phallic sexuality, he naturally comes to desire his mother as a sexual object and perceives his father as a rival for his mother's attention. At this stage, the boy desires to possess his mother and get rid of his father. Since the father is both physically strong and endowed with authority, Freud believed that the boy would fear castration by his father as punishment for his mother-love and father-hatred. Then, "under the impression of the danger of losing his penis, the Oedipus complex is abandoned, repressed and, in the most normal cases, entirely destroyed, and a severe super-ego is set up as its heir."[50] Fear of castration is thus the catalyst for the development of the boy's superego.

Freud believed that girls' development differs significantly from that of boys. "They notice the penis of a brother or playmate, strikingly visible and of large proportions, at once recognize it as the superior counterpart of their own small and inconspicuous organ, and from that time forward fall a victim to envy for the penis."[51] This envy "will leave ineradicable traces on their development and the formation of their character and which will not be surmounted in even the most favourable cases without a severe expenditure of psychical energy."[52] Realizing that her mother shares the same lack, a girl turns her attention to her father. Like the boy, the girl recognizes the power and authority of the father; rather than fear it, Freud claimed that she takes comfort from it, believing that her lack of a penis can be compensated by a "penis-baby" given to her by her father. "The feminine situation is only established, however, if the wish for a penis is replaced by one for a baby."[53]

A key difference between the psychological development of girls and boys in this Freudian account is that the boy both hates and fears his father during the Oedipal stage, but the girl neither hates nor fears her mother. "It is only in the male child that we find the fateful combination of love for the one parent and simultaneous hatred for the other as rival."[54] Freud explained that since the girl is like the mother, she realizes that her role is not to possess the father, but rather to be possessed by him. So the mother represents not the girl's rival, but her limitation. The goal of the Oedipal stage for the girl, then, is to become passive instead of active. The girl resolves her Oedipus complex through a feminine attitude of passive love for the father, as opposed to the boy's active attempt to possess his mother. The boy wishes to possess; the girl wishes to be possessed.

According to Freud, the Oedipal experience is quite different for girls than it is for boys. It is a place of refuge for the girl, where she finds comfort from the pain caused by her recognition of her lack of a penis, and which contains the promise of a substitute—a baby. The boy, however, finds that the Oedipal stage carries with it the castration complex, a fear so great that there is strong motive to abandon the Oedipal phase through development of the superego. The girl, Freud explained, having experienced the anxiety of believing that she has been castrated previously, finds only refuge in the Oedipal stage, and has little motive to repress it and replace it with the superego. "The girl is driven out of her attachment to her mother through the influence of her envy for the penis and she enters the Oedipus situation as though into a haven of refuge. In the absence of fear of castration the chief motive is lacking which leads boys to surmount the Oedipus complex. Girls remain in it for an indeterminate length of time; they demolish it late and, even so, incompletely. In these circumstances the formation of the superego must suffer."[55]

Having posited the incomplete development of the superego in woman, Freud argued that this has significant effects on woman's character and abilities, including a larger amount of narcissism and vanity, a need to be loved that is stronger than the need to love, a predominance of envy, weakness in social interests, and a weakened capacity for the sublimation of instincts.[56] Accepting the position that morality requires a sense of justice and the ability to replace instinct with duty, Freud concluded that woman's inability to surmount the Oedipal stage condemns her to moral inferiority. A sense of justice requires transcendence of envy, he explained, and woman's lack of a penis results in a sense of envy that she is incapable of fully controlling.[57] Thus, woman is tied to the instincts and feelings and only man is capable of overcoming them to reach the moral stage.

Despite his radically different account of the cause of woman's moral inferiority, Freud's conclusions echo those of earlier theorists. In fact, Freud interpreted this similarity as a confirmation of his theory. "Character-traits which critics of every epoch have brought up against women—that they show less sense of justice than men, that they are less ready to submit to the great exigencies of life, that they are more often influenced in their judgments by feelings of affection or hostility—all these would be amply accounted for by the modification in the formation of their super-ego which we have inferred above."[58]

Freud's views on sublimation are also relevant to his account of woman's inferior moral development. According to Freud, the works of civilization—putting the good of the community before the good of the individual—require sublimation of the instincts. But because women "represent the interests of the family and the sexual life" (that is, they work for individual goods), they have little concern for the good of the community. Only men are capable of the sublimation necessary for action based on duty.[59] Freud also argued that woman's weaker capacity for sublimation results in part from the greater labor involved in her ego formation: the process of developing gender identity is more difficult for girls in that it involves two additional stages.

By Freud's account of the earlier phallic phase, sexual attention in both sexes is concentrated on the penis or, in the girl, the "penis-equivalent," the clitoris, Freud insisted that during the evolution to the Oedipal stage, the girl must change her erogenous zone. "With the change to femininity the clitoris should wholly or in part hand over its sensitivity, and at the same time its importance, to the vagina."[60] The boy's development is simpler since he retains the same erogenous zone, the penis, throughout the various stages. "The more fortunate man has only to continue at the time of his sexual maturity the activity that he has previously carried out at the period of the early efflorescence of his sexuality."[61]

In addition to this transfer of sexual attention from the clitoris to the vagina, a girl must also make her father, instead of her mother, the object of her attraction. Given Freud's assumption that women are the primary caretakers of children, a child's first object of love will be her or his mother. So, the Oedipal stage occurs in the boy without any transfer, for he continues to see his mother as his primary love object. But a girl must shift from her mother to her father as a love-object in order to enter the Oedipal stage. Thus a girl's development is more complex than that of a boy, for she must change both the location of sexual attention and her love object.

Freud concluded that the complexity of a girl's psychological development inhibits the full development of her superego, making her less capable of sublimation. In addition, the passivity that a girl adopts in entering the Oedipal stage further undercuts her ability to sublimate, since ego development requires an active, individuating subject. And even if a girl successfully attains gender identity by changing both the object of her love and her erogenous zone, the very identity she has worked so hard to develop, femininity, precludes full ego development! The girl is clearly in a no-win situation. Freud concluded that woman is "little capable" of instinctual sublimation.[62] This inability ties woman to the realm of the passions and inhibits her full moral development.

Man's development of the superego and his fuller ego development enable him to come to terms with the sexual and to overcome it. Since woman is unable to overcome the sexual through her own abilities, she must be brought up to suppress it. We see here Freud's theory repeating the millennia-long fear of woman's "rampant" sexuality. Even his mechanism for repression is similar to earlier accounts. Freud held that girls must be raised in such a way that any sexual curiosity is immediately condemned as unnatural and sinful, and they must be frightened into avoiding their natural interests in sexuality, so that sex is viewed with fear and repugnance.[63] In this way, Freud believed, women would avoid the excesses of sexuality that they are otherwise incapable of controlling.

Interestingly, Freud also attributed woman's intellectual inferiority to this repressive upbringing. He posited no innate impediment to woman's intellectual development; rather, he explained that in the process of being forbidden any intellectual curiosity about sexuality, girls "are scared away from *any* form of thinking, and knowledge loses its value for them."[64] So woman's intellect is suppressed along with her sexuality. Instead of condemning the sexual repression of woman because of this result, Freud argued that such inhibition of thought is necessary for the good of society, since woman's sexual instincts cannot be otherwise controlled.

We thus see in Freud's account a number of themes that have been repeated by theorists for centuries. He posits the male as the ideal. It is the masculine personality that represents the completion of human psychological development, while the female remains an incomplete male. Lacking both the physiological and psychological capacities of the male, she is identified through her incapacities.

Normal femininity is defined as undeveloped in comparison to masculinity. Woman is seen as more tied to the instinctual, the emotional, and the sexual. She is less capable of controlling her desires, and so must be controlled by man for her own good and for the good of society.

Therefore, woman's inferior moral sense results from a deficiency. Often it is an intellectual deficiency, which is traced to a defect in heat or to some otherwise arrested development. The cause of woman's moral inferiority was frequently associated with her sexual passions, but throughout the centuries it was ultimately tied to woman's role in the family and in reproduction. Whether theorists posited a physiological mechanism (the amount of energy expended in reproduction) or a psychological one, the conclusions were the same: woman's moral sense, is, at best, the result of inclination or training. Only man is capable of the highest stage of morality in which acts are based on duty or justice. Woman is the less noble sex.

FIVE

The Hysteria of Woman

Beliefs about reproduction are a central and generative factor in images of woman's nature. Woman's arrested development, woman as a natural mutation, her weaker cognitive abilities, her inferior moral sense, her greater propensity for sin—all these are intimately related, in complex ways, to the conclusion that the reproductive process takes a greater toll on woman than on man. This premise has been largely responsible for the idea that woman's reproductive organs play a more significant role in her physical and mental health than do those of man.

Classical scientists saw the uterus as having such a major impact on a woman's physical health that any uterine disorder could endanger her seriously. This womb/well-being correlation remained a part of medical theory well into the twentieth century. However, between the seventeenth and nineteenth centuries, there was a shift in perception of the potential effects of woman's sexual organs on the mind as well as the body. Earlier, medical theorists stressed the ways in which disorders of the womb affected woman's physical health. But by the beginning of the nineteenth century, theories were focused more on their effects on woman's mental health.

WANDERING WOMBS

Classical medical theory defined "hysteria" as a disorder of woman caused by disturbances of the womb. This view is reflected in the etymology of the term, since its root is the Greek word *hystera*, which means uterus.[1] Some physicians believed that the uterus could become dislocated and move around in the body, causing various maladies. They offered numerous explanations for this wandering womb phenomenon.

Scientists of the classical period viewed intercourse as a necessary part of humans' physical well-being. The majority of physicians argued against continence on the grounds that it would result in disease. Since the condition of the womb was considered central to a woman's general health, these physicians frequently prescribed intercourse and pregnancy as cures for women's ills. According to Hippocrates (460?–?377 BCE), a lack of intercourse would result in the uterus becoming dry and cold. "The womb is not damp of its own accord (as, for example, in the case of a woman who does not have coitus) and there is empty space for the womb (as, for example, when the belly is more empty than usual) so that the womb is displaced when the woman is drier and more empty than normal."[2]

Male seminal fluids were seen as necessary for the health of the uterus, since they provide this needed moisture. Hippocrates claimed that the womb, deprived of such fluids, would dry up and, especially when it was "heated" from exertion, would go in search of moisture within the woman's body: hence, a wandering womb. This would cut off respiration and hamper the function of the liver.

> If suffocation occurs suddenly, it will happen especially to women who do not have intercourse and to older women rather than to young ones, for their wombs are lighter. It usually occurs because of the following: when a woman is empty and works harder than in her previous experience, her womb, becoming heated from the hard work, turns because it is empty and light. There is, in fact, empty space for it to turn in because the belly is empty. Now when the womb turns, it hits the liver and they go together and strike against the abdomen—for the womb rushes and goes upward toward the moisture, because it has been unduly heated by hard work, and the liver is, after all, moist. When the womb hits the liver, it produces sudden suffocation as it occupies the breathing passage around the belly.[3]

While viewing intercourse as necessary for a healthy womb, classical theorists did prescribe moderation. Physicians believed that too much sex could result in the displacement of the womb as easily as too little. Aristotle explained this was often the case, "owing to excessive desire, arising either from youthful impetuosity or from lengthened abstinence, prolapsion of the womb takes place and the menses appear repeatedly, thrice in the month, until conception occurs; and then the womb withdraws upward again to its proper place."[4] Like Hippocrates, Aristotle prescribed intercourse in "moderate" doses and pregnancy as the cure for female illnesses.[5]

The Hippocratic theory was perpetuated by many classical writers. Plato, in the Timaeus, depicted the womb as an animal with desires and emotions. "The animal within them is desirous of procreating children, and when remaining unfruitful long beyond its proper time, get discontented and angry, and wandering in every direction through the body, closes up the passages of the breath, and, by obstructing respiration, drives them to extremity, causing all varieties of disease."[6] Aretaeus, the first-century Greek physician who wrote an influential text on the cause, symptoms, and treatment of acute and chronic diseases, also characterized the uterus as an erratic animal. "In the middle of the flanks of women lies the womb, a female viscus, closely resembling an animal; for it is moved of itself hither and thither in the flanks . . . in a word, it is altogether erratic."[7]

Aretaeus believed that the womb, being like an animal, would delight in and follow fragrant smells, and be repelled by fetid smells. Thus, he advised that if a woman's uterus had traveled upward, rubbing fragrant oils, like cinnamon, into the female parts would attract it. If the woman partially recovers, "she is to be seated in a decoction of aromatics, and fumigated from below with fragrant perfumes."[8] This would cure "sluggishness in the performance of her offices, prostration of strength, atony, loss of the faculties of her knees, vertigo, and the limbs sink[ing] under her; headache, heaviness of the head."[9] If the uterus had traveled downward, this could be remedied by applying fetid smells to the genital region, which would cause the womb to run back to its original position. These were Aretaeus's cures for "pulse intermittent, irregular, and failing; strong sense of choking; loss of speech and sensibility; respiration imperceptible and indistinct; a very sudden and incredible death."[10]

HYSTERICAL FITS

Careful attention to anatomy belied the womb's ability to wander freely around the body, and by the end of the classical period this view had been generally rejected. Although the practice of science is an intricate part of the social and cultural context in which it is practiced, the beliefs and values of scientists are always subject to empirical evaluation; indeed, this complex evidential relationship serves as one of the limits of science. Some theories fit the data better than others, and recalcitrant data can lead to theory revision.[11] The case of classical anatomical studies of the structure of the uterus is a good example of how empirical investigations result in theory revision. The tenet that the uterus was a free-floating organ was rejected because of careful observations. However, although the anatomical error was corrected, many of perceptions related to it were maintained. The uterus continued to be seen as a cause of numerous ills, including hysterical fits.

Soranus of Ephesus, a second-century physician whose *Gynecology* would influence gynecological tradition well into the seventeenth century, explicitly attacked medical theories that conceive of the uterus as an animal, to be attracted or repelled by smells. "We, however, censure all these men who start by hurting the inflamed parts and cause torpor by the effluvia of ill-smelling substances."[12] Soranus denied that the uterus moves because of any desire for a smell or even for moisture, but acknowledged that it could be displaced—"it is drawn together because of the stricture caused by the inflammation."[13] He argued that inflammation of the uterus could result in hysterical suffocation, causing seizures similar to those of epilepsy or apoplexy. Interestingly, he also argued that frequent pregnancies, especially when fetuses are large, would result in atony (weakness) of the uterus. This, in turn, might cause "melancholic madness and mania."[14]

Although until the nineteenth century emphasis was upon the physical ailments to which women were prone because of their sexual organs, a connection between the uterus and madness had been established almost two millennia earlier. The second-century physician and anatomist Galen of Pergamon, for example, also attributed hysterical fits to diseased uteri. He argued that retention of female semen would result in a corruption of the blood, which in turn caused a cooling of the body and an irritation of the nerves that would then manifest itself in a fit. Aulus Cornelius Celsus, writing in the first century CE, described such a fit in *On Diseases of the Womb*. "Females are subject to a malignant disease of the womb: and next to the stomach, this organ is highly susceptible of being affected either in itself, or by sympathy affects the rest of the body. Sometimes this affection deprives the patient of all sensibility, in the same manner as if she had fallen in epilepsia. Yet with this difference, that neither the eyes are turned, nor does foam flow from the mouth, nor are there any convulsions: there is only a profound sleep."[15]

Medical theory remained strongly influenced by such views well into the eighteenth century. Dame Trotula of Salerno, author of an eleventh-century medical handbook on the diseases of women, adopted an Aristotelian view of woman's physical inferiority. She held that since women were "by nature weaker than men it is reasonable that sickness more often abound in them especially around the organs involved in the work of nature."[16] Trotula noted that when the womb is choked or otherwise suffocated, it causes various maladies, including vomiting, fainting, and convulsions. Her explanation of the cause parallels that of Galen: "This happens to women because too much spoiled seed abounds in them and it changes to a poisonous character. Especially does this happen to those who have no husbands, widows in particular and those who previously have been accustomed to make use of carnal intercourse. It also happens in virgins who have come to marriageable years and have not yet husbands for in them abounds the seed which nature wished to draw out by means of the male."[17]

A similar view was offered in the early fifteenth century by Anthonius Guainerius, a professor of medicine at the University of Pavia. He claimed that serious illnesses would result if women did not accept the "proper" feminine role; a woman should be married, avoid luxury, and have regular intercourse with her husband. Like Galen and Trotula, Guainerius believed that failure to release seed periodically would poison the womb and cause suffocation. He also warned that illnesses also could be caused by "superfluous exercises" or "immoderate accidents of the soul—exceeding wrath, excessive sadness or worries."[18]

Popular opinion concerning "hysterical fits" shifted during the time of the witch-hunts. Such fits, with their resulting paralysis and blindness, were seen as a result of demonic possession rather than a symptom of a diseased uterus. But sixteenth-century medical theory still continued to support views similar to those of the classical period. Paracelsus, for example, argued in his treatise *Diseases that Deprive Man of His Reason* that disorders of the uterus could result in hysterical fits that take "away all reason and sensibility."[19] He theorized that wombs deprived of proper nourishment lose their right nature and become cold, and this coldness results in a spasm of the lining of the womb that passes to the limbs and veins of the rest of the body. "If such contraction takes place in the veins of the whole body, vapor and smoke come out of the womb to the organs around it, and if it touches the heart the convulsion is similar to epilepsy with all its symptoms, and no other organ but the heart is affected with it."[20]

Reginald Scott (1538?–1599) employed a similar theory to directly attack popular opinion about witches. He argued that women were prone to melancholy, particularly after menopause, "upon the stopping of their monethlie melancholike flux or issue of bloud."[21] He explained that failure to expel such blood would cause foul vapors to arise, affecting these women's brains and depraving their senses and judgment. This, he claimed, caused them to have visions and to imagine themselves capable of witchcraft.

Another sixteenth-century theorist, Ambroise Paré, accepted a Galenic explanation of hysteria, seeing it as the result of the strangulation of the womb caused by "gross vapours and humours" contained within it. "Moreover, the womb swells, because there is contained or inclosed in it a certain substance, caused by the defluxion either of seed or flowers, or of the womb or whites, or of some other humour, tumour, abscess, rotten apostume, or some ill juice, putrefying, or getting or engendering an ill quality, and resolved into gross vapours."[22]

Paré claimed that these vapors distend the uterus, causing compression of the lungs. He listed five signs of hysteria: foolish talking, madness, loss of speech, contraction of the legs, and coma. Notice that by the sixteenth century, mental illness was as commonly associated with hysteria as was physical illness. Like earlier theorists, Paré believed that hysteria was, in part, the result of celibacy. Explaining that hysteria seldom afflicts women who "use copulation familiarly," he claimed that it was to be found "in those women that have not their menstrual flux as they should, and do want, and are destitute of husbands, especially if they are great eaters, and lead a solitary life."[23]

During the seventeenth and eighteenth centuries, woman's reproductive organs were perceived as rendering her more susceptible to physical illness (although theorists allowed, as had Paré two centuries earlier, that they sometimes affected woman's mental health). The physician Thomas Sydenham (1624–1689), for example, argued that woman's role in reproduction makes her much more inclined to hysteria than is man. He believed that "very few women . . . are quite free from every assault of this disease."[24] His list of symptoms include both physical and mental ailments: apoplexy, convulsions, violent beating of the heart, vomiting, coughs, pain, anguish of mind, and dejection of the spirits.[25] The English physician Thomas Arnold (1742–1816), in his treatise on insanity, claimed that a difficult childbirth could lead to insanity if blood retained in the body after delivery "be diverted, by some accidental, and imperceptible cause, to the brain."[26] He further argued that there was a "sympathy" between the womb and the brain, so that an irritation or disability of the womb could precipitate hysterical symptoms. But until the nineteenth century, hysteria was generally viewed as a physical rather than a psychological ailment.

WOMB MADNESS

By the nineteenth century, physicians were labeling hysteria a mental condition. Rather than the suffocation and liver displacement talked about in earlier centuries, medical theorists elaborated on the notion of a hysterical fit, viewing it as a mental imbalance and associating it with a nervous condition. The uterus was seen as connected to the central nervous system in such a way that disorders of the reproductive organs could cause pathological reactions throughout the body. In addition, medical views shifted the origin of hysteria from the uterus to the sexual organs in general, and scientists began to debate the possibility that men could also be hysterics.

But even those theorists who allowed for the possibility of male hysteria insisted that woman was much more susceptible. Nineteenth-century physicians perceived woman's reproductive organs as having a far greater impact on her than man's did on him. In the words of the U.S. physician John Wiltbank,

> Destined to increase and multiply her species, and to keep up an uninterrupted succession of generations, upon her devolve conception, gestation, parturition and lactation, with all the accidents and contingencies resulting from such complicated processes. With her, therefore, the reproductive organs are pre-eminent. They exercise a controlling influence upon her entire system, and entail upon her many painful and dangerous diseases. They are the source of her peculiarities, the center of her sympathies, and the seat of her diseases. Everything that is peculiar to her, springs from her sexual organization.[27]

The theory of physiology underlying this perception is what nineteenth-century physicians referred to as "reflex action." They held that the human body was a closed system containing a fixed quantity of energy; if energy in one part of this system was expended, there must be a corresponding depletion in another part. Other medical scientists of the time also saw reproductive forces as having the greatest impact on woman's physiology. According to the renowned English neurophysiologist Thomas Laycock, the "influence which the generative organs must exert over the whole animal economy, may be easily inferred from the general fact, that the final cause of all vital action is the reproduction of the species."[28]

These scientists believed that woman's animal economy is far less stable than man's due to her "periodicity"—the cycles of menstruation and pregnancy. Add the belief that "the nervous system of the human female is allowed to be sooner affected by all stimuli, whether corporeal or mental, than that of the male," and the conclusion of woman's greater pathology is unavoidable.[29] In the words of Dr. Isaac Ray (1807–1881), "with women, it is but a step from extreme nervous susceptibility to downright hysteria, and from that to overt insanity. In the sexual evolution, in pregnancy, in the parturient period, in lactation, strange thoughts, extraordinary feelings, unseasonable appetites, criminal impulses, may haunt a mind at other times innocent and pure."[30]

Accepting the theory of reflex action, nineteenth-century medical science depicted all women as prone to hysteria. Woman's "normal" state was perceived as internally unstable, and thus prey to imbalances of the nervous system. Although some medical theorists like Laycock were willing to accept the possibility of male hysteria ("in a vast majority of cases" hysterics are women, and "its occurrence in males may be considered an exception to the general rule") many others continued to view hysteria as a female malady.[31]

Frederick Hollick (1813–1900), in his *Diseases of Women,* rejected the position that hysteria could be caused by any of the sexual organs. He claimed instead that the uterus controlled and directed a woman's body, and was thus the source of her mental imbalances. "The Uterus, it must be remembered, is the *controlling* organ in the female body, being the most excitable of all, and so intimately connected, by the ramifications of its numerous nerves, with every other part."[32] Seeing the uterus as the "hub" of the body, Hollick insisted that symptoms resulting from an imbalance of the uterus would be "multitudinous and diverse," and would affect a woman's entire character. With this focus on the uterus, Hollick denied that hysteria could be a male malady.

There was much controversy among theorists concerning which of the sexual organs were most responsible for woman's susceptibility to hysteria. Some continued, like Hollick, to blame the uterus. An example is Horatio Storer (1830–1922), a surgeon at St. Elizabeth's and St. Francis' Hospitals for Women in Boston. In *Reflex Insanity in Women,* Storer claimed that the "excited" uterus is the cause of grave mental and physical derangement, and insisted that it was "at the foundation, physiologically and pathologically, of much of the mental derangement that occurs in women."[33] Others, like Laycock, implicated the ovaries, viewing them as "the most essential of all the organs of generation."[34] Laycock argued that during menstruation, woman's entire nervous system is put in a "state of excitement" by the ovaries, rendering her susceptible to nervous disorders.

Other theorists shifted focus from a specific organ to the "bad blood" hypothesis, thereby implicating menstruation as the source of woman's ills. George Tate, in his *Treatise on Hysteria,* argued that irregular or defective menstruation was the cause. By examining numerous cases of hysteria, Tate claimed to "prove, conclusively, that defective menstruation is solely accountable for all these manifestations."[35]

Despite their differing views on which organ was primarily responsible for woman's susceptibility to hysteria, nineteenth-century physicians and psychologists generally agreed that a woman was most susceptible during her menstrual period. Storer labeled woman a "victim of periodicity" and insisted that menstruation was a time of "infirmity" as well as "temporary insanity."[36] A. O. Kellogg (1818–1888), in an article published in the *American Journal of Insanity,* also implicated female periodicity, claiming that during the menstrual cycle, woman has far less mental ability and less control over her emotions. Even when the menstrual function is healthy, Kellogg believed, it could make a woman, especially one of a "nervous, excitable temperament . . . morose, taciturn, wayward, fidgety, and impatient, frequently manifesting a certain nervous irritability bordering on hysteria."[37] Given this, an imbalance of the menstrual functions was sure to bring on insanity. And for those women who were truly insane, the U.S. physician Alexander Walker (1779–1852) claimed that "delirium increases and suicide occurs most frequently at the catamenial period."[38]

Walter Johnson, in his *Morbid Emotions of Women,* agreed that "the menstrual epoch is one peculiarly exposed to the incursions of disease."[39] According to him, woman's menstrual cycle is exceedingly liable to disturbance, so that the slightest physical ailment or mental or moral agitation is sufficient to induce "baleful results." Such agitations, causing either an excess or deficit of bleeding, result in minor to violent fits, excitability, feebleness of volition, and unconquerable impulses.[40]

Given that Johnson subscribed to the notion of the animal economy,[41] it should be no surprise that he claimed that:

the grand cause of hysteria—that which puts out the eyes and lames the limbs, and distorts the features of the young and beautiful; that which prompts the canine bark, obstructs the breath, and wrings the brow with anguish; that which melts the women of England into powerless babes, lulls them into months of slumber, deforms the moral beauty of their souls, and shatters their intellect; that which stretches them moaning and struggling on the ground, or petrifies into living statues; that which will sometimes freeze every faculty of the soul and sense, and, by destroying reason, level them with those that chew the cud—this grand traitor and foe to humanity is Polite Education. First, the boarding school, then the salon, the theatre, the opera— these are the focus of infection, the very den of hysteria.[42]

Woman's nature, her supposedly greater role in reproduction, makes her more vulnerable to insanity. But any attempt on her part to defy her "nature," perhaps by striving for an education equal to that of man, will also bring about a mental breakdown.

The diseases caused by such imbalances of woman's sexual organs were believed to be primarily of a mental nature. Although a woman's physical health might also be impaired, nineteenth-century theorists emphasized the gravity of the effect upon her mental health. Given this shift, descriptions of hysterical fits changed, and the earlier lists of physical ailments gave way to catalogs of psychological ills. Compare the former descriptions of a hysterical fit with this one from Charles Meigs:

The hysterical woman, like the highly electrified thunder cloud, requires but the point to draw the flash. She sits, like Tam O'Shanter's wife, "Gathering her brows, like gathering storm, / Nursing her wrath to keep it warm;" when, suddenly and unexpectedly, some word, sign or gesture, or the failure of some word, sign or gesture, gives the occasion; and we have reproaches, tears, screaming, laughter, sobs, wringing of hands, tearing of hair, clonic convulsions, tonic spasms, stupor, stertor, smiles like a May morning, loud laughter again, floods of tears, and then a gradual return to a state of gentle composure, wherein the tenderest affections of the female heart come to resume, with unusual supremacy, their wonted sway over the soul.[43]

For nineteenth-century theorists, not only was woman's individual development arrested by her role in reproduction, but she was daily at the mercy of her sexual organs. This view of woman as a slave to her sexual organs was a central metaphor in the writings of Charles Meigs. In his texts, which became classics of the new specialty of gynecology, he advised pupils to concentrate on the sexual organs of woman, insisting that doing so would clarify her whole nature. He charged his students to study the influences of her reproductive organs "not on the body alone, but on the heart, the mind, and the very soul of woman."[44]

To illustrate the delicacy of woman's sexual organs and the impact of even the slightest imbalance, Meigs offered as an example the case of a young woman who, upon preparing for a dance, discovered that she had begun to menstruate. Since young women were expected to rest and avoid all exercise at the onset of their monthly courses, the woman complained to her servant regarding her ill luck. The servant responded that the woman could stop her flow by bathing in cold water. Following this advice, the young woman took a cold bath and went to the ball. Meigs reported that she returned early with a "blinding headache, was attacked with a brain fever, lost her bloom, and her embonpoint; and now, at the age of near fifty years, still feels the miserable effects of such a scandalous dereliction on the part of the favorite and confidential servant."[45]

Meigs also held the popular view that the nervous system of woman is directly connected to her sexual organs. The power of these organs is well illustrated in his explanation of the consequences of the infamous bath:

> The uterus and the ovaria, and all the branches of the hypogastric, the sciatic and ovaric arteries, were full—it was full tide with all that system of vessels—the accompanying nerves were all ripe and rife with the periodical excitement. The cold hip-bath produced instantly a spasmodic closure of the excreting orifices in the womb, and the uterus and ovaria became instantly the seats, not of an out-flowing affluxion, but of intense engorgement, which, reacting as a disturbing force upon the cerebrospinal system, laid at once the train for years of ill health. That lady's whole life was rendered a scene of bitterness—of vapours and caprices by that single hip-bath. It shocked her nervous system ruinously.[46]

Meigs's correlation of the sexual organs and the nervous system was an accepted tenet of nineteenth-century medicine. George Man Burrows, head of the English Association of Apothecaries and Surgeon-Apothecaries, insisted that "everybody of the least experience must be sensible of the influence of menstruation on the operations of the mind. In truth, it is the moral and physical barometer of the female constitution . . . the functions of the brain are so intimately connected with the uterine system, that the interruption of any one process which the latter has to perform in the human economy may implicate the former."[47] G. Fielding Blandford, president of the psychiatric section of the British Medical Association and author of numerous texts on insanity, claimed that the "sympathetic connection existing between the brain and the uterus is plainly seen by the most casual observer."[48]

Since theorists accepted the premise that woman's reproductive organs dictated her nature and well-being, it is no surprise that they believed that she would be more prone to nervous disorders than man. Woman's reproductive cycles—puberty, menstruation, pregnancy, childbirth, lactation, and menopause—were all times when she was subject to the nervous disorder labeled "reflex insanity," the nineteenth-century term for hysteria. Woman was a "victim of periodicity" and thereby subject to a range of mental disturbances that had "neither homologue nor analogue in man."[49]

These theories reified centuries-old beliefs about the proper relations between the sexes.[50] Woman was to bear and raise children. Any attempt to deny this role would lead to physical and mental distress. But this role, though her purpose, took a toll on woman, both physically and mentally.

SEXUAL DESIRE AND HYSTERIA

As nineteenth-century medical opinion shifted hysteria from an organic to a mental disorder, the link between hysteria and sex was emphasized. Classical theo-

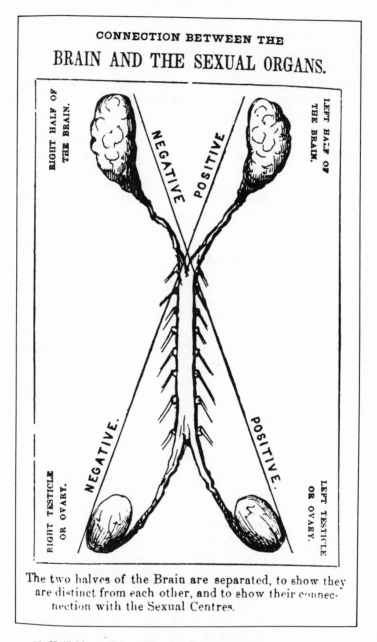

CONNECTION BETWEEN THE
BRAIN AND THE SEXUAL ORGANS.

RIGHT HALF OF THE BRAIN.

LEFT HALF OF THE BRAIN.

NEGATIVE

POSITIVE

NEGATIVE.

POSITIVE.

RIGHT TESTICLE OR OVARY.

LEFT TESTICLE OR OVARY.

The two halves of the Brain are separated, to show they
are distinct from each other, and to show their connec-
nection with the Sexual Centres.

12. Hollick's rendition of the direct connection between the brain
and sexual organs is representative of nineteenth-century scientific views. Frederick Hollick, *The Marriage Guide, or Natural
History of Generation.* New York: T. W. Strong, 1850.

rists had believed that a lack of intercourse would lead to various physiological imbalances, such as a wandering womb, which in turn could result in hysteria. In the nineteenth century scientists implicated an individual's sexual habits, arguing that certain practices, such as masturbation, could precipitate psychological disorders, including hysteria and neurasthenia.

Robert Brudenell Carter, author of an influential study of hysteria, provides an excellent model of this association of sex and mental illness. In *On the Pathology and Treatment of Hysteria,* Carter argued that the predominance of women hysterics was in large part due to the socially enforced repression of woman's sexual passions. Men, he explained, married or single, have "facilities for its gratification," for sexual mores allowed a man recourse to mistresses and prostitutes. The same mores, however, dictated that unmarried women be "compelled to restrain every manifestation of its sway."[51] Thus the unmarried or widowed woman has no outlet for what Carter claimed to be the most "violent" female emotion— sexual passion.[52] Not only is a woman often lacking acceptable channels for them, she is, on Carter's account, more prone to sexual emotions than a man. Arguing that repressed emotions lead to psychological disorders, Carter had only to allude to the commonly accepted belief in woman's untempered, unchanneled sexual passions to account for her heightened sensitivity to hysteria.

Interestingly, although Carter insisted that repressed sexual needs resulted in hysteria, he saw no acceptable outlet other than marriage for woman's sexual desires. Although Carter supported prostitutes as a "proper channel" for an unmarried man's sexual desire, he attacked the use of the speculum for medical examinations, since its use would "indulge" a woman's sexual feelings. Women, he protested, "find out by observation that the speculum becomes more grateful to their feelings the oftener it is applied, and that the wish for it is in some degree excited by each successive dose of the medicine."[53] He paints a picture of young, unmarried women "reduced, by constant use of the speculum, to the mental and moral condition of prostitutes," their passions so aroused by a medical examination that they resort to the "terrible vice" of masturbation and go to doctor after doctor asking them to "institute an examination of the sexual organs" in order to satisfy their passions.[54] The unmarried woman is thus caught between hysteria and masturbatory addictions—clear scientific "proof" of the unnaturalness of the unmarried state for woman.

While repression of the sexual drives was believed to be a cause of hysteria in woman, unfettered sexuality was equally condemned. Augustus Gardner (1821– 1876), in his *Conjugal Sins Against the Laws of Life and Health,* argued that extended sexual contact could result in a woman's organs becoming so sensitive and irritated that nothing could appease them. "The natural nervous character of females is heightened and intensified, and local congestions and weakening discharges are the direct result of the exciting erethisms so thoughtlessly employed."[55]

Man's physical capacity for sexual gratification was limited, according to Gardner, so he was not prone to sexual excesses. However, Gardner saw woman as possessing an almost unlimited capacity for sexual gratification, a situation that seems to have made him very uncomfortable. He condemned woman's sexual capacity as being too easily overstimulated, leading to the loss of her moral and mental capabilities. "The unnatural irritation sometimes cannot be appeased, and these manifestations of disease may proceed from the complicity of simple nervous local irritation with some general sympathies, until it reaches the grand ganglion and the throne of reason itself trembles and is shattered."[56] Gardner concluded that hysteria is more often "the result of excess in venery than as connected with its entire absence."[57] This conclusion was also supported by E. Curtis in his popular text *Manhood: The Causes of its Premature Decline,* which sold over half a million copies between 1848 and 1869.

The image of woman's Pandora-like insatiable sexual appetite held sway over the minds of nineteenth-century medical scientists. They saw the arousal of this appetite as the greatest danger to woman's mental well-being (and perhaps their own greatest fear). Their prescription was that woman should not deviate from her proper role of wife and mother in order to protect her mental well-being. Laycock, for example, agreeing that an imbalance of sexual activity— either abstinence or indulgence—causes hysteria, offered a solution he credits to Hippocrates: "the best cure of hysteria is for the patient to marry and bear children."[58]

PSYCHOSURGERY: CONTROLLING WOMAN'S SEXUALITY.

Whatever the psychological source of their negative reactions to woman's sexuality, nineteenth-century medical theorists viewed both woman's sexual organs and sexual passions with suspicion. While the organs themselves were the instruments through which woman satisfied her biological purpose of procreation, they were also the seat of disease and derangement. With the rapid development of the specialty of gynecology in the nineteenth century and the concurrent improvement of surgical and anesthetic techniques, the obvious step for many doctors was to remove the source of woman's ills. Beginning in the late 1860s and throughout the rest of the century, a number of doctors advocated surgical treatment for the psychological disorders of women.

Prior to the mid-nineteenth century, standard treatment for hysteria often consisted of attempts to relocate the displaced uterus. Doctors had, since the classical period, recommended fumigation of the uterus, using either ill- or good-smelling vapors to attempt to coax the uterus back into place. Through the centuries, doctors added to this the practices of bleeding the hysteric, placing pessaries in the womb, using leeches on the vulva or the neck of the uterus, injecting various liquids, and cauterization.

In the middle of the nineteenth century, medical practitioners began to encourage the surgical removal of the offending organ. To cure female hysteria, in 1858 the English gynecologist Isaac Baker Brown introduced the removal of the clitoris. Arguing that the mental afflictions of woman are often the result of undue irritation of the nerves "arising originally in some branches of the pudic nerve, more particularly the incident nerve supplying the clitoris," Brown concluded that once such irritation has begun, the only effective cure is the destruction of the nerve through clitoridectomy.[59] The practice of clitoridectomy did not become popular in England; in fact, it was used more frequently in the United States until it was superseded by the practice of female circumcision (removal of all or a portion of the hood of the clitoris).[60] These operations were seen as particularly important, for such surgery was believed to "control" woman's unlimited sexual appetite, as described by Gardner and other physicians. The surgery was performed on women whose sexual appetites were believed to be "unbalanced," with masturbation seen as the primary symptom of this "disease."[61]

In 1869 Robert Battey, a founding member of the American Gynecological Society, originated the most common form of surgical intervention. Arguing that the ovaries, rather than the uterus, are the cause of insanity and epilepsy, Battey prescribed their removal. He even advocated renaming hystero-mania "oophoro-mania," because "disorders are dependent upon a nervous irritation proceeding from the ovaries and not from the uterus."[62] By the middle of the nineteenth century, a number of physicians began to emphasize the importance of the ovaries on the constitution and character of woman. W. W. Bliss, for example, in his text *Woman and Her Thirty Years' Pilgrimage*, talked of "the gigantic power and influence of the ovaries over the whole animal economy of women," insisting that they are the most powerful agents of woman's mental, moral, and physical qualities, and stressed the destruction they could cause when disordered.[63] Henry Maudsley (1835–1918), an English psychiatrist, similarly argued that the "monthly activity of the ovaries which marks the advent of puberty in women has a notable effect upon the mind and body; wherefore it may become an important cause of mental or physical derangement."[64]

Influenced by this view of the power of the ovaries, "Battey's operation," as it was termed by the U.S. gynecologist J. Marion Sims, became popular in America between 1880 and 1910.[65] Despite numerous protests that such surgery deprived women of their role in life while also depriving society of countless ova, more than 150,000 such operations were performed in the United States alone by 1906, according to the estimates of E. van de Warker.[66] Battey countered the objections by insisting that the subjects of his surgeries, although their ovaries appeared normal, were either infertile or would have given birth to defective children. Near the end of the century hysterectomies began to be performed for psychological disorders, presenting an alternative to ovariotomy. Physicians justified these procedures by arguing that they were necessary to stem the tide of woman's overpowering sexual desires, desires that could result in the loss of all self-control and modesty.[67]

Initially, the main candidates for such surgery were women from the middle- and upper-income groups. Believing that the working woman was not a fit subject for gynecological surgery, doctors limited their practice to women "so situated in life as to be able to conserve her strength and, if necessary, to take a prolonged rest, in order to secure the best results" of such surgery.[68] However, by the turn of the century ovariotomy was widely prescribed for epileptic and insane women. Robert Kitto, in an article published in the *Journal of the American Medical Association* supported the widespread use of ovariotomy on the grounds that "hundreds of unfortunate women are today languishing in insane asylums, who might be cured by a similar operation."[69]

The belief that such women should not be allowed to reproduce enhanced the popularity of this "treatment" even when its curative powers were questioned. William Goodell, a professor of gynecology at the University of Pennsylvania, insisted that "if the operation be not followed by a cure, the surgeon can console himself with the thought that he has brought about a sterility in a woman who might otherwise have given birth to an insane progeny. In fact, I am not sure but that, in this progressive age, it may not in the future be deemed sound political economy to stamp out insanity by removing the ovaries of insane women."[70] Eventually, protests against the widespread use of gynecological surgery as a cure for insanity led to its demise, with opponents arguing that the surgery was experimental, illegal, brutal, and inhumane.

But even after sexual surgery fell out of fashion, the medical and psychological establishments continued to implicate woman's sexual organs in what they perceived as the female proclivity to hysteria. After the discovery of sex hormones, theorists turned their attention from the organs themselves to the hormones secreted by them. William Blair Bell, cofounder and first president of the British College of Obstetricians and Gynaecologists, indicted ovarian secretions as the cause of "sexual insanity" and melancholia in woman. "When excessive sexuality, amounting perhaps to sexual insanity, exists in women we must look for an excessive ovarian secretion as the primary cause of the condition; and contrariwise we find that a deficient ovarian secretion may lead to melancholia, probably indirectly."[71]

Medical views of woman's illnesses, both mental and physical, were clearly influenced by the accepted theories concerning woman's nature. Woman's nervous instability was an unquestioned axiom, stemming from the belief that woman's reproductive role placed a strain upon her entire system, often directly resulting in physical disorders as well as causing an earlier arrest of her entire development. Biases concerning woman's greater emotionality were explained by this arrested development, which in turn was cited to account for woman's susceptibility to certain mental disorders.

The view of woman's reproductive organs as the seat of her physical and mental health is simply one perspective of the complex image of woman built up around her uterus. We see here the extent to which both social and cultural assumptions concerning woman's nature affected the practice of science. These scientific theories incorporated untested and often nonempirical axioms about woman's nature—that woman's purpose is bearing children (for what other reason would God have created a woman rather than a man as a helpmate?) and that this function requires vast expenditures of energy. Scientists' experiences with, observations of, and views about woman's nature have a crucial impact on their assumptions and theories.

The view that woman is far more affected by reproductive forces than man had a wide-ranging impact on the social roles deemed appropriate for woman. Woman's reproductive role was used to account for her intellectual deficiencies and her incompatibility with advanced education. Woman's heightened emotionality and unlimited capacity for sexual gratification, as well as her inability to develop an appreciation of the sublime or to understand the abstract notion of justice, were seen as stemming from the same source. Both philosophers and scientists seem obsessed by this image of woman as mother.

III

Creativity's Soil

The *man* is the source of life—the one who mounts.
She, like a stranger for a stranger, keeps
the shoot alive unless the god hurts the roots.
I give you proof that all I say is true.
The father can father forth without a mother.
Here she [Athena] stands, our living witness.

Aeschylus (513?–?456 BCE), *Oresteia*

In order to defeat the mother, the male must prove
that he is not inferior, that he has a gift to produce.
Since he cannot produce with a womb, he must produce in another fashion; he produces with his
mouth, his word, his thought.

Erich Fromm (1900–1980),
The Forgotten Language

Children of the Gods

For centuries, Western science accounted for woman's perceived inferiority by referring to her role in reproduction. Scientists implicated gestations, births, lactations, and menstruations in causing her to be less developed, less evolved, less moral, less capable of rational thought, less divine. But what of the procreative realm? Surely this is one function in which we would expect woman to be judged man's equal, if not his superior.[1] It seems unreasonable to say that man, who does not gestate, bear, or lactate, possesses reproductive capacities superior to those of woman. But this is exactly what we find. Man's procreative superiority is inscribed upon the science of embryology and the religious metaphysics of creation. Religious cosmogonies postulate the male as the essential creative force, while biological theories assign a greater importance to the male role in generation—another example of the way in which religion and science are mutually reinforcing.

This chapter examines some of the most influential religious creation myths in Western cultures. These myths share a common metaphorical understanding of the nature of the creative force that has important implications for conceptions of female generative powers.[2] In the following chapter I will illustrate the ways in which embryological theories reflect this same imagery.

LET THERE BE: GENESIS AND CREATION

At the heart of Western images of the origin of the universe is the biblical story of creation. God's bringing all that exists into being has been viewed as the epitome of creativity. The account of primeval history found in Genesis has been the dominant creation myth in Western culture for over 1,800 years.

To understand the impact and importance of the Genesis account of creation, one must look carefully at its metaphors and images.

> In the beginning God created the heavens and the earth. The earth was without form and void, and darkness was upon the face of the deep; and the Spirit of God was moving over the face of the waters.
>
> And God said, "Let there be light"; and there was light. And God saw that the light was good; and God separated the light from the darkness. God call the light Day, and the darkness he called Night. And there was evening and there was morning, one day.
>
> And God said, "Let there be a firmament in the midst of the waters, and let it separate the waters from the waters." And God made the firmament and separated

the waters which were under the firmament from the waters which were above the firmament. And it was so. And God called the firmament Heaven. And there was evening and there was morning, a second day.

And God said, "Let the waters under the heavens be gathered together into one place, and let the dry land appear." And it was so. God called the dry land Earth, and the waters that were gathered together he called Seas. And God saw that it was good. And God said, "Let the earth put forth vegetation, plants yielding seed, and fruit trees bearing fruit in which is their seed, each according to its kind, upon the earth." And it was so. The earth brought forth vegetation, plants yielding seed according to their own kinds, and trees bearing fruit in which is their seed, each according to its kind. And God saw that it was good. And there was evening and there was morning, a third day. (Genesis 1:1–13)

The most salient aspect of the nature of the creative force as depicted in Genesis is that it is masculine. In the role of creator, God is referred to with the masculine "Elohim" (אלהים), and the verb is in the masculine singular (". . . the waters that were gathered together he [קרא] called Seas" [Genesis 1:10]). All that exists issues from a masculine source. A creation myth that identifies the creative force as male will have a crucial impact on a culture's images of the creative abilities of woman and man. If we believe that the universe is created by a male god, the creativity of males is given initial credibility and priority. And indeed, the Genesis creation myth has had this effect on Western culture. In fact, the metaphors used to describe the acts of creation in Genesis recur often in scientific views of human procreation.

The language of the Genesis creation myth is the language of the craftsperson.[3] The order of creation evinces a molding or modeling image: as a potter or sculptor would first organize her or his raw materials, God's first act was to create the raw material of the universe, the earth that was without form or life and the darkness that covered the deep. Like a craftsperson or artist, God used this lifeless, unorganized, and undifferentiated raw material to create his masterpiece, to separate light from darkness and the waters under the firmament from those above.

When each creative act was completed, God looked over his creation and pronounced it "good," verifying that it was sound or well-designed, as "And God saw that the light was good" (Genesis 1:4). Pronouncing a product sound was an action required by law of Mesopotamian craftspeople before products left their shops. Similarly, an artist, upon completing a masterpiece or executing a difficult procedure, might step back and survey her or his work to make sure that it is properly done and aesthetically pleasing.[4]

We also see craftsperson imagery in the creation of man in the second Genesis creation myth. In it, man is created by God as a potter would form a vessel. God took clay and molded it into the shape of a man: "Then the Lord God formed man of dust from the ground" (Genesis 2:7). Man, hā'ādām, was formed by the divine potter from the ground, 'ādhāmah. Even his name reflects his origins. This metaphor of the creator as potter and humans as product is repeated in Romans, when Paul employs the same image to admonish his audience: "But who are you, a man, to answer back to God? Will what is molded say to its molder, 'Why have you made me thus?' Has the potter no right over the clay, to make out of the same lump one vessel for beauty and another for menial use?" (Romans 9:20–22).

Like a craftsperson, God gave form to matter. But unlike a craftsperson, God gave form by naming. Just as we use language to transform the chaos of undifferentiated sense perceptions into the ordered world of things and activities, God gave the unformed raw material of his initial creation its definition. The linguistic act, the act of naming, brings order to chaos. "God called the light Day, and the darkness he called Night. . . . And God called the firmament Heaven. . . . God called the dry land Earth, and the waters that were gathered together he called Seas" (Genesis 1:5–10).

Also unlike a human craftsperson, God created the very materials to which he gave form. The world was created *ex nihilo*, out of nothing. God did not give form to already present but formless matter; rather, he produced all that is from nothing.[5] And as God gave form through naming, he created by calling into being. Each act of creation in Genesis begins with a calling forth. That which is given form through the name is evoked through the word. "And God said, 'Let there be light. . . .' And God said, 'Let the earth put forth vegetation. . . .' And God said, 'Let the earth bring forth living creatures' " (Genesis 1:3–24).

There is, then, a fourfold pattern of creation in Genesis: evoking, separating, naming, and seeing that it is good. In the words of Tertullian (160?–230?), the African church father, "God devised the whole universe by Word, by Reason, by Might."[6] God brought forth substance, divided it and classified it, and thereby gave it form.[7]

Before considering the implications of the Genesis metaphor of the craftsperson who creates from nothing, it would be helpful to contrast this image with other creation metaphors. There are three basic metaphors, the first being the Genesis image of creation *ex nihilo*. The second metaphor is that of giving form to already existing matter, and the third is the image of giving birth. The second creation metaphor can be found in the Akkadian creation epic *Enuma Elis*, while the third metaphor is the guiding image of the *Theogony*, the ancient Greek myth of creation.

BIRTHING THE WORLD: HESIOD'S *THEOGONY*

Hesiod's *Theogony* contains a description of the birth of the gods and the creation of the universe. The metaphor of birth is central to this creation story.

> Chaos was born first and then after her came Gaia
> the broad-breasted, the firm seat of all . . .
> Chaos gave birth to Erebos and black Night;
> then Erebos mated with Night and made her pregnant
> and she in turn gave birth to Ether and Day.
> Gaia now first gave birth to starry Ouranos,
> her match in size, to encompass all of her,
> and be the firm seat of all the blessed gods.

> She gave birth to the tall mountains, enchanting haunts
> of the divine nymphs who dwell in the woodlands;
> and then she bore Pontos, the barren sea with its raging swell.
> All these she bore without mating in sweet love. But then
> she did couple with Ouranos to bear deep-eddying Okeanos,
> Koios and Kreios, Hyperion and Iapetos,
> Theia and Rheia, Themis and Mnemosyne,
> as well as gold-wreathed Phoibe and lovely Tethys.[8]

In this birth image of creation, all that exists issues forth from the body of the creators. Rather than bringing into being out of nothing, the gods *bear* their off-spring. They do not impose a form upon unformed matter, as in the craftsperson image of Genesis, but rather generate beings out of their own bodies. This image is one of form evolving as it gestates in the bodies of the gods.

Also unlike Genesis, the primordial forces in the *Theogony*, Chaos and Gaia (Earth), are female. They are born, though Hesiod gives us no explanation of the nature of their births, and it is from these two female gods that all else comes.[9] The initial creation is parthenogenetic. Chaos, without partner, gave birth to Erebos (Underworld) and Night. From the body of Gaia alone came Ouranos (Heaven), as well as the mountains and the sea. Thus the female is the sole force in the initial acts of creation.

After giving parthenogenetic birth to a number of male gods, Erebos, Oura-nos, and Pontos (Sea), the majority of subsequent births result from the joint contributions of female and male gods. Here the human procreative act is the model of creation. A female god is attracted to a male god, they copulate, and the female becomes pregnant and gives birth. Gaia first gave birth parthenogeneti-cally to Ouranos, then coupled with him and gave birth to nineteen children.[10] Later she lay with another of her parthenogenetic offspring, Pontos, and gave birth to four more gods.[11] Gaia's last child was born of a coupling, "goaded by Aphrodite"; Gaia lay in love with Tartaros (the darkest place of the underworld) and bore her youngest child, Typhoeus.[12]

Chaos never mated in sweet love. She gave birth parthenogenetically to a male god, Erebos, and a female god, Night. These offspring mated and gave birth to Ether and Day. Neither Night nor Erebos mated again, though much later, Night, "having lain with no one," gave birth parthenogenetically to a host of gods and forces, many of which are negative forces.[13]

In the *Theogony*, the gods, the physical universe, and the variety of forces that exist are portrayed as having been birthed into being. The language of creation in the *Theogony* has no crafting metaphors. All images are of mating and birthing: "Chaos gave birth; Erebos mated with Night and made her pregnant / and she in turn gave birth; Baneful Night bore; loathsome Strife bore; Pontos lay with Gaia and sired; this bright-eyed maiden lay in love with Typhaon . . . and impregnated by him she bore."[14]

Before comparing a birth image of creation to a craft image, let us consider an example of the second form of creation metaphor, in which form is given to al-ready existing matter.

BETWEEN EVOKING AND ISSUING: *ENUMA ELIS*

The *Enuma Elis* provides an account of creation that contains metaphors of both issuing and evoking. This Akkadian epic dates back to the Old Babylonian period, the early part of the second millennium BCE, and it was recited annually as part of the New Year's festival. In this myth, creation results from a god giving form to an already existing substance.

The *Enuma Elis* opens with, "when on high the heaven had not been named," from which the title *Enuma Elis* (*When On High*), originates.[15] When on high—when neither the heaven nor the earth had been named—primordial Apsu (the sweet-water ocean) and Tiamat (the salt-water ocean) were concerned about their children, the gods. Because of their clamor and boisterousness, Apsu decided to destroy them, a plan Tiamat protested. However, before either could act, the young gods killed their father. Tiamat, angry at the loss of Apsu, planned to avenge his death by killing the young gods. And Tiamat, mightier than Apsu, would be far more difficult for the young gods to stop. In fact, only one god, Marduk, was brave enough to fight her.

When Tiamat came to attack the gods, Marduk confronted her and challenged her to a duel. During the course of the battle, she opened her mouth to swallow him. But Marduk "drove in the Evil Wind that she close not her lips" and shot an arrow through her mouth which tore her belly and split her heart.[16] In this way he extinguished Tiamat's life.

The creation of the universe begins at this point. After killing Tiamat, Marduk

> paused to view her dead body,
> That he might divide the monster and do artful works.
> He split her like a shellfish into two parts:
> Half of her he set up and ceiled it as sky. . . .
> [Taking] the spittle of Tia[mat]
> Marduk created [. . .] . . . .
> He formed the c[louds] and filled (them) with [water].
> The raising winds, the bringing of rain (and) cold,
> Making the mist smoke, piling up her poison:
> (These) he appointed to himself, took into his own charge.
> Putting her head into position he formed the[reon the mountai]ns,
> Opening the deep (which) was in flood,
> He caused to flow from her eyes the Euphr[ates (and) T]igris,
> Stopping her nostrils he left . . . ,
> He formed at her udder the lofty m[ountain]s,
> (Therein) he drilled the springs for wells to carry off (the water).
> Twisting her tail he bound it to Durmah,
> [. . .] . . . Apsu at his foot,
> [. . .] her crotch, she was fastened to the heavens,
> (Thus) he covered [the heavens] (and) established the earth.[17]

After creating the universe, Marduk's heart prompted him "to fashion artful works," and he decided to create creatures—humans—to ease the life of the gods: "The ways of the gods I will artfully alter."[18] Marduk killed one of the gods who had urged Tiamat to attack her children after Apsu's murder, and "out of his blood they [the gods] fashioned mankind."[19] These beings were charged with providing sustenance for the gods, thereby freeing the gods from such ordinary work.

The *Enuma Elis* stands midway between the Genesis myth and the *Theogony* myth in a number of interesting respects. Its initial creation, the creation of the gods, is like that of the *Theogony* in that it involves a birth metaphor. Apsu is referred to as the "begetter" of the gods; Tiamat's epithet is "she who bore them all"; and the younger gods are referred to as the "first-born" of Tiamat and Apsu. The creative forces are both female and male, and birth metaphors are prominent in descriptions of the children of Tiamat and Apsu. This account of the creation of Marduk provides one example. "He who begot him was Ea, his father; / She who bore him was Damkina, his mother. / The breast of goddesses he did suck."[20] However, the line before these suggests a different metaphor: "In the heart of holy Apsu was Marduk created."[21] This image is one of creation through thought or desire. In his heart, Apsu had the idea for a son, and through this desire Marduk was created. Still, the prominent metaphor for the process of the creation of the gods remains that of birth.

The image of creation of the universe, however, is significantly different. Although the universe is formed from the body of a goddess, the underlying metaphor is not one of birth. The created world is not generated from the living body of the goddess, but rather is carved out of her dead flesh. Marduk is neither consort nor lover; he is an artisan. In this image of creation, the male becomes the sole creative force. The female serves only to provide the matter upon which the male imposes form.

The account of the creation of the universe in the *Enuma Elis* is similar to that of Genesis, for Marduk is portrayed as an artist or craftsperson. He intends to "divide" the body of Tiamat and use it for "artful works." Just as the god of Genesis separates in order to create, so too does Marduk divide Tiamat in order to create. Just as Marduk imposed form upon the flesh and fluids of Tiamat to create the sky, mountains, and rivers, the god of Genesis imposed form upon the dust of the earth to create man. In fact, the *Enuma Elis* and Genesis share a similar account of man's creation. Although formed from different materials, in both accounts man is fashioned by the gods as a vessel might be fashioned by a potter.

One difference between the Genesis myth of creation and that of the *Enuma Elis* is found in the roles of creation *ex nihilo* and through the word. Although the Akkadian creation myth does not explicitly depict Marduk giving form through naming, as does the God of Genesis, this image plays a part in the *Enuma Elis*. Its opening lines indicate a view very similar to that of Genesis: "When on high the heaven had not been named, / Firm ground below had not been called by name."[22] According to the myth, heaven and earth were created only after Marduk slew Tiamat and divided her body. Prior to that time they did not exist, for, as the opening lines say, they had not been named.

The *Enuma Elis* contains an image of creation through the word that involves the theme of creation *ex nihilo*. This occurs when the gods are testing Marduk's powers. The assembly of gods convened to judge Marduk's ability to fight Tiamat. To prove his power, Marduk was to destroy and then create again, by his word, a piece of cloth the gods had given to him. The gods claimed that Marduk's "word shall be supreme"; they told him to "open thy mouth" and make the cloth vanish, and then to "speak again" and make it whole once again. "At the word of his mouth" the cloth vanished, and when "he spoke again" it was restored. When the gods saw "the fruit of his word," they declared him king.[23] To prove the efficacy of his word and thereby earn the support of the gods, Marduk had to demonstrate his ability to create out of nothing as well as his power to destroy.

The *Enuma Elis* contains all of the creation images found in both the *Theogony* and Genesis. In addition it contains a fourth image of the universe as forcibly formed from the dead flesh of the goddess.

MYTHS, METAPHORS, AND VALUES

Each of these creation myths embodies a variety of metaphysical values—deeply held beliefs that constitute world views and are often tied to religious systems. Such values give order to the world we experience and form part of the background out of which social institutions develop. There is, however, no unique or necessary connection between any particular metaphysical value and a certain type of social institution, for there are a variety of other influential factors—economic, political, and the like. Still, the metaphysical values of each myth do offer insight into the attitudes their believers are most likely to have about the creative act.

In the myth of the *Theogony*, the female is the initial creative principle. Three of the first gods, as well as the mountains and seas of the earth, arise parthenogenetically from the primordial goddesses Chaos and Gaia. Later creations issue from the mating of female and male gods. Hence, a metaphysical value arising from this portion of the *Theogony* is the importance of the female principle in creation.

The *Enuma Elis* does not deny potency to the female principle, but it depicts the creative act as complete only after the female principle, Tiamat, has been destroyed.[24] Thus, although the *Enuma Elis* recognizes a female principle in creation, it is the male principle that is ultimately given priority.

Genesis acknowledges only a male creative principle. No female divinity is involved in the act of creation—neither actively, as are Chaos and Gaia, nor passively, as is Tiamat when Marduk divides her. The notion of birth plays no role in the creation myth of Genesis.[25] Creation is through word or act. Creativity is therefore associated only with a male principle, and the source of creation will be the word or reason, rather than birth or flesh.[26]

The conception of form also differs in each of these myths. Since the *Theogony* contains a birth metaphor, form will evolve or grow out of the body of the goddess or the union of the female and male principles. In Genesis, form is imposed on matter by the god. The *Enuma Elis* contains both images: in the creation of the gods, form evolved from the union of the female and male principles, while the creation of the universe involved the imposition of form upon matter by a god.

Each of these myths encourages a different concept of the relationship between the gods and their creations. In the *Theogony*, everything that exists is the offspring of the gods; each thing is engendered from the body of a god. The gods are thus likely to be perceived as being a part of all that is; they are *in* the world. The god of Genesis is distinct from his creation, which is not of him. This image encourages a perception of the divine being as transcendent and thus separate from his own creation.[27] In the *Enuma Elis*, although the world is created from the body of a god, it does not evolve from her living being, but is rather carved out of her dead flesh. So creation is perceived as part of the divine, but, in an important sense, the created world will lose its vigor and its spirit.

Both the *Theogony* and the *Enuma Elis* contain metaphors that put metaphysical value on a female force in creation and on sex, birth, and flesh. That which exists is born or formed from the bodies of the gods, and the union of the female and male is seen as essential to the creation of the universe. The sexual act, at least at the level of the gods, will be valued as sacred, as the source of all things. But the sexual act plays no role in the Genesis creation myth, which places no value on the union of female and male. Since the universe was evoked through the word, that process receives value from this myth, and reason is seen as sacred.

A number of scholars have argued that study of early creation myths reveals a pattern of demotion of female gods.[28] Comparing the creation myths of the *Theogony*, the *Enuma Elis*, and Genesis shows how the female principle in the act of creation can be either valued, devalued, or denied. Despite the fact that the female has obvious involvement in human creation, by downplaying or rejecting a birth metaphor, creation myths can minimize or deny altogether the importance of any female creative principle. Scientific theories, developed in the context of cosmogonic depreciation of the female role in creation, similarly minimize the female role in human creation. This will be discussed in the next chapter.

It has been argued that this pattern of demotion of the female creative force is well documented in the *Theogony*. The classical scholar Apostolos Athanassakis, for example, claimed that "since Zeus, the male Sky god, is ultimately descended from Mother Earth, we have here [in the *Theogony*] the record of an evolutionary process that takes us from the physical to the nonphysical, and from female dominance to male dominance."[29] Since the *Theogony*, of the three creation myths examined, places the highest value on the female creative principle in the origin of the universe, it is important to trace this evolutionary process.

THE OLYMPIAN GODS: THE DEMOTION OF THE FEMALE

FOUR GENERATIONS OF GODS.

The *Theogony* contains an account of four divine generations: (1) Chaos and Gaia; (2) Gaia and Ouranos, and Night; (3) Rheia and Kronos, and Strife; and

(4) Zeus. In the beginning, neither Gaia (Earth) nor Chaos had mates. The sky (Ouranos), the sea (Pontos), and the mountains were born from Gaia parthenogenetically. Chaos gave birth to Erebos and Night apart from any male element. The first divine generation is thus female.

In the second generation, Gaia coupled with Ouranos and gave birth to a host of gods: Okeanos, Koios, Kreios, Hyperion, Iapetos, Theia, Rheia, Themis, Mnemosyne, Phoibe, Tethys, Kronos, Kyklopes, Brontes, Steropes, Arges, Kottos, Briareos, and Gyges. But all of these children hated Ouranos "from the day they were born, / for as soon as each one came from the womb, / Ouranos, with joy in his wicked work, hid it / in Gaia's womb and did not let it return to the light."[30] Gaia, "groaned within herself / and in her distress she devised a crafty and evil scheme" to punish Ouranos for this deed.[31] She produced iron and from it made a huge sickle, and showed it to her children, intending that they use it to punish their father. "Fear gripped them all." Only Kronos agreed to help his mother in this deed. She "confided in him her entire scheme," made him sit in ambush, and placed the sickle in his hands.[32] Kronos was in Gaia's womb, where Ouranos had imprisoned him, and there he waited for his father. Ouranos, "longing for Gaia's love," lay upon her. Kronos waited until Ouranos had entered Gaia and then "reached out from his hiding place and seized him / with his left hand, while with his right he grasped / the huge, long, and sharp-toothed sickle and swiftly hacked off / his father's genitals."[33]

The power of the female creative principle is still very strong in this second generation. Although Gaia's issue resulted from the conjunction of female and male principles, the female element remained the most powerful. When Ouranos, the male principle, attempted to thwart creation by putting the children back into her womb, the active and powerful Gaia was able to devise a plan to stop him.

The second generation issuing from Chaos also continues to illustrate the power of the female principle. Erebos and Night, the parthenogenetic children of Chaos, had initially coupled and given birth to Ether and Day. After the castration of Ouranos, Night gave birth to "hideous Moros and black Ker, / and then to Death and Sleep and to the brood of Dreams."[34] She then gave parthenogenetic birth to Momos, Oizys, the Hesperides, Keres, the Moirai, Klotho, Lachesis, and Atropos, Nemesis, Deception, Passion, Old Age, and Strife. The female creative principle remained powerful, although some of Night's children represent negative forces in human life.

In the third generation descended from Gaia, Rheia "succumbed to Kronos's love and bore him illustrious children": Hestia, Demeter, Hera, Hades, Earthshaker, and Zeus.[35] But Kronos, to prevent any of his children from usurping his power, swallowed them as they were born. Knowing from experience that he was not sufficiently protected from their power by imprisoning them within their mother's womb, he enveloped them within his own body where, as part of him, they could do no harm. By swallowing the children, Kronos caused Rheia endless grief, so when she was pregnant with Zeus, she begged her parents, Gaia and Ouranos, to help her save him. They agreed, and just as she was about to give birth sent her to Crete, where Gaia could hide Zeus and care for him. When Kronos came to Rheia demanding his child, "she handed [him] a huge stone wrapped in swaddling clothes. / He took it in his hands and stuffed it into his belly."[36] Under Gaia's care, Zeus grew swiftly, "and, as the year followed its revolving course, / sinuous-minded Kronos was deceived by Gaia's / cunning suggestions to disgorge his own offspring— / overpowered also by the craft and brawn of his own son."[37]

A pattern repeats itself in these two succession myths, but with a very interesting variation. In the second generation, Ouranos attempted to obstruct the full creation of his children by forcing them to return to Gaia's womb. In this way, he inhibited the development of their powers in order to ensure his reign. Kronos acted in a similar fashion. Like Ouranos, he wished to prevent any of his children from usurping his power. But rather than placing the children back into their mother, he placed them *inside himself.* Kronos employed the same technique as Ouranos: obstructing the development of his children's powers by not allowing them to separate from their parent. However, instead of imprisoning the products of creation within the female parent's body, Kronos enveloped them within his own body. Although the children still issue from the body of the mother, in the succession myth of Kronos the products of creation are contained within the body of the father.

This variation on the pattern stems from a gradual increase in the power of the masculine principle, which is paralleled by a decrease in the power of the female principle. In the first succession myth, Gaia devised the scheme to free her children, with her son Kronos playing an important but secondary role. In the second myth, Rheia is passive. She was unable to devise a plan of her own and required the help of her parents, Gaia and Ouranos.

The third generation descended from Chaos shows a similar demotion of the female principle. One of the children of Night's parthenogenetic creation, Strife, bore offspring in turn. Since no mate is mentioned, Strife appears to have had her children parthenogenetically. Although the female principle is powerful enough to give birth independently of any male force, the offspring of such births are, with each successive generation, increasingly negative. Night's parthenogenetic offspring, part of the second generation, are a mixture of good (Hesperides, Moirai, Klotho, Lachesis, and Atropos) and bad (Momos, Oizys, Keres, Nemesis, Deception, Passion, Old Age, and Strife). Strife's offspring, the third generation, are all negative forces: "Ponos, the bringer of pains, / Oblivion and Famine and tearful Sorrows, / the Clashes and the Battles and the Manslaughters, / the Quarrels and the Lies and Argument and Counter-Argument, / Lawlessness and Ruin whose ways are all alike, / and Oath, who, more than any other, brings pains on mortals / who of their own accord swear false oaths."[38]

Zeus is the fourth generation descended from Gaia. He, like Kronos before him, knew of the prophesy that a son would take his power. Zeus married Metis (Resourcefulness, Wisdom), "a mate wiser than all gods and mortal men,"[39] and Metis became pregnant with a daughter, Tritogeneia (Athena), "who in strength and wisdom would be her father's match."[40] Metis's second child was destined to be a son who would rule over gods and men. When she was about to bear Tritogeneia, Zeus, desiring to continue his reign, "deceived the mind of Metis with guile / and coaxing words, and lodged her in his belly."[41]

Again, like Kronos, Zeus contrived to thwart the birth of his prophesied successor by swallowing him. But he devised a plan that surpassed Kronos's: Zeus swallowed Metis, the female principle herself, rather than the products of their mating. The female principle and her offspring could no longer pose a threat to the male principle. By enveloping the principle within himself, Zeus assimilated her power and assured his own supremacy. Metis, lodged in Zeus's belly, advised him on matters good and bad.[42] The female creative principle is thus subsumed by the male and takes on the secondary, more passive role of advisor.

The fourth generation of gods brings a complete demotion of the powers of the female creative principle. Zeus not only enveloped within himself female wisdom: by swallowing the pregnant Metis, he also acquired the expressly female power to give birth. Zeus bore his gray-eyed daughter, Athena, "from his head."[43] Thus the male principle has taken within himself all of the powers of the female. Moreover, there is no fourth generation descended from Chaos, for Strife's offspring are barren, containing in themselves no creative spark. The generation of Chaos have become impotent. The powers of Gaia are now controlled by Zeus. The male principle reigns.

BIRTH REVERSALS.

Through these four generation of gods in the *Theogony* we see a gradual displacement of the female principle's role in creation. Originally the primal creative force, the female principle is ultimately demoted to very minor participation; the key image in this demotion is the reversal of the birth process. The central metaphor of creation in the *Theogony* is that of birth, and the male gods achieve power by reversing its normal course.

The first reversal occurred when Ouranos forced his children to remain in the womb of their mother, Gaia. Rather than the children becoming separate from the mother after birth, Ouranos reversed the process by placing the children back in the womb. Kronos similarly reversed the normal process, but his reversal was twofold. Not only were the children placed back inside the body after birth, they were placed in the male body instead of the female body. Kronos thus not only reversed the internal/external birth order, he also inverted the internal location from the female body to the male.

The image of swallowing or enveloping is central to all of these birth reversals. Ouranos forced Gaia to re-envelop her children. Kronos swallowed his own children. Most dramatically, Zeus swallowed his children's mother, Metis. Unlike both Ouranos and Kronos, Zeus did not allow the normal birth process to occur prior to his reversals. By swallowing Metis, Zeus accomplished his first reversal—the female creative principle was enveloped by the male creative principle, and thereby made less powerful. Through this act of assimilation, Zeus guaranteed his reign by gaining control over the very process in which he was created and received his power.

Zeus's reversals do not end here, for his swallowing of Metis results in three subsequent birth reversals. Although Zeus assimilated Metis, Athena continued to live within him. Like Kronos, Zeus also reversed the birth process by carrying his offspring within him. And there is a second birth reversal when Zeus gives birth to Athena: the child now issues from the male rather than the female. In the third reversal, Zeus gives birth through the head rather than the womb. This is a final, important reversal, since the head, associated with reason, is seen as the opposite of the womb, associated with passion.[44]

The birth reversals of Zeus were popular images of classical mythology. The story of Athena was retold or mentioned in such works as the *Hymns* of Orpheus, *The Oresteia* of Aeschylus, the Homeric *Hymn to Athena*, Apollodorus's *Library*, the *Odes* of Pindar, and Homer's *Iliad*. Most of these emphasize Athena's emergence from Zeus's head. Orpheus referred to Athena as she "of splendid mien," who "sprung from the head of Jove."[45] Pindar elaborated on the myth by explaining that Zeus was assisted in this birth by Hephaistos, the god of the crafts and technology, who made a breach in Zeus's skull through Athena could pass. "By the artifice of Hephaistos, / at the stroke of the bronze-heeled axe Athene sprang / from the height of her father's head with a strong cry."[46] Hephaistos is the god of *techne*, of art and artifice. With Pindar's addition of his role in the birthing of Athena, the craftsperson metaphor of creation is wedded to a birth metaphor!

Some of the implications of Athena's birth reversal are clearly illustrated by Aeschylus. In his *Oresteia*, Aeschylus told how Agamemnon, on return from his victory in the Trojan War, was killed by his wife Clytemnestra, as revenge for his earlier sacrifice of their daughter Iphigenia. Orestes, the son of Clytemnestra and Agamemnon, then followed the command of Apollo, and killed Clytemnestra to avenge his father's death. Chased to the shrine of Apollo at Delphi by the Furies, Orestes was forced to stand trial for matricide, the most terrible of crimes. Athena presided over the trial; Apollo pleaded Orestes's case. Apollo argued that Orestes was not guilty of killing his parent, on the grounds that the true parent is the father, not the mother. Apollo insisted that *"man* is the source of life," while woman is simply "a nurse to the seed."[47] To prove his claims, he gave the example of Athena, father-born, she who is without a mother.

Aeschylus's Apollo voices a perspective that becomes important in classical conceptions of human reproduction. His words express the belief that the true parent is the father, for the male seed is the primary creative force. The woman is like a plowed field that merely provides nourishment for the fertile seed.[48]

SPERM CHILDREN.

This theme—that the male seed is the primary source of creation—is repeated frequently in classical mythology. Male seed was perceived as being so powerful that it could generate a child when placed in fertile surroundings. We will see the ways in which science mirrored this idea in the next chapter.

The birth of Erichthonius, child of Hephaistos, illustrates this belief in the potency of the male seed. Athena went to the forge of Hephaistos to ask him to make her a set of weapons. Poseidon, angry at Athena for rejecting his advances and wishing to cause trouble for her, told Hephaistos that Athena was attracted to him and was coming to express her desire. Believing Poseidon, Hephaistos thrust himself at Athena when she entered the forge. Athena wanted to remain a virgin and attempted to flee, but Hephaistos caught her and embraced her. Although Athena continued to fight off his advances, Hephaistos was so aroused that he ejaculated against her thigh. Athena wiped off her thigh with a piece of wool, which she threw to the ground. When the seed of Hephaistos mixed with the earth, Erichthonius was produced.[49]

In this story, male seed is potent enough to create life when it is placed in nourishing surroundings. The earth is an obvious source of nourishment, and in many stories of sperm children, the male seed falls to the earth. The sea is an alternate source of nourishment. For example, when Kronos cut off Ouranos's genitals with Gaia's sickle, he threw them into the sea.[50] After a time, a "white foam rose from the god's flesh, and in this foam a maiden / was nurtured."[51] The maiden was Aphrodite, and she is "fond of a man's genitals, / because to them she owed her birth."[52] Like Erichthonius, Aphrodite was born of man alone.[53]

The relative weakness of the female creative force reinforces this image of the potency of the male creative force. There are very few myths in which a being arises from the mixture of earth and the female force. An example is the story of Medusa, one of the Gorgons, who was raped by Poseidon in the temple of Athena. Enraged that her temple would be so desecrated, Athena changed Medusa into a winged monster with glaring eyes, huge teeth, protruding tongue, brazen claws, and serpent locks.[54] Athena made her so ugly that anyone who looked upon her face would be turned to stone.[55] But Perseus killed Medusa by cutting off her head, which he took with him. While flying over the Libyan desert (wearing the winged sandals of Hermes), Perseus spilled some of Medusa's blood onto the desert sand. These drops bred a swarm of venomous serpents.[56]

The blood of Medusa produces neither god nor mortal, but a crop of dangerous snakes, for the creative power of female blood is viewed as far inferior to that of male sperm. Furthermore, the *Theogony* depicts male *blood* as highly potent. When Kronos cut off Ouranos's genitals, Gaia saved all the bloody drops that spattered off and used them to bear "the potent Furies and the Giants, immense, / dazzling in their armor, holding long spears in their hands, / and then she bore the Ash Tree Nymphs of the boundless earth.[57] Male blood is capable of producing wonders, while female blood produces vipers.

The parthenogenetic offspring of Hera also illustrate the perceived inferiority of the female creative force. According to classical sources, Hera has two such children, Hephaistos and Typhaon. Hephaistos is Hera's first parthenogenetic child. In the Homeric "Hymn to Pythian Apollo," Hera is depicted as despising her son Hephaistos because he is defective. She is angry because Zeus has just given birth to Athena, whose perfection (particularly in comparison to Hephaistos) is the source of her anger. "Now apart from me he gave birth to a grey-eyed Athena, / who excels among all the blessed immortals. / But my son, Hephaistos, whom I myself bore / has grown to be weak-legged and lame among the blessed gods. / I took him with my own hands and cast him into the broad sea."[58]

Zeus, the male creative principle, gives birth to a perfect offspring, Athena, one of the most important and respected of the Olympian gods. Hera, the female creative principle, can produce only a defective being. Hephaistos's defective gait and his frequent cuckoldings by his wife, Aphrodite, are the source of jokes and laughter among the gods.[59] Zeus's child is honored by the gods; Hera's child is laughed at.

Angered by all of this, Hera decided to bear another child parthenogenetically. "And now, I shall contrive to have born to me / a child who will excel among the immortals. / And to our sacred wedlock I shall bring no shame, / nor visit your [Zeus's] bed, but I shall pass my time / far from you, among the immortal gods."[60] Hera then struck the earth her hand, crying out for help from Earth and Sky to bear a child stronger than Zeus.

> Thus she cried out and lashed the earth with her stout hand.
> Then the life-giving earth was moved and Hera saw it,
> and her heart was delighted at the thought of fulfillment.
> From then on, and until a full year came to its end,
> she never came to the bed of contriving Zeus. . . .
> But when the months and the days reached their destined goal,
> and the seasons arrived as the year revolved,
> she bore dreadful and baneful Typhaon, a scourge to mortals,
> whose aspect resembled neither god's nor man's.
> Forthwith cow-eyed, mighty Hera took him and, piling evil
> upon evil, she commended him to the care of the she-dragon.
> He worked many evils on the glorious races of men.[61]

So Hera's second parthenogenetic birth was even less perfect than her first. Typhaon, far from being outstanding, was a monster neither human nor divine. As with Hephaistos, Hera rejected this defective offspring, giving it to the she-dragon (Typhoeus). But Typhaon was even more imperfect than Hephaistos, for this child was both evil and mortal. The female creative force, although not entirely impotent, is perceived as defective in comparison to the male creative force—a theme mirrored in scientific theories of reproduction for many centuries.

PANDORA.

Hesiod's detailed account of Pandora's creation reinforces that demotion of the female principle of creation. Zeus decided to create Pandora to punish man for Prometheus's twofold deception: the trick involving the sacrificial ox, and the theft of the fire. And so Pandora was fashioned as a trap for man, like Prometheus's first trick—desirable on the outside, repulsive on the inside.

In order to create Pandora, Zeus ordered Hephaistos, Athena, Aphrodite, the Graces, Persuasion, the Seasons, and Hermes to assist him by giving Pandora gifts. The gifts of the male gods are strikingly different from those of the female gods. Zeus ordered Hephaistos "to mix earth with water / with all haste and place in them human voice / and strength," for Hephaistos was to give this being a face as beautiful as that of a goddess and the figure of a lovely maiden.[62] Hermes was ordered by Zeus to "put in her the mind of a bitch and a thievish nature," and Hermes "placed in her breast / lies, coaxing words, and a thievish nature."[63] The gifts of the two male gods thus provide Pandora with all that is essential to her being. Her body and its shape and strength, her face and its countenance, her voice, her mind, and her nature were all crafted by male gods.

Although there are far more female than male gods involved in the creation of Pandora, their gifts are far less substantial. Athena "was to teach her skills and intricate weaving."[64] She also clothed her and "adorned her body with every kind of jewel."[65] Aphrodite was to "pour grace round the maiden's head, / and stinging desire and limb-gnawing passion."[66] The Graces and Persuasion gave her golden necklaces to wear, while the Seasons crowned her with spring flowers.[67]

The female gods' gifts are relatively insignificant in comparison to those of the male gods. Whereas the latter gave Pandora such essentials as her body and her mind, the former gave her primarily external ornaments. Only Athena's skills and Aphrodite's grace and passion add to Pandora's basic nature. The rest—her clothes and jewels—are merely finery that will, at best, augment the beauty given to her by Hephaistos. Hesiod's description of the creation of Pandora reinforces the view that the female contribution is not essential, for the male gives form to that which is created.

BIRTH REVERSALS IN THE CHRISTIAN TRADITION

EVE AND MARY.

Birth reversals similar to those depicted in classical myths are also found in biblical literature. The Genesis story of the creation of the universe solely from a male source emphasizes the primacy of the male creative principle. The second version of the story of human creation, in which man is formed out of dust and woman from his rib, contains many images parallel to those of Hesiod. As Hephaistos formed Pandora from clay and Hermes placed a mind or soul within her, the god of Genesis formed the first man from the dust of the ground and breathed life into him. The created beings in both stories owe their existence to male gods.

There is also a birth reversal similar to those found in the *Theogony* in the Genesis story of the creation of woman. God caused man to fall into a deep sleep and took from him one of his ribs. "And the rib which the Lord God had taken from the man he made into a woman" (Genesis 2:22). The Genesis image of woman's creation inverts the biological birth process as the created being comes out of the body of the male. Creation is represented as craft or art, the imposition of form upon matter, and woman is formed by God from matter taken from the male. In the Genesis story, the male is thus both the material and formal cause of woman's being. Through such reversals, the creative function of woman is given to man.

The Genesis creation myth not only posits an exclusive role for the male creative force in the generation of the universe, it also emphasizes that, despite woman's earthly role in reproduction, she originally emanated from man. As we saw earlier, man is treated as the ultimate cause of woman: he provides the material out of which she is formed, and is also her end and her purpose. Woman is created to be his helpmate: " 'It is not good that the man should be alone; I will make a helper fit for him' " (Genesis 2:18). Woman arises out of man's body and is bent to man's needs.

The biblical story of the birth of Jesus also reflects the image of the primacy of the male creative force. Although not involving a birth reversal, the myth of the Virgin Mary emphasizes the role of male in conception. The Gospel of Luke is the most complete biblical rendition of this myth. According to Luke, an angel was sent to Mary when she was still a virgin to announce the miracle that was to take place. "And the angel said to her, 'Do not be afraid, Mary, for you have found favor with God. And behold, you will conceive in your womb and bear a son, and you shall call his name Jesus' " (Luke 1:30–31). When Mary protested that this could not be, since she had no husband, the angel explained that " 'the Holy Spirit will come upon you, / and the power of the Most High will overshadow you; / therefore the child to be born will be called holy, / the Son of God' " (Luke 1:35).

The biblical myth was augmented in later centuries by theological speculations on the nature of this miraculous conception. According to the received view, Jesus, the son of God, existed from the beginning of time, and was placed in Mary already divinely formed, in order to be united with human flesh. Mary was to provide only the flesh of his being. Pope Leo I (390–?461), for example, explained that "the Son of God came into this world below, coming down from His heavenly seat and without losing His paternal glory, by a new order and a new nativity . . . from the mother the Lord received the nature of flesh but not the guilt."[68]

Thus Mary comes to be seen as fertile earth that provides nourishment for the divine seed of Christ. This metaphor was used extensively by St. Ephrem: " 'Thy husbandman needs no seed: Himself coming down will sow Himself in thy womb, from thee will He spring up as the herb, and will satiate the world's hunger.' "[69] The female role is minimal: Mary provides only the soil out of which the flesh of Jesus is formed, while his nature is divinely crafted. Thus, the male creative force determines form and soul; the female provides only the flesh. "On the branch of the Virgin Mary, God, coming down from on high, hung the fruit."[70] That fruit is already formed, and Mary is merely the tree that supports its growth.

Both central female figures in the Bible, Eve as well as Mary, are associated with myths concerning the potency of the male creative force. Since the sole creative principle of the universe in the Bible is male, it is not surprising that woman, man, and the son of God, central figures in the divine plan of the universe, are all created by male forces.

SOPHIA.

A similar privileging of the male creative principle was reflected in many writings of the Gnostic tradition, which involved a blend of Christian, Greek, and Zoroastrian views. By the second century CE there were numerous Gnostic sects. The metaphysics of Gnosticism interpreted the universe in terms of basic dualities or opposite forces: light and darkness, good and evil, man and woman. This Gnostic tradition differed somewhat from the Christian in that female cre-

13. The Campin altarpiece depicts the baby Jesus, already formed by God, flying to Mary. Notice his descent in the upper left corner of the panel, between the two round windows. Robert Campin, *Merode Altarpiece*, c. 1425–1430. The Metropolitan Museum of Art, The Cloisters Collection, 1956. (56.70)

ative principles sometimes played a role. Although the female creative principle was often far stronger in the Gnostic tradition than in the Christian, the Greek and Christian influences carried with them the usual depreciation of female creativity. The *Apocryphon of John* is an excellent example of the Gnostic blend, viewing the female creative principle as important yet inferior to the male creative principle.

The *Apocryphon of John* dates back to the second century CE. Its themes involve the origin of evil and the means by which humans can escape the evils of the world. According to this myth the ultimate creative force is male. It is referred to as the "Perfect One," "the spring of the water of life," and the "Father." However, with the first thought of the Perfect One, the female principle appeared. "And [his Ennoia performed a] deed and she came forth, [namely] she who had [appeared] before him in [the shine of] his light."[71] The female principle is referred to as "the first [power which was] before all of them."[72] Like Athena, she came "forth from his [the Father's] mind, and her light resembled that of the Father."[73] "Her light [is the likeness of the] light, the [perfect] power which is [the] image of the invisible, virginal Spirit who is perfect . . . [she] is the first thought, his image; she became the womb of everything for she is prior to them all."[74]

There is an interesting mixture of images here. The female principle is not primordial, but is dependent upon the Perfect One, the male creative principle that is eternal. She issues from the thought or the mind of the Father, and like Metis in the belly of Zeus, she gives counsel to the Perfect One. It is at her request that the Perfect One creates the four principles of foreknowledge, indestructibility, eternal life, and truth.[75]

At this point the Father unites with the female principle, Barbelo, to create Christ. "And he looked within Barbelo with the pure light which surrounds the invisible Spirit and (with) his spark, she conceived from him. He begot a spark of light with a light of blessed likeness."[76] This version of the creation of Christ is similar, at a metaphorical level, to the Christian depiction. Both involve a union of the male and the female principles, and in both it is the male principle that is active, for it is the Father who enters. The female principle merely conceives, while the Father begets. Furthermore, the perfection of Christ is due to the Father: "And he anointed it with his goodness until it became perfect."[77]

Up to this point, the female creative principle, though less potent than the male, is not viewed as defective. That image emerges after the creation of Sophia, one of the host of beings created after Christ, who is depicted as having brought evil into the world. Sophia "conceived a thought." She wanted to "bring forth a likeness out of herself without the consent of the Spirit—he had not approved—and without her consort and without his consideration."[78] Like Hera, she brought forth a child by herself. And like Hera's parthenogenetic offspring, Sophia's child was defective. "Her thought did not remain idle and a thing came out of her which was imperfect and different from her appearance, because she had created it without her consort."[79] Just as Hera gave birth to the monster Typhaon, Sophia conceived a "lion-faced serpent."[80] Again like Hera, "she cast it away from her, outside that place, that no one of the immortal ones might see it, for she had created it in ignorance."[81] She named her child Yaltabaoth. In addition to other defects, Yaltabaoth was both ignorant and insane.

The female creative force, it seems, functions properly only when passive and acting in harmony with the male creative force. On her own, the female force creates defective children—monsters and madness.[82]

We thus see a set of themes common to classical, Christian, and Gnostic versions of the creation story. All of them credit the male principle as the primary creative force. The male actively forms his offspring; the female merely receives what is placed in her by the male and nurtures it. The male seed provides form and purpose; the female provides only the material of creation. This perception of the primacy of male creative power had a strong influence on classical scientific views of reproduction, which in turn influenced scientific theories of generation well into the eighteenth century.

SEVEN

The Weaker Seed

Western religious conceptions of the creation of the universe uniformly ascribe primacy to the generative powers of the male principle. With the strong influence of the Genesis story, the most prevalent metaphor of creation has been that of a craftsperson imposing form upon unformed matter. Embryological theories gave expression to, and elaborated on, both the craftsperson metaphor and the tenet of the primacy of the male principle. Although the female role in generation was never fully discounted by any scientific theory, it was consistently perceived as making a less important contribution than the male. Woman furnished the unformed matter upon which man crafted human form and nature. He was the master artist of human generation; she merely supplied the raw materials for his work.

THE PRIMACY OF MALE GENERATIVE POWERS: CLASSICAL VIEWS

While scientific theories of human generation in the classical period agreed on the primacy of the male role, they disagreed on the exact nature of the female contribution. Aristotle insisted that the female provided only matter, nourishing the fetus formed in her by the male seed. To support his view, Aristotle even attempted to prove that the male alone contributed seed to generation. While Hippocrates and Galen held that both male and female produced seed, they agreed that female seed was less potent than male seed.

WOMAN'S IMPOTENT SEMEN: ARISTOTLE.

Aristotle acknowledged both female and male principles in generation: the male contains "the efficient cause of generation," while the female contains "the material of it."[1] And he believed that there are four factors involved in creation: "first, the final cause, that for the sake of which; secondly, the definition of essence (and these two we may regard pretty much as one and the same); thirdly, the material; and fourthly, that from which the source of movement comes."[2] Limiting the female role in reproduction to the material cause of generation, Aristotle attributed the remaining three causes to the male. "What the male contributes to generation is the form and the efficient cause, while the female contributes the material."[3]

So Aristotle maintained that the female gave nothing to the form or function of the created being, but merely supplied the blood upon which the male imposes form. He supported this position by arguing that the female provides no seed in the act of generation. The equation of woman's menstrual fluids with man's semen was a central premise in Aristotle's proof of woman's defect in heat, and he used this same argument to prove that woman is impotent. To review briefly: by Aristotle's account, human semen is formed from blood. Male semen, however, does not resemble blood. Aristotle claimed that semen's whiteness proved that it had been well "cooked" or concocted by the superior heat of the male, which concentrated the potency of the blood and changed its appearance.

Aristotle then argued that "menstrual discharge is a residue, and that it is analogous in females to the semen in males."[4] His primary justification for this view was the observation that the menstrual flow begins in woman about the same time that semen begins to appear and be emitted in man. Similarly, woman goes through menopause about the same time that "the generative power fails" in man.[5] Aristotle assumed that female seed would be visibly emitted, like that of males. Since menstrual fluid "is what corresponds in the female to the semen in the male, and since it is not possible that two seminal discharges should be found together, it is plain that the female does not contribute semen to the generation of the offspring. For if she had semen she would not have the menstrual fluid; but, as it is, because she has the latter she has not the former."[6] In other words, woman's menstrual fluid is the blood that would be turned into potent semen if she had sufficient heat to concoct it.

The untenability of this view rests on the equation of menstrual with seminal fluids. Men have nothing that corresponds to menstrual fluids, and there are striking differences between menstrual fluids and semen. The most obvious is that menses occur only once a month and are not associated with intercourse or genital stimulation, while male seminal fluid is emitted whenever there is sufficient stimulation for ejaculation. It would have been logical for Aristotle to consider whether females also emit a fluid during intercourse or other genital stimulation that is analogous to male semen, and in fact, such a view was popular enough that he did attempt to refute it. "Some think that the female contributes semen in coition because the pleasure she experiences is sometimes similar to that of the male, and also is attended by a liquid discharge."[7]

Aristotle raised three objections against this position. First, he claimed that this discharge did not occur in all women, but appeared only "in those who are fairskinned and of a feminine type generally, but not in those who are dark and of a masculine appearance."[8] (He gave no explanation of how he arrived at this conclusion.) Since some women do not have this discharge, yet all can conceive, Aristotle concluded that it cannot constitute woman's seminal fluid.

Second, Aristotle noted that "the pleasure of intercourse is caused by touch in the same region of the female as of the male; and yet it is not from thence that this flow proceeds."[9] Aristotle appears to be arguing that it would be incorrect to associate this discharge with male semen, for unlike men, it does not issue from the place of stimulation.

It should be obvious by now that these arguments are contrived, and that Aristotle is straining against observation in attempts to support his own theory. All women have lubricating fluids. These fluids can be produced in a woman by stimulating the vulva or vagina, causing them to issue from the place touched. Furthermore, a male can ejaculate from stimulation of areas other than his penis, in which case the flow proceeds from a region other than that touched.

Only one of Aristotle's objections is not contrived. His third objection was that the association of lubricating fluids with female semen is fallacious because women often conceive without the sensation of pleasure in intercourse.[10] Since a woman can conceive without emitting such fluids, these fluids cannot be seminal. While acknowledging the strength of this piece of reasoning, one must also notice that Aristotle does not deal with the parallel fact that men may ejaculate during intercourse without pregnancy resulting. This gives us good reason to believe that the male ejaculate alone is not sufficient for conception; otherwise, we would expect a pregnancy every time a man ejaculated into a woman's vagina. Aristotle failed to mention this anomaly. Had he dealt with it, he might have arrived at speculation about the existence of a female seed that is only periodically emitted.

Aristotle's tenet that woman produces no semen had numerous ramifications for his understanding of human creation. He supported the view that the fetus is contained within the male, who places it in the female. "By definition the male is that which is able to generate in another . . . the female is that which is able to generate in itself and out of which comes into being the offspring *previously existing in the generator.*"[11]

Careful attention to Aristotle's theory reveals that the offspring should not be thought of as existing preformed in the body of the male. Rather, the male imparts the form of the fetus to the female. The metaphor Aristotle used to explain this process was very similar to the craftsperson metaphor of Genesis, for he compared the process of conception to that of a carpenter carving out a bed. In conception, the woman provides the raw material, just as the tree provides the wood. But it is the man who, like the carpenter, determines the function of the object to be produced and gives it its form. The female body becomes the workplace and source of raw material out of which the male crafts a human life.[12] Just as the god of Genesis imposed form on the dust of the earth and breathed life into it, the seed of the male imposes the nature of a human being on the blood of a woman's womb.

A value underlying this metaphor is that the female's role in generation, though necessary, is relatively unimportant, since she merely provides the raw material out of which a fetus will be formed. For Aristotle, the material cause involved the least degree of being or perfection of all the four causes: "the first efficient or moving cause, to which belong the definition and the form, is better and more divine in its nature than the material on which it works . . . for the first principle of movement, whereby that which comes into being is male, is better and more divine, and the female is matter."[13] Woman is thus relegated to the least significant of all the causes. Man, in providing the form and motion of the fetus, is far more responsible for its generation.

Aristotle reinforced his thesis of the excellence of the male contribution to generation by arguing that it involved nothing material; he thus made the assumption that nonmaterial substance has a higher degree of perfection than material substance. Using the analogy of the carpenter, Aristotle depicted male semen as a tool that moves upon the material within the womb and imparts form and motion, but does not become a part of the fetus. "While the body is from the female, it is the soul that is from the male, for the soul is the substance of a particular body."[14]

The female, like Tiamat, provides only the flesh upon which the male imposes form and imparts soul; the female contribution is again held to be inferior. "For the female is, as it were, a mutilated male, and the menstrual fluids are semen, only not pure; for there is only one thing they have not in them, the principle of soul."[15] Aristotle echoes the words of Aeschylus's Apollo: "the woman you call the mother of the child / is not the parent, just a nurse to the seed, / the new-sown seed that grows and swells inside her. / The *man* is the source of life."[16]

WOMAN'S LESS POTENT SEMEN: HIPPOCRATES AND GALEN.

Aristotle's view of the primacy of the male principle of creation was consistent with both the metaphysical views of his time and other scientific theories of generation. His embryological theory, however, was extreme in holding that only the male contributed seed. Many classical theorists, including Anaxagoras, Empedocles, Hippocrates, and Parmenides, believed that the fetus was the result of a combination of male and female semen. But although they gave woman a role in the creation of the form as well as the material of the fetus, they uniformly held that her contribution was less potent.

Hippocrates, for example, believed that both woman and man produced seed.[17] According to his account, there are two types of seed: female and male. Although woman and man produce both kinds of seed, he held that woman produced feebler seed. So although woman contributes to the form of the offspring, her contribution is inferior to that of man.

Hippocrates also believed that generation could result in six types of individuals, depending on the particular combination of seed. A mix of male and female seed would produce a man if the male seed dominates. If the father contributes the male seed and the mother the female seed, the offspring will be courageous. But if the dominant male seed is from the mother and the female seed from the father, the resulting individual will be a hermaphrodite. A mix of male and female seed where the female seed dominates will result in a female. If the dominant female seed originates from the father, the daughter will be "bold yet graceful," but if it originates from the mother, she will be "brazen and mannish." If both the mother and the father contribute male seed, the offspring will become a man who is "brilliant in soul and strong in body." The sixth possible individual would result from a mixture of female seed from both parents and would be the "most female and very well-endowed."[18] Notice that the characteristics resulting from dominant female seed are less perfect than those resulting from dominant male seed—a sign of woman's less potent seed.

Galen, although strongly influenced by the Aristotelian worldview, agreed with Hippocrates on the issue of woman's semen. However, he went beyond the Hippocratic position in offering a biological explanation of the inferiority of woman's semen. Galen insisted that woman's genitals are less formed, and thus less perfect, than those of man, and since her organs of generation are not fully formed, the obvious inference is that her semen is also imperfect. "The female must have smaller, less perfect testes, and the semen generated in them must be scantier, colder, and wetter (for these things too follow of necessity from the deficient heat)."[19]

Galen claimed that female seed, whether produced by woman or by man, is inferior to that of male seed. Not only is the semen produced by woman weaker than that produced by man, the seed out of which a female is conceived is also less perfect than the seed out of which a male is conceived. In order to prove this second point, Galen accepted the popular classical view that male seed is produced in the right testis and female seed in the left. According to this theory, a girl would be produced when seed from the left testis of the male combined with seed from the left testis (ovary) of the female and implanted in the left side of the uterus, for the left side of the uterus was believed to provide nourishment that results in female characteristics. The Hippocratic permutations are determined both by the testis from which the seeds originate and by the side of the uterus in which the mixture of seeds implants.

On the basis of his idea of seed origination, Galen was able to construct a biological explanation of the inferiority of female seed. Using very creative anatomy, Galen explained that the spermatic and ovarian artery and vein going to the right testis and right side of the uterus arise directly from the vena cava and the aorta below the level of the renal vessels, thus carrying blood already cleansed by the kidneys. The corresponding veins and arteries of the left testis, however, arise from the renal vessels going to the left kidney, and thus carry uncleansed blood.

We now know that the veins and arteries of both sides arise from the vena cava and aorta, but Galen's mistake proved to be a very convenient explanation of the cause of woman's biological inferiority. Holding that they are fed from veins that pass to the kidneys, Galen stated that "the left testis in the male and the left uterus in the female receive blood still uncleansed, full of residues, watery and serous, and so it happens that the temperatures of the instruments themselves that receive [the blood] become different."[20] In other words, the blood going to the left side is impure. And because of its impurity, such blood contains less heat, which will result in production of imperfect seed. The male seed, however, fed from pure blood, is able to achieve complete development and is thus more perfect than the female seed.

Galen's anatomical error provides the explanation, missing from the Aristotelian account, of why woman is deficient in heat. Although Aristotle based all of woman's imperfections on this defect, he failed to provide any account of the mechanism that causes it. Galen's creative anatomy provides this mechanism: the impurity of the blood out of which female seed is generated accounts for woman's inferior heat. Since woman is conceived out of impure blood, she is colder than man. Due to this defect in heat, her organs of generation are not fully formed, and the seed produced by them is imperfect.

Religion postulated a male being—Marduk, Elohim, Zeus—as the ultimate creative force to account for the primacy of the male creative principle. Science pointed to the anatomy of the testes.

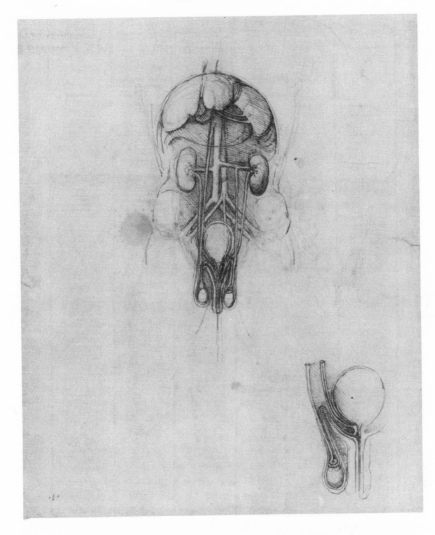

14. Leonardo da Vinci's rendition of the anatomy of the veins to the testicles. da Vinci, Genito-urinary system of the male (19099r/Q III 5r). By permission of Her Majesty the Queen. Windsor Castle, Royal Library. © Her Majesty Queen Elizabeth II.

THE PERPETUATION OF MALE GENERATIVE PRIMACY

Aristotelian biology, corrected by the work of Galen, remained authoritative for many centuries. Aristotle's claim that man provided the primary causes of generation, and Galen's explanation of woman's imperfection and the related weakness of her creative powers, were repeated by scientists well into the sixteenth century. Although the elegance of Galen's account might partially explain the popularity of this position, the fact that it is based on an anatomical error suggests an alternate reason. Scientific theories reflect the values and attitudes of their authors. One would expect that the Apollonic and Jahwistic metaphysics informing thought from the classical period through modern time would influence scientific explanations as well as observations.

CONCEPTION AND THEOLOGY.

Christian theorists in the Middle Ages, believing that the creative principle was male, had little trouble accepting Aristotle's view that the male was the primary creative force in human generation. Saint Gregory of Nyssa, adopting this theory, argued that the embryo was implanted by the male in the female.[21] Aquinas compared the generation of humans to the creation of the world: just as God alone can produce a form in matter, "the active force is in the semen of the male." Only the "foetal matter is provided by the female." This matter "is transmuted by the power which is in the semen of the male, until it is actually informed by the sensitive soul."[22] Woman is capable of only the passive, less perfect role of providing the matter upon which the male semen will act.

The views of Jewish commentators also reflect the influence of Aristotelian and Galenic biology. In fact, the Midrashic image of generation is identical to that of Aristotle. Man's sperm acts on woman's menstrual blood, causing it to come together and giving it form. "Job said 'Hast Thou not poured me out like milk and curdled me like cheese, . . .' (Job 10:10–12). A mother's womb is full of standing blood, which flows therefrom in menstruation. But, at God's will, a drop of whiteness enters and falls into its midst and behold a child is formed. This is likened unto a bowl of milk: when a drop of rennet falls into it, it congeals and stands; if not it continues as liquid."[23]

The Jewish view often denied either the existence or the potency of woman's seed. "For, although she has 'eggs' [ovaries] like the eggs [testicles] of the man, either she creates no seed there or that seed . . . has nothing to do with the foetus."[24] At best, when woman was seen as sharing in the formation of the embryo, the less perfect parts were attributed to her role. From the woman's contribution "is formed his [the fetus'] skin, flesh, hair, and black of his eye." From the man's contribution "are formed the child's bones, sinews, nails, brain, and the white in his eye."[25]

PERPETUATING GALEN: THE ANATOMICAL TRADITION, 1200 TO 1700.

The embryological views of Christian and Jewish theologians continued to be supported by contemporary scientific theories of generation. In his *Anatomia Vivorum*, the anatomist Ricardi Anglici (1180–1225) relied on Aristotle's authority and supported a view identical to that of Aquinas. Like Aristotle, Anglici believed that male and female semen are intended for different purposes. He identified female semen with menses, and supported the Aristotelian position that female semen is so imperfectly developed that it can provide only the least perfect of all the causes of generation—the material cause. "The purpose of the male sperm is to give form in the likeliness of that from which the sperm comes; the purpose of the female sperm is to receive the likeness of that from which the sperm comes. From the male sperm, therefore, come spirit and creative power and form; from the female sperm come foundation, generation, and material."[26]

Anglici employed a molding metaphor rather than Aristotle's carpenter to describe the mechanism by which man's sperm gives form to woman's sperm. "The male and female sperms mingle in the uterus, and the male sperm acts upon the female, for the male sperm naturally tends to impress the form of that from which it comes, and the female sperm tends to receive form."[27] Once again the male seed is perceived as active, the female seed as passive.

Albertus Magnus (1206?–1280), whose ideas were very influential and frequently copied, deviated from the Aristotelian view in holding, with Galen, that the female produces seed in addition to her menstrual fluids. But although he accepted the existence of seed in woman, Albertus allowed it only a secondary role in generation. The seed of the man remained the active and formative agent, while the woman's seed had a role only in "preparing and enabling matter [the menstrual fluids] to receive the action from the operator, that is, man's sperm."[28] While rejecting Aristotle's view that the female provides no seed, Albertus attributed to woman the same diminished role in conception as had Aristotle. "The semen is twofold, namely effective and material."[29] The female semen consists only of the latter. "Generation materially is from what is called the woman's sperm."[30] The male sperm, endowed with the primary creative force, or what Albertus called "formative virtue," imparts to the female seed and the menstrual blood its form and end.

Using imagery similar to Anglici's, Albertus offered the metaphor of imprinting to depict the generative process. Upon entering the womb, the male sperm "receives first the female sperm and then also the menstrual blood in which it stamps and imprints the creature's form and members."[31] Like Marduk forming the mountains and rivers out of the flesh of Tiamat, or Elohim giving form to the unformed earth, the male seed informs the blood and seed of the female.

The Galenic modification of Aristotle's views on conception was not, however, uniformly accepted. Giles of Rome (1243–1316) opposed this position in his *De Formatione Corporis Humani in Utero.* He argued that the female seed was not a true seed, and provided neither movement nor form. Its only purposes were to irrigate the womb, thereby moderating its temperature, and to attract the male seed into the uterus. But the male seed alone provided motion and force, and thereby "truly conveys human nature to the offspring." Giles believed that a single agent is required to give form to matter; to have both male and female seed provide a formative function would be superfluous. Given the need for only one motivating agent, Giles argued that this agent could not be the female, for then she would be capable of parthenogenetic generation. Therefore, this function must be only provided by the male seed.[32]

The Galenic explanation of the cause of the weakness of female seed, and ultimately the cause of woman's inferior role in generation, was accepted by the

majority of theorists in the fifteenth and sixteenth centuries, during which one of
the most influential medical texts was *Aristotle's Masterpiece*. This book provided
information concerning generation, as well as contraceptive and midwifery techniques. Its authors, clearly influenced by the writings of Aristotle, also incorporated more recent theories. One of these was Galen's rendition of the anatomy
of the female reproductive system. "The preparatory [spermatic] Vessels differ
not in Number from those in Men, for they are likewise four, two veins and two
arteries; their Rise and Original is the same as in Men, differing only in their
Largeness, and Manner of Insertion; the right Vein issuing from the Trunk of the
hollow vein descending, and the left from the emulgent Vein."[33]

Similarly, Alessandro Achillini (1463–1512), the Italian anatomist and philosopher, maintained that the sperm for the generation of the female passes through
the left emulgent vein, which is "full of watery blood" that has yet to be cleansed
in the kidney. Achillini's anatomical theory was not based simply on authority, for
he claimed to have performed, on two separate occasions, anatomical examinations in which he observed the left seminal vessel arising from the left emulgent
vein. Like Galen, Achillini argued that the sperm for the generation of the male
issues from the right vessel "because that vessel arises full of clean blood from
the vena cava, that is, after the kidney sucks at the watery part, also because
the branch of the artery is mingled with the right hand vessels and thus carries
a more copious spirit."[34] Woman, generated from unclean blood that lacks a
"copious spirit," cannot reach the perfection of being that is found in man.

Allesandro Benedetti (1450?–1512), a professor of medicine and anatomy at the
University of Padua, developed a theory of generation with an unusual blend of
Aristotelian and Galenic premises. Similarly to Aristotle, he insisted that woman's semen was "useless and vitiated." However, rather than identifying menses
with woman's semen, Benedetti sided with Galen in claiming that woman has semen in addition to menstrual fluids. He equated woman's semen with what he
called "genital female whiteness."

Benedetti also differed from Aristotle in holding that woman has a formative
role in generation. "The members of the foetus are formed from both the male
and the female and the spiritual life is produced from both, but the principal members are constituted from the male seed and the other more ignoble ones from
the female seed, as if from purer matter, just as the spiritual vigor is created."[35]
So, although Benedetti elevated woman's role in generation by allowing that she
participates in the form of the offspring, her role remains clearly inferior to that
of the man, for what she provides is less pure and produces only secondary members of the body.

The Spanish anatomist Andres de Laguna (1499–1560) supported a position
identical to that of Galen. "The vessels which come to the left testis take their
origin from the emulgent veins that are carried to the left kidney. Those which
reach the right testis derive beyond doubt from the vena cava and the dorsal artery. For this reason the right testicle must be warmer than the left and the right
side of the matrix warmer than the left side, especially since the more impure
and serous blood always distills into the left testicle."[36] According to de Luguna,

female seed is produced in the left testis, where the impurity of the blood corrupts the seed, resulting in the imperfection of the new being. This imperfection is manifested in the female organs of generation, de Laguna argued, for a woman produces little semen, and the little she does produce is much colder than that of man. Again the female creative principle, though necessary, plays a secondary role in generation.

Until the sixteenth century dissection was generally used to illustrate either the treatises of Galen or those of the Islamic physician Avicenna (980–1037). However, as numerous discrepancies between these traditional texts and the conditions found in the cadavers were uncovered, there was a gradual realization among anatomists that the subject needed revision. The anatomist Andreas Vesalius of Brussels (1514–1564) is widely recognized as central to this movement that questioned the tradition of authority, and his work is credited with founding modern anatomical practices.

Despite this new atmosphere, many anatomists persisted in the view that female seed was defective because of the impure blood that fed it. Although careful attention to the actual structure of the veins and arteries of the testicles and ovaries would refute them, anatomists continued to overlook this error. Even Vesalius did not perceive it. Notice in his depiction of woman's reproductive organs (shown in figure 15) that the vessel feeding the left ovary (e) originates in the renal artery (v) that carries uncleansed blood, while the right ovary is fed from the cleansed blood of the dorsal artery (d). This anatomical misconception was in no way the result of ignorance of human female anatomy, for Vesalius based his drawings of the female reproductive system on dissections of at least nine women's bodies.

It is not surprising that even an anatomist as careful as Vesalius would perpetuate such an error, for the scientific theory he had inherited demanded this "fact." The belief that female seed arose from the "serous, salty, and acrid" blood of the left testis was the only viable explanation of the perceived differences between woman and man.

Niccolo Massa (1485–1569), the Italian doctor and anatomist, provides an interesting case study of the power of such a bias. Massa appears to have recognized Galen's anatomical error, for in his *Introductory Book of Anatomy,* he claimed that the vessels feeding the left ovary and testicle originate from the same source as those that feed the right. "You will note, however, that often this left-hand vessel does not originate from the emulgent vein but from the trunk of the great chilis vein [vena cava] and also from the trunk of the aorta artery, just as the right-hand vessel does, as was said in the anatomy of the seminal vessels in males."[37]

Notice how explicitly he rejects the view that there is an anatomical difference between the right and left testicles and ovaries. Yet Massa continued to insist that female seed is weaker than male seed. And amazingly, his explanation of the imperfection of female seed is identical to that of Galen! "I also know that to the left testicle of the woman as well as of the man a watery blood is sent from the emulgents. From this a sperm is created which is not very strong."[38] Although

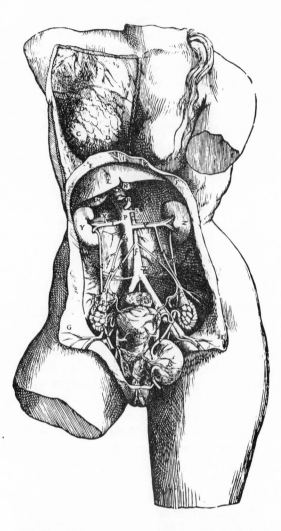

15. Vesalius's anatomical drawing of the veins
and arteries feeding the ovaries. Andreas Vesalius, *De humani corporis fabrica*. Rome: Per Ant.
Salamanca et Antonio Lefrerj, 1560.

able to see the error of Galen's anatomy, Massa was unable to perceive its implications. He continued to support Galen's theoretical explanation of woman's
inferiority even as he undercut the physiological basis for it.

The pervasive image of woman as an incomplete or inferior man contributed to
the persistence of Galen's explanation for the cause of this difference. Despite
the "corrections" of anatomists like Massa, it would take over a century for Galen's error to be generally recognized. For example, Herman Boerhaave, at the

end of the seventeenth century, admitted that he was initially "seduced" by authority. Although acknowledging the mistake, he proceeded to "explain" it with yet another piece of creative anatomy, claiming that the veins and arteries of the left ovary and testicle are wrapped in a "capsule" or "tunic" that makes their point of origin more difficult to see than that of the right ovary and testicle.[39] Simply put, the belief in female generative inferiority was so strong that it dictated observation for centuries.[40]

THE PERFECT MASCULINE SEED: ALCHEMY

While the sciences of medicine and anatomy adopted Galen's modifications of Aristotle's generation theory, the European alchemical tradition from the thirteenth to the seventeenth centuries generally accepted the original Aristotelian view that only the male produced seed. Alchemists depicted the female role in reproduction as that of nurturing and providing sustenance for the seed placed in her by the male. This image of generation is reflected in their texts in three areas: metaphysics—the interactions of the male and female forces in nature and in alchemical processes, biology—human generation, and psychic phenomena—spiritual generation.

THE METAPHYSICS OF LUNA AND SOL.

Since alchemists viewed the final form of their creation as masculine—the red king or the philosophers' stone—it is hardly surprising that they would conceive of the male as the superior creative principle. The masculine creative principle in the metaphysics of alchemy was the sun or Sol; the female creative principle was the moon, Luna.

In the alchemical tradition, Luna was the counterpart of Sol, and the characteristics of each were in accord with the Aristotelian scheme. Sol was hot, dry, brightly shining, spiritual, active, and masculine. Luna was cold, moist, feebly shining or dark, corporeal, passive, and female. One of the most important stages of the alchemical process was the wedding, or *conjunctio*, of the masculine and feminine principles. Alchemists believed that bringing these two forces together, what they called "coitus," was a necessary step in producing the "philosophical child"—the philosophers' stone.

The feminine principle had an indispensable role in the generation of the philosophers' stone, but this role was clearly secondary to that of the male principle. Luna, the female principle, was labeled the "vessel of the sun," the "universal receptacle," or the *"infudibulum terrae"* (the earth's funnel), each epithet reflecting her role in the generation of the philosophical child. Sol, the male principle, was conceived of as a fountain that poured forth "universal form and natural life." It was Luna's role as vessel to receive these powers and then, as funnel, to transmit them to the earth. Luna received the "universal seed of the sun," and nurtured it in the "quintessence" or the "belly and womb of nature."

This alchemical metaphysic is similar to that of Aristotle. Both view the female creative principle as less perfect than that of the male, and the imperfection is

EMBLEMA XXIII.   *De secretis Naturæ.*

Aurum pluit, dum nascitur Pallas Rhodi, & Sol concumbit Veneri.

EPIGRAMMA XXIII.

R Es est mira, fidem fecit sed Græcia nobis
          Ejus, apud Rhodios quæ celebrata fuit.
Nubibus Aureolus, referunt, quòd decidit imber,
     Sol ubi erat Cypriæ junctus amore Deæ:
Tum quoque, cùm Pallas cerebro Jovis excidit, aurum
     Vase suo pluviæ sic cadat instar aquæ.

                              N 3   AURUM

16. The generation of Athena. Michael Maier, *Atalanta Fugiens:
Emblemata nova de secretis naturae chymica.* Omenheimii: John
Theodori de Bry, 1618. Emblem XXIII.

reflected in the passive, nurturing role of the female in the transmutation process. "The seminal seed masculine / Hath wrought and won the Victory / Upon
the menstrualls worthily, / And well converted them to this kind."[41] The male
seed is active, providing the form of the creation; the passive female merely
nourishes the seed planted in her by the male, and ultimately is assimilated in the
process of transformation.

Alchemical emblems reinforce this view in their depictions of the male as the
source of creation. Images of Zeus giving birth to Athena and of Eve being born

EMBLEMA VI.   *De fecretis Naturæ.*

Seminate aurum veſtrum in terram albam foliatam.

EPIGRAMMA VI.

R Uricolæ pingui mandant ſua ſemina terræ,
    Cum fuerit raſtris hæc foliata ſuis.
Philoſophi niveos aurum docuère per agros
    Spargere, qui folii ſe levis inſtar habent :
Hoc ut agas, illud bene reſpice, namque quod aurum
    Germinet, ex tritico videris, ut ſpeculo.

E   PLATO

17. The male inseminating the fertile earth. Michael
Maier, *Atalanta Fugiens: Emblemata nova de secretis nat-
urae chymica*. Omenheimii: John Theodori de Bry, 1618.
Emblem VI.

out of Adam were common alchemical emblems. Another popular image was that
of a man planting seeds in the ground—the male inseminating the fertile earth.
Such emblems testify to the metaphysical valuation of the male over the female
in the alchemical worldview.

Michael Maier's alchemical text *Atalanta Fleeing* provides an intriguing example of this assumption of male primacy. Since Maier wrote accompanying epi-
grams, we can examine more fully the values contained within each of his

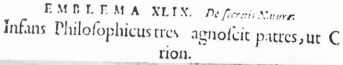

EPIGRAMMA XLIX.

EPIGRAMMA   XLIX.

F *Abula narratur, Phœbus, Vulcanus & Hermes*
  In pellem bubulam femina quod fuerint;
Tresque Patres fuerint magni fimul ORIONIS:
  Quin Sobolem Sophiæ fic tripatrem effe ferunt:
SOL. etenim primus, Vulcanus at effe fecundus
  Dicitur, huic præstans tertius arte pater.
                                              T

18. The generation of the philosophical child. Michael Maier, *Atalanta
Fugiens: Emblemata nova de secretis naturae chymica.* Omenheimii: John
Theodori de Bry, 1618. Emblem XLIX.

emblems. Emblem XLIX, for example, depicts five men, three of them holding
onto an ox skin, the other two looking on. The epigram reads:

> The Philosophical Child acknowledges three fathers,
>   just as Orion.
> According to the legend Phoebus, Vulcan and Hermes
>   gathered their sperm in an ox-hide;

And all three equally became the father of the great Orion.
Truely, it is said, the child of Wisdom proceeded likewise
   from three fathers;
For Sol is its first father, Vulcan its second, as is said,
And its third father excels in art.[42]

One version of the classical myth of Orion relates directly to this emblem. Zeus and Hermes, disguised as poor mortals, visited an old beekeeper by the name of Hyrieus, who offered them food and drink and shared with them all his comforts. To repay him for his generous hospitality, Zeus and Hermes asked Hyrieus what he most desired. He replied that he wanted a son. The gods instructed him to sacrifice a bull, but to save its hide. He was then to ejaculate onto the hide and bury it in his wife's grave. He did so, and nine months later a son, whom he named Orion, was born to him.[43]

This emblem presents the male seed as the primary source of creation, with woman's role merely that of the earth in which the seed is "planted." Like the birth of Orion, the ultimate goal of the alchemical process—the philosophers' stone—is seen as generated from three fathers: Sun, Vulcan, and Hermes. In his discussion of this emblem, Maier claimed that the unspeakable force of Sol affected a certain matter "as if that matter were in the womb of a woman" and, in doing so, "generated a Son equal to himself." Sol then "hands him over to Vulcan and to the artist that they may perfect him and multiply his forces," so they too become the "father of the Child of the Philosophers."[44] The female plays no part in the generation of the philosophical child.

HUMAN GENERATION.

The preceding view of male primacy in alchemical creation applies also to the alchemists' view of human creation. Indeed, their logic would support this. Since man is the microcosm of the macrocosm, and woman is the microcosm of man, the generation of humans must mirror the generations of all things in the universe. Thus, alchemists thought that humans, like Orion, could be generated from a man's seed when it was given the proper nourishment. This view was held by many alchemists, including Paracelsus, who went so far as to offer directions for generating a child.

Paracelsus claimed that man, not woman, contains the *liquor vitae* from which life is generated. According to his theory, this fluid originates in the brain and travels through the nerves to the testicles. It "contained the nature, quality, character, and essence of beings" and it "may be looked upon as an invisible or hidden man." "This semen, however, is not the sperma or the visible seminal fluid of man, but rather a semi-material principle contained in the sperma, or the *aura seminalis,* to which the sperma serves as a vehicle . . . [the semen is] the essence of the human body containing all the organs of the latter in an ideal form."[45]

The female role in reproduction is merely to provide, like the earth and the dead body of Hyrieus's wife, the soil of generation. "Woman, however, being nearer to Nature, furnishes the soil in which the seed of man finds the conditions required for its development. She nourishes, develops, and matures the seed

19. Alchemist with homunculus.
Kelley, *Tractatus de Lapide Philosophorum*, 1676.

without furnishing any seed herself. Man, although born of woman, is never derived from woman, but always from man."[46] The woman merely provides the nourishment that enables the seed of man to "ripen." In this view, it is quite reasonable to hold that such seeds could ripen outside of a woman.

Paracelsus not only believed it was theoretically possible to generate a human outside of a woman's womb, he claimed to have done so himself. His contention was that the generation of "beings like men or women" without the assistance of a female organism was one of the greatest secrets of alchemy, and he called such beings "Homunculi." Although insisting that this knowledge should remain a secret "until the days approach when all secrets will be known," he provided the reader with the following recipe for producing a homunculus:

If the sperma, inclosed in a hermetically sealed glass, is buried in horse manure for about 40 days, and properly "magnetized," it may begin to live and to move. After such a time it bears the form and resemblance of a human being, but it will be transparent and without a corpus. If it is now artificially fed with the *arcanum sanguinis hominis* until it is about 40 weeks old, and if allowed to remain during that time in the horse manure in a continually equal temperature, it will grow into a human child, with all its members developed like any other child, such as may have been born by a woman, only it will be much smaller.[47]

Despite viewing the female role in human creation as secondary and dispensable—if one only has a bit of manure!—it is the female who is blamed for any defect in the creation itself. According to alchemists, the seed of a man, as well as the seed of Sol, is perfect and without blemish. When the offspring has any imperfection, it must be due to some flaw in the womb of the woman or of the earth or mercury in which the seed was placed. "And mark that Nature in the beginning of her origin intends to make the Sun or the Moon, but cannot, because of Venus, [who is] a corrupt [and] mixed quicksilver, or because of the foetid earth. Wherefore, as a child in its mother's womb accidentally contracts a weakness and a corruption by reason of the place, although the sperm was clean, [and] the child is nevertheless leprous and unclean because of the corrupt womb, so it is with all imperfect metals, which are corrupted by Venus and the foetid earth."[48]

Spiritual Generation.

Alchemists believed that humans were capable of spiritual as well as biological generation. Paracelsus, for example, held that the former occurred in the "aquastric fissure." The nature of the sex differences at work in spiritual generation reflects the general alchemical denigration of female creative powers.

The location of the important aquastric fissures is different for woman and man. Woman's is located at the back of her head, while man's is on his forehead. Man, like Zeus with Athena, is able to give birth through this fissure "not cagastrically but necrocomically, to the necrocomic *Animam vel spiritum vitae microcsmi.*"[49] Necrocomica are telepathic phenomena or events indicative of the future. Through this fissure, men are able to have telepathic connection with the spirit of the microcosm. They can communicate with the "illiastric spirit of life in the heart," which Paracelsus identified as the "true soul" or "breath of god."

Woman's fissure is very different from that of man. Located in the back of her head rather than in the front, it is connected to demonic possession rather than telepathic creation. Woman's fissure permits access not to the necrocomic aquaster, but rather to the cagastric aquaster. The necrocomic aquaster enables telepathic connection with the living spirit of the universe, while the cagastric aquaster permits possession by diabolical spirits. Therefore, men are able to commune with the breath of god and thereby learn the secrets of the world, but women are liable to become witches!

Paracelsus believed in the existence of witchcraft, and accepted the common view that women were more likely to practice it. To him, witchcraft was an evil art in which the powers of creation are perverted. Women, having no creative power of their own, collect male semen and extract from it a "powerful Mumia," that is then "transformed into evil things; or it [the Mumia] may decompose and become a strong poison, furnishing life to innumerable invisible existences, by which epidemics and plagues may be caused."[50] Paracelsus warned that convents, monasteries, and houses of prostitution should be carefully watched, for they are often the places in which men are sexually enticed by witches who wish to collect their semen.

The presupposed element in Paracelsus's image of witchcraft is that women have no creative power. In order to "create," women must steal the power of men—their semen. Since women do not have understanding either, their acts pervert the creative power of the semen and have evil results.

These two images of creation are a powerful study in opposites. The alchemist "renders perfect what Nature has left imperfect, and purifies all things by the power of the spirit that is contained in them."[51] The witch steals the creative power, makes it impure, and uses it to deform and destroy the life spirit. Man, connected to the spirit of the universe, engenders perfect creation; woman, connected to evil forces, perverts creation.

The seed of the male is so potent that, when placed in fertile surroundings, it gives rise to perfectly developed individuals—homunculi or Aphrodite. But woman's impotence hinders her from generating anything other than monsters or defective beings—demons or Yaltabaoth. Woman at best serves as nourishing earth for the seed man plants in her. Again, it is the male who is the true parent, the active creative force.

THE SEEDS OF CREATION: PREFORMATION DOCTRINE

For almost two thousand years, scientists consistently viewed woman's contribution to human generation as less potent than man's. In the seventeenth century, a new theory took hold that had significant effects on the science of embryology.

From Aristotle to William Harvey, early embryologists believed that new life was produced through gradual development from unorganized matter, what we now call an epigenetic theory of development. Form was seen as evolving from the actions of the male semen upon the blood of the uterus, or from the mixture of the semen of the two parents. But the idea of an evolution of complexity from unstructured material lost favor toward the end of the seventeenth century, because of the general scientific commitment to a mechanistic worldview and the insufficiency of mechanical explanations for the gradual development of living organisms.

Once rejected, the epigenetic view was replaced by the thesis that development was the result of the growth or unfolding of preexisting structures—preformation doctrine. This theory was formulated initially in the works of Nicholas Malebranche, Claude Perrault, and Jan Swammerdam, who claimed in 1669 that "there is never generation in nature, but only a lengthening or increase in parts."[52] Fetal development was likened to the enlargement of the little leaves in a bud: the structures of the entity were all there from the beginning, and growth increased only the size, never the complexity, of the preexisting parts. For approximately one century, beginning in the last quarter of the 1600s, preformation doctrine supplanted epigenetic theory.

According to early versions of this theory, the spot in the center of a chicken's egg contained, preformed, all of the essential structures of a chick, although its parts were far too small to be seen. The anatomist Marcello Malpighi (1628–1694), utilizing microscopic magnification, supported preformation in his study of chick embryos. He prepared plates showing the early states of the heart, liver, vertebrae, and other structures. Malpighi observed that a small but fully formed heart was visible in the embryo well before it began to beat, thus lending credence to preformation.[53]

If it is not possible for an entity to increase in complexity, then embryos *must* exist fully formed within the parent. In fact, carried to its logical conclusion, the theory of preformation would require that each seed itself must contain within it the seeds of subsequent generations. This view came to be known as encase-ment, and it was held that Adam and Eve contained all humanity in their loins, each generation encased in the seed of the previous generation.

An important consequence of preformation theory is the belief that the seed of subsequent generations could reside in only a single parent; generation could no longer be the result of a mixture of semen. The only question was whether the miniature being was in the female egg (ovism) or the male sperm (animalculism). Preformationists initially saw the female as the source of this seed, arguing that the male parent provided only a stimulus that caused the outermost seed to begin its growth. However, by 1680 a version of preformation that viewed the male par-ent as the source of seed was offered.

Chicken eggs had long been a popular subject of study because they were large enough to allow observation, as well as readily and cheaply available. Many em-bryologists, from Aristotle to Malpighi, had grounded much of their empirical knowledge of embryology on the study of chick embryos. Given this, it is not sur-prising that preformationists first turned to the female as the source of encased seed. Spermatozoa had yet to be observed in any animal, while scientists had numerous examples of female animals that contained visible eggs.

The situation changed when Louis Dominicus Hamm, the assistant of Anton van Leeuwenhoek (1632–1723), saw "spermatic animalcules" while looking at hu-man seminal emissions under a microscope. In a series of correspondences with the Royal Society beginning in 1677, Leeuwenhoek claimed to have confirmed Hamm's discovery and concluded that these animalcules were the source of em-bryos. To counter the arguments of ovists, he also studied female ovaries, and declared that these mammalian organs were useless ornaments. Echoing centu-ries of tradition, Leeuwenhoek insisted that nourishment of the masculine seed was the sole function of the female. To account for the generation of two sexes, Leeuwenhoek claimed to have observed two kinds of spermatozoa, one that would give rise to males, the other to females.[54]

Nicolaus Hartsoeker (1656–1725) was the first scientist to illustrate the ap-pearance of a fetus contained within a spermatozoon. Hartsoeker did not pretend to have seen such a being himself, but claimed that if we could see through the skin that hides it, we might see it as represented in his illustration. Plantade, writing under the name of Dalenpatius in 1699, did claim to have seen an animal-cule. "For while I was examining them all with care one appeared which was larger than the others, and sloughed off the skin in which it had been enclosed, and clearly revealed, free from covering, both its shins, its legs, its breast, and two arms, whilst the cast skin, when pulled further up enveloped the head after the manner of a cowl. It was impossible to distinguish sexual characters on ac-count of its small size, and it died in the act of uncovering itself."[55]

Those theorists who supported animalculism (the animal or all the essential structures of the animal preformed in the spermatozoon) over ovism (the animal preformed in the egg) saw the egg as simply a temporary habitation for the sper-matic animalcule, one that provided it with food, shelter, and warmth. From this perspective, an organism's entire structure resides in the sperm, but the female

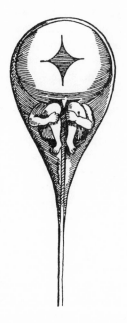

20. Spermatozoon with homunculus. Nicolaus Hartsoeker,
Essai de Dioptrique, 1694.

egg is still necessary as a nutritive mass. Animalculists argued that only the
sperm that is able to find the egg and pierce it will begin the growth process.

Although ovists were initially without rivals, their theory quickly went out of
favor once the male analog to the egg was observed. Within two decades, animalculism was the favored view, and continued to be held for almost a century.[56]
By 1730, ovism was almost uniformly rejected, although it was revived for a short
period (1760–1780) by John Haller, Charles Bonnet, and Lazarro Spallanzani, just
before the return to epigenetic theories. By the end of the eighteenth century,
epigenetic theory replaced preformation doctrine.[57]

What is especially fascinating about the history of preformation doctrine is the
general popularity of animalculism over ovism. Clearly, some of the popularity of
animalculism was rooted in the centuries-old bias of male primacy in generation.
In the ovist view, the male merely provides the stimulus that initiates the unfolding process; it is the female who contains the formed being—a theory that
lends itself to viewing the female as contributing more to generation than the
male. There were, to be sure, problems with both theories. Ovists were faced
with the difficult question of how a female egg could travel from the ovary to a
Fallopian tube, as well as how it could pass through the initial narrows into the
uterus. The animalculists had to solve an even more serious problem than the
ovists, namely the huge numbers of spermatozoa in each emission. To believe

that each spermatozoon contained a miniscule individual, itself encasing generations of such individuals, meant that hundreds had to be sacrificed in order for even one to achieve the conditions necessary for growth; it was difficult to understand why a divinely designed universe would permit such waste. The popularity of animalculism in the face of this difficulty indicates the strength of the bias toward male primacy in creation.

Although animalculist theory was in sharp contrast to Aristotelian embryological theories in its rejection of epigenesis for preformation, its premises sound surprisingly similar to those of Aristotle. The seventeenth-century animalculist George Garden argued that the egg, although essential to development, provided none of the form of the fetus. The ovum supplied only the nutrients necessary for the unfolding of the embryo that was already fully formed in the sperm.[58] "The Animalcules of the male Semen contain," according to the animalculism of Herman Boerhaave, "the future Rudiments of the whole body." The female supplies the "nidus," or egg, that will offer nourishment and warmth, enabling the animalcule to unfold itself "so as to display the latent Parts, of which [it is] composed."[59]

Martin Frobenius Ledermuller (1719–1769) claimed that "the small seminal animalcule develops in the mother just as the seed does in the field."[60] In 1762, John Cooke compared animalcules to the seeds of plants, for they are nourished by the egg as seed is fed by the "juices of the earth." In an image echoing those of the *Theogony,* Cooke insisted that animalculism is "confirmed by the natural Instinct of Mankind (for the Children are not denominated from the Mother, which if the Stamina had preexisted in her Eggs, and not in the Male Sperm, they in Strictness ought to have been); but they are, as in Justness they should be denominated from the Father, as proceeding first of all out of his Body, before by Birth they came out of the Body of their Mother."[61] Cooke argued that the spermatozoa carried by a man "are no less than his own little Pupilla, Images, or Pictures in Parvo, wrapt up very securely, Insect like, in a fine exterior Bag, Covering, or Wrapper."[62] Woman continues to play a role in generation, but it is simply feeder/caretaker of the growing animalcule.

Even as late as 1794, Erasmus Darwin (1731–1802) held that the male provides the form or rudiment of the embryo, while the female provides only the oxygen, food, and nidus. To support his position, Darwin pointed to the larger size of the male, insisting that because of this he "should contribute as much or more towards the reproduction of the species." Since the female provides food and oxygen, she could not also provide part of the embryo, or her contribution would be greater than that of the male. Based on these imaginative premises, Darwin concluded "that the embryo is produced by the male, and the proper food and nidus by the female."[63]

Even scientific popularizers adopted this imagery. In a passage that Apollo might have quoted during the trial of Orestes, J. M. Good stated that "every man who pretended to the smallest portion of medical science, was convinced that his children were not more related, in point of actual generation, to his own wife, than they were to his neighbours."[64] And as late as 1869 we find William Holcombe claiming that "paternity and not maternity is the crowning phenomenon and wonder of nature."[65]

In an interesting deviation from the Aristotelian carpenter metaphor, animalculists used a molding metaphor to account for the fact that some children resemble their mothers. Jean Astruc (1684–1766) argued that "the worm which is the germ of the foetus, comes from the father only; the mother has no part in it . . . in the little nich of the ova of women, there is a concave impression; that resembles every woman; and is placed in every nich, on the same side, as where the end of the cord is: which must be the ground of the resemblance of children to their mothers."[66] As in the creation of Pandora, the female generative principle was given a role only in the external appearance of the new being. All else was attributed to the male.

The history of embryology from Aristotle to the preformationists illustrates the ways in which cultural values shape the process of scientific investigation.[67] The accepted belief in woman's inferiority affected the process of observation, the interpretation of data, and the justification and defense of theory. Belief in the primacy of male generative power was such a fundamental tenet of cosmogony that it permeated embryology for centuries.

Aristotle set the basic orientation for the next two thousand years of embryological thought. His arguments, supplemented by the work of Galen, were retained even in the face of growing evidence of their untenability. The underlying presence of birth reversal imagery can be seen throughout this tradition. There were basically two lines of development: (1) Aristotle and the denial of female seed, and (2) Galen and the role of inferior female seed. The anatomical tradition followed Galen; the alchemical tradition of the sixteenth and seventeenth centuries supported an Aristotelian view; the preformationists adopted a synthesis of Aristotelian and Galenic themes. But throughout, the belief in the primacy of the male remained unchallenged.

The history of Western views of human generation provides more than a chronicle of the legacy of Aristotle and Galen. The tenacious defense of belief in the primacy of male generative powers, even in the face of growing evidence against it, reveals the deep-rooted nature of this conviction and the emotional valence attached to it. Aristotle and Galen were key figures, but part of their prominence came through their articulation of a systematic explanation that preserved and defended this popular belief. Their influence cannot be explained solely in terms of their roles as authoritative figures.

It is important to recognize that the survival and renewal of Aristotle's and Galen's view were, to a significant degree, due to their legitimation of the deeply-held belief in woman's inferiority. It is most important to remember that scientists do not possess a disembodied or dispassionate viewpoint, for they are individuals living in a particular time and place. When they walk into the "laboratory," they carry their personal, cultural, and social values with them. The task of historians of science is to identify these values and their sources, and trace their impact.

IV

The Beautiful Evil

It is evident that the man, possessing reasoning faculties, muscular power, and courage to employ it, is qualified for being a protector: the woman, being little capable of reasoning, feeble, and timid, requires protection. Under such circumstances, the man naturally governs; the woman naturally obeys.

Alexander Walker (1779–1852), *Woman Physiologically Considered*

EIGHT

In Man's Control

Salimbene, the thirteenth-century Franciscan, collected sayings about women in his autobiography. One of these presents a shockingly negative view of woman: "What else is woman but a foe to friendship, an unescapable punishment, a necessary evil, a natural temptation, a desirable calamity, a domestic danger, a delectable detriment, an evil of nature, painted with fair colours!"[1] Man's fear of woman, illustrated by this adage, is a common theme of Western thought. Woman's biological, spiritual, and moral weaknesses were all seen as making her far more prone to acts of injustice, particularly those resulting from the passions and desires. A woman uncontrolled was one of the greatest dangers to mankind.

The recognition of the potential danger of all women was reflected in classical literature in a repeated wish for a world without them. In the *Medea*, Euripides's Jason gives voice to this desire: "What we poor males really need / is a way of having babies on our own— / no females, please. / Then the world would be / completely trouble free."[2]

Jason's statement articulates a sentiment frequently repeated in the next two thousand years: with the exception of her function in reproduction, woman adds little of value to man's life. She is necessary only for bearing children. But this necessity carries with it great danger. Woman, like Pandora, not only brings children into the world, she also brings misery to man. Although a world without women was a common dream of the classical man, the belief that woman is a necessary evil leads to a more practical solution. In the words of Hippolytos, "women are a huge natural calamity, / against which men must take / strenuous measures."[3] Woman can be a helpmeet only if her passions are domesticated and her energy is channeled into the well-being of her family. Given that woman's rational and moral faculties were perceived as inadequate for such a task, the conclusion was obvious. Woman must always be in Man's control.

THE DOMESTICATED WOMAN

The Greeks believed that the natural order dictated man's control of woman. A central theme of classical philosophy and biology was that the rule of mind or soul over body, and of the rational element over the passionate, was both natural and expedient. Aristotle's biology documented and explained woman's inability to control her passions through reason, for although he allowed that woman had some sense of justice, Aristotle argued that she was unable to master her desires sufficiently to lead a good life. Thus, woman, left on her own, would be led astray by her passions, particularly her sexual passions, and in turn would cause great suffering to man. It was clear to Aristotle that man must serve as the rational influence over the uncontrolled passions of woman.

Aristotle's explanation for the consequences of woman's defect in heat, in combination with popular images of woman as unruly and lascivious, reinforced the view that man must rule over her. "Again, the male is by nature superior, and the female inferior; and the one rules, and the other is ruled."[4] By serving as woman's rational soul, guiding and controlling her, man would ensure that woman's potential for evil was nullified. From this perspective, man's control of woman is dictated by biology, not social convention. It is the natural order, not education or training, that results in the male being "by nature fitter for command than the female."[5] If woman is not so governed, she is a danger to the happiness of man and the good of society.

The Greeks believed that the animal passions inherent in woman's nature could best be tamed through marriage. A proper union would domesticate woman by ensuring that her passions were properly controlled and directed toward the welfare of her family. Her sexuality would be limited to her husband; her passions would be directed to the care of her children. Stability would be attained. The proper marriage thus required the subordination of the will of the wife to the governance of her husband. In this way, woman would be a helpmeet to man, a crown to him.

In the *Oeconomicus* of Xenophon (434?–?355 BCE), this Greek historian and essayist provided an elaborate image of the domesticated woman, the good wife. The main character of the dialogue, Ischomachos, describes the role of a wife and gives an account of her proper training.

Ischomachos brags that he trained his wife himself. He proudly explains that when his wife first came to him, she could not have known anything because "she was not yet fifteen."[6] The belief that a woman should be married when she was young, and married to a man significantly older than she, was widely supported by classical theorists. Plato thought that a woman should be married when she was between sixteen and twenty, while a man should wait until he was thirty to thirty-five to wed.[7] Hesiod instructed men to marry when they were "only a few years younger than thirty, / or just a few years older," and to marry a woman "five years past puberty" (about eighteen).[8]

Hesiod also instructed men to "marry a virgin," but his emphasis here is that a woman should be so naive that her husband could mold her character according to his own beliefs and values: "Marry a virgin so you can teach her right from wrong."[9] Ischomachos is in complete agreement with Hesiod. A wife should be like a lump of clay, ready to be molded by her husband. To ensure this, it is not sufficient that a suitable bride be young; she must also be raised throughout childhood "under diligent supervision in order that she might see and hear as little as possible and ask the fewest possible questions."[10] Woman, like the passions, must be kept in abeyance until she has a ruling faculty, a husband, who can serve as the rational element that will teach her proper order.

Ischomachos taught his wife that the roles of husband and wife were designed by the gods. He explained to her that man and woman were brought together to ensure the perpetuation of the human race. However, "the way of life of human beings" requires shelter; "someone is needed to work in the open air" and some-one must "do the works that need shelter."[11] Ischomachos makes a clear gender division between the roles of woman and man, insisting that this division is part of the natural order. "The god directly prepared the woman's nature for indoor works and indoor concerns," making her less capable of enduring physical hard-ships, implanting in her the nourishment of newborns as well as a stronger af-fection for them, and giving her a greater share of fear.[12] The god equipped man in body and soul with a greater capacity for enduring hardships and with a large share of boldness, "and so has ordered him to the outdoor works."[13]

Ischomachos's ideal wife devotes her energy to the home and family. In fact, her life is confined to the private realm. She is to "remain indoors" and care for the children, rule over the maidservants, receive what is brought in and distrib-ute it, make clothes, fix food, and tend sick servants.[14]

The domestication of woman is necessary not only for the harmony of the fam-ily, but also for the good of society. The Roman statesman Cato (234–149 BCE) warned that the failure of individual men to "maintain the prerogative and author-ity of a husband" in their own households would disrupt the social order. He ex-plained that it is "not proper that women should perform any, even private, business, without a director." By not providing such control, men would be giving women "the reins to their intractable nature, and their uncontrolled passions." Such untamed women would not only become tyrants in the home, but would also demand control of the forum.[15]

ADAM'S EVE

The belief that woman must be in man's control received strong support from Jewish and Christian theologians. The myth of Adam and Eve was taken as proof that the rule of man over woman is divinely ordained. The second version of the creation story, in which woman is created from man's rib, was frequently used to justify the rule of husband over wife. Philo's writings are a good example of such a correlation.

Philo argued that God formed woman from man's rib rather than from the earth in order to guarantee that man would rule over woman, and that she in turn would serve him. "Third, he [God] wishes that man should take care of woman as of a very necessary part of him; but woman, in return, should serve him [man] as a whole."[16] The proper relationship between man and woman is to mirror that between mind and passion—the two are to act in harmony, but there is to be a clear dominance of mind over passion. Man is to have "the authority of a master," while woman is to take "the rank of servant" and be "obedient to his life."[17]

Philo believed that the nature of the creation of woman and man revealed both that gender roles are divinely ordained and that wives should be younger than their husbands. Noting that woman was created after man, Philo concluded that it was God's will for a wife to be younger than her husband. Those men who marry women who are no longer young are, according to Philo, "destroying the laws of nature."[18] He also offered a scriptural justification for a sexual division of labor, explaining that the passage in Genesis in which woman is compared to a building (Genesis 2:22) should be interpreted to mean that a man without a woman is "homeless." "For to man are entrusted the public affairs of state; while to a woman the affairs of the home are proper."[19] Philo used scriptural evidence to arrive at the same conclusion as Xenophon four centuries earlier: woman's place is in the home.

Paul, in his letter to the Ephesians, argued for a benevolent rule of husband over wife, comparing their relationship to that of Christ and church. "As the church is subject to Christ, so let wives also be subject in everything to their husbands" (Ephesians 5:24). Although Paul claimed that husband and wife should be "subject to one another," the nature of this subjection differs (Ephesians 5:41). A woman is to respect her husband and accept that he is her head, while a man is to love his wife and sanctify her. Paul envisions the husband as a benevolent ruler, but a ruler nonetheless.

This rule of husband over wife is also likened to political order. St. John Chrysostom held the view that the first government God created on earth was that of Adam over Eve, and argued that because this hierarchy was created by God, it was part of the natural order. St. John interpreted the statement that man was created in God's image to mean that man had the ability and divine right to govern all other earthly creation, including woman. He explained that man received this role because of woman's error in listening to the words of the serpent. "For the woman taught the man once, and made him guilty of disobedience, and wrought our ruin. Therefore because she made bad use of her power over the man, or rather her equality with him, God made her subject to her husband."[20]

St. John Chrysostom concluded that man is naturally suited for the public sphere, while woman's sphere is limited to the private realm of home and family. Man, as head of the family, contributes spiritual qualities to the marriage, while woman provides the material services appropriate to her role. Any attempt to modify these relations is, in St. John's account, a rebellion against God and nature. "Thou seest how great an evil it is not to master pleasure, to upset the ruling principle in nature, and for a man to be a slave of women."[21]

Theologians offered three basic scriptural "proofs" that woman must be subject to man. One of these proofs is based on woman's defect in reason, and that this imperfection was the cause of her deception by the serpent. Augustine, for example, insisted that only Eve was seduced by the serpent, that only woman and not man believed its lies. Adam, Augustine explained, agreed to eat of the fruit of the forbidden tree not because he believed what the serpent said, but rather because of his love for Eve. "We cannot believe that Adam was deceived, and supposed the devil's word to be truth and therefore transgressed God's law, but that he by the drawings of kindred yielded to the woman, the husband to the wife, one human being to the only other human being. For not without significance did the apostle say, 'And Adam was not deceived, but the woman being deceived was the transgression'; but he speaks thus, because the woman accepted as true what the serpent told her, but the man could not bear to be severed from his only companion, even though this involved a partnership in sin."[22]

Augustine interpreted woman's fatal error of listening to the serpent as proof that she had to be subordinated to man. Woman is, because of the sex of her body, less able to perceive the truth, and thus requires guidance and control. "Just as in man's soul there is one part which rules by taking thought and another part which is subject to obedience, so for man, also corporeally, a woman was created to have a nature equal to his in mind and rational intelligence, but to be in sex subjected to the masculine sex in the same way as the appetite which leads to action is subjected to the skill, mentally derived, of acting rightly."[23] For correct order to reign, woman requires external governance—the rule of man. Aquinas agreed with Augustine, explaining that "good order would have been wanting in the human family if some were not governed by others wiser than themselves. So by such a kind of subjection woman is naturally subject to man, because in man the discretion of reason predominates."[24]

The second scriptural proof equates woman's creation from man's rib with her subjection to him. Gratian embraced this line of reasoning to justify man's control of woman: "For woman is the body of man, has come from his rib and is placed in subjection to him, for which reason also she has been chosen to bear children. The Lord says, 'He will rule over her.' Man has lordship over the woman since he is also her head."[25]

The third type of scriptural proof is based on God's punishment of woman for her disobedience. " 'I will greatly multiply your pain in childbearing; / in pain you shall bring forth children, / yet your desire shall be for your husband, / and he shall rule over you' " (Genesis 3:16). Luther's arguments for the necessity of a husband's rule were based on this passage. He insisted that woman and man were originally created as equals, but after woman disobeyed God, she was subjected to man as punishment for her sin. "For the punishment, that she is now subjected to the man, was imposed on her after sin and because of sin."[26]

Luther further concluded that this punishment entailed the exclusion of woman from the public realm of politics. "If Eve had persisted in the truth, she would not only not have been subjected to the rule of her husband, but she herself would also have been a partner in the rule which is now entirely the concern of males. . . . However, they cannot perform the functions of men, teach, rule, etc."[27]

Although theologians relied on different portions of the myth of the creation and fall of humans to document the proper relation between woman and man, their conclusions were the same. Woman was to be subject to the rule of man.

LOVING SUBJECTION

The power of a creation myth comes from the metaphors or models it provides for understanding relationships—those between humans and the divine, between humans and the rest of creation, and between woman and man. Theologians employed the Genesis myth to define the latter, justifying man's rule over woman. But the power of this particular myth is not limited to religious images of the proper relations between the sexes. Its influence can be found in philosophical discourses on the same subject, as well as in scientific thought.

The impact of the Genesis creation myth on Western philosophy is well illustrated in the political theory of John Locke (1632–1704). He supported the subjection of woman to man, basing his argument on an interpretation of the Genesis story of Eve and Adam. Locke, like Luther, emphasized God's punishment of woman for her disobedience; the rule of man over woman is "a punishment laid upon *Eve.*" And this punishment is the "Subjection they [women] should ordinarily be in to their Husbands," which consists of "the Power that every Husband hath to order the things of private Concernment in his Family, as Proprietor of the Goods and Land there, and to have his Will take place (before that of his wife) in all things of their common Concernment."[28]

In *Two Treatises of Civil Government*, Locke attempted to refute the position of his contemporary, Robert Filmer, an influential critic of social contract theory, concerning the source of man's power over woman. Filmer had also argued for the subjection of woman to man, but he had grounded that power in law—in this case, the law of God.[29] Locke rejected Filmer's attempt to locate man's rule in any kind of law, reminding his readers that in Genesis 3:16, when God cursed woman and thereby made her subject to man, God spoke *only* to woman. The words "were not spoken to *Adam,* neither indeed was there any Grant in them made to *Adam.*"[30] Locke thus denies Filmer's claim that God's curse contains "the original grant of government"; he sees the curse not as *establishing* woman's subordination to her husband, but *predicting* it.

Locke explained that it is not law that binds woman to the pain of childbirth, nor is it law that subjects her to the rule of her husband. Just as the pain that woman experiences in childbirth is due not to convention, but is a fact of nature arising out of God's punishment for disobedience, so too, the subjection of a wife to her husband is not the result of any arbitrary social structure. Woman's subordination to man has "a Foundation in Nature."[31]

For Locke, this assumption of natural dominion carried with it differences between the abilities of woman and man. He presupposed that man's rule in the private realm would be guaranteed by his natural superiority. In the second book of the *Treatise,* this presupposition is made explicit. Arguing for the authority of the husband within the family, Locke noted that decisions relating to the family, in particular the disposition of property, would have to be made. Although these decisions would be of joint concern, sometimes the marriage partners would not be in agreement, and final say must rest with one of them.[32] "But the Husband and Wife, though they have but one common Concern, yet having different understandings, will unavoidably sometimes have different wills too; it therefore being necessary, that the last Determination, i.e., the rule, should be placed somewhere, it naturally falls to the Man's share as the abler and the stronger."[33] Locke here reiterates his belief in woman's natural inferiority, and uses it as a foundation for supporting the necessary subordination of a woman to her husband concerning family property.[34]

One of Locke's primary reasons for arguing against Filmer's position is that he believed it granted too much authority to the husband. Locke was opposed to viewing the relationship of husband and wife as parallel to that of monarch and subject, which would give the husband "power of life and death" over his wife.[35] Nevertheless, his attempt to justify the husband's authority within the family was, in large part, based on a presupposition of man's superiority over woman.

This bias is further revealed by a tension in Locke's position. When discoursing on political power, Locke acknowledged that there would be natural differences in the abilities of different men. However, he did not think that such differences would preclude equality. Locke believed that the natural state of man is one of perfect freedom, "wherein all the Power and Jurisdiction is reciprocal, no one having more than another."[36] Locke thus posited a natural right of all men to be equal in freedom from the dominion of any other person. He is clear in insisting that equality does not require "sameness"; men's inborn abilities and talents may vary, but their claim to freedom will not.

This same premise breaks down when applied to women. Even in this envisioned "natural estate," Locke claimed that the inherent differences between the sexes would override any claims women might have to the freedom and equality that men enjoyed. Thus, Locke assumed from the outset that women are not independent individuals with full rights. For him, political authority was based on consent, while the authority of the husband over the wife was based on the natural superiority of male over female.[37]

One of the striking features of the history of political theory is the general concurrence on the "proper" roles of woman. With centuries of scientific theories documenting woman's inferiority, and powerful theological warnings of her dangers, this agreement is hardly surprising. Like Locke, many political theorists accepted such beliefs as axioms upon which they developed their ideas. Upon these foundations, they constructed conclusions that can be traced throughout the history of political theory: woman's activities are to be limited to the private realm of home and family, and are to be governed by man.

If one looks carefully and reads between the lines, belief in the danger posed by woman can be found underlying arguments that justify the "duties" of husbands to protect and govern their wives. The danger of woman lies in the strength of her passions. Rousseau argued that without the impediments of modesty and shame, woman would openly express her desires.[38] Rousseau also explained that if woman expressed her passions, "men would be tyrannized by women. For, given the ease with which women arouse men's senses and reawaken in the depths of their hearts the remains of ardors which are almost extinguished, men would finally be their victims and would see themselves dragged to death without ever being able to defend themselves."[39] Notice the Pandora-like image of woman expressed here—passions so strong they can roast a man long before his time.

With his view of "untamed women," it is no surprise that Rousseau, like Xenophon before him, focused a girl's entire education on her "domestication." All her training must be aimed at suppressing these passions that he feared. Girls "ought to be constrained very early. This misfortune, if it is one for them, is inseparable from their sex, and they are never delivered from it without suffering far more cruel misfortunes. All their lives they will be enslaved to the most continual and most severe of constraints—that of the proprieties. They must first be exercised in constraint, so that it never costs them anything to tame all their caprices in order to submit them to the wills of others."[40]

But Rousseau is also well aware that the harshness of such training will break woman's spirit, rendering her dependent upon man's constant care. "From this habitual constraint comes a docility which women need all their lives, since they never cease to be subjected either to a man or to the judgments of men and they are never permitted to put themselves above these judgments."[41]

Rousseau concluded that the good of society, as well as the continuation of the human race, requires that woman be subjugated to man so that she will please rather than arouse him. He reinforced this position by arguing, as did Locke before him, that authority in the family cannot be shared between the spouses, but must rest with the one who will have the final decision-making voice. Insisting that in the family "there must be a single government, and when opinions are divided, there must be a dominant voice that decides," Rousseau found male superiority so obvious that he did not even attempt to argue against the possibility of a cooperative relationship between spouses.[42] The spouse in whom this authority will be vested is, of course, the husband.

Rousseau offered two justifications for the husband's command, the first being that woman has necessary periods of inaction. Rousseau insisted that "however slight the incapacitations peculiar to the wife are thought to be," these times are sufficient to preclude a wife's primacy.[43] Although he does not spell out the nature of this "inaction," we can safely interpret that Rousseau perceived reproduction and/or menstruation as intervals when a woman would be physically unable to command.

The second justification involves paternity—a theme so common to men's political theory that it is difficult not to see it as an obsession. Rousseau argued that a husband must be able to "oversee his wife's conduct, because it is important to him that the children he is forced to recognize do not belong to anyone other than himself."[44] With both the institution of patrilineal inheritance and the belief that woman is subject to the dictates of her passions, particularly her sexual passions, the conclusion is inescapable: woman must be in man's control.

Rousseau recognized, along with Locke, that the subjugation of woman precludes her full humanity, although it was a central tenet of his philosophy that all people are born "equal and free."[45] In *On the Social Contract,* Rousseau claimed that renouncing one's liberty is tantamount to denying "the rights of humanity and even its duties."[46] But independence is a "consequence of *man's* nature."[47] The goal of a girl's education is to train her to submit to the will of others, and thus to renounce the liberty that makes one fully human.

Rousseau's views on woman blinded him to this tension within his own theory, which disappears when he discusses the natural state. For Rousseau, the original state is not the family, but rather the independent individual who immediately "gratifies whatever sexual desire presents itself to consciousness when *he* happens to encounter a *female*."[48] Even when Rousseau discussed the origins of the family, women are curiously absent; we hear only of children and their fathers: "The most ancient of all societies, and the only natural one, is that of the family. Yet children remain bound to the father only as long as they need him for self-preservation. As soon as this need ceases, the natural bond dissolves. The children, exempt from the obedience they owed the father, and the father, exempt from the care he owed the children, all return equally to independence."[49]

Given Rousseau's views on the liability of reproduction for woman, we have good reason to think these independent children are all sons. A boy becomes a man by gaining independence. A girl becomes a woman by forfeiting even her desire for independence.

Kant similarly emphasized the dependence of woman: "*Children* are under tutelage for natural reasons, and their parents are the natural guardians. A *woman*, regardless of her age, is under civil tutelage [or incompetent to speak for herself (*unmundig*)]; her husband is her natural curator."[50] Kant claimed that this "tutelage" is a duty of man and a corresponding right of woman, rather than a liability. According to Kant, it is man's role to protect the "weaker sex" and his duty to take her under his protection. In turn, woman "rightfully demands that man be her protector."[51] Despite Kant's protests, he based this "right" on what he perceived to be a natural liability—woman's role in reproduction. He claimed that, because of woman's childbearing role, she will experience "fear in the face of *physical* harm and timidity in the face of physical dangers."[52] Kant concluded that woman's fear and timidity cause her to need man's protection.

Kant supplemented this position by voicing the view held by Locke and Rousseau about the nature of the marriage relationship—the husband must govern. "If a union is to be harmonious and indissoluble, it is not enough for two people to associate as they please; one party must be *subject* to the other and, reciprocally, one must be the *superior* of the other in some way, in order to be able to rule and govern him."[53] Although Kant argued that in a state of peace, government would consist of cooperation among men, he, like Locke and Rousseau, rejected this possibility in the marriage relationship. "For if two people who cannot dispense with each other make *equal* claims, self-love produces nothing but wrangling."[54] He later cautioned that "we cannot count positively on the harmony that is based on equality."[55]

Kant attempted to soften his position by explaining that although the husband will "govern," the wife will "reign." "Who, then, should have supreme command in the household?—for there can be only one person who coordinates all occupations in accordance with one end, which is his. I would say, in the language of gallantry (but not without truth): the woman should *reign* and the man *govern;* for inclination reigns and understanding governs."[56]

Upon examination, however, reigning turns out to be a very hollow role. Kant likened the reign of the wife to that of a "monarch who thinks only of amusement," explaining that the husband should be compliant with his wife's desires, but since only he is capable of judging which actions are best, *he must tell her what her will consists of!*[57] "The monarch can do all that he wills, but on one condition: that his minister lets him know what his will is."[58] As with Ischomachos and his wife, the will of a good woman is dictated by her husband.

THE EVOLUTION OF THE GOOD WIFE

While philosophers stressed the proper relationships between husbands and wives, scientists emphasized domesticity as woman's natural lot. In his text on female diseases, Charles Meigs explained that woman's role in the private realm of family and her exclusion from the public realm are not arbitrary—that is, due to restrictions on educational or career opportunities. Rather, women's "lot is cast for them; men did not make it; God made it. They cannot, in the present state of the world, and probably never will, participate in the affairs of nations or municipalities, because, by the very nature of their moral and physical constitution, they are bound to the horns of the family altar."[59]

In the nineteenth century, the voices of scientists were frequently raised in opposition to those who were arguing for women's rights and equality with men in the public realm. Often scientists would stress the physical and psychological damage that would result to the woman who attempted to participate in the toils of higher education, or who tried to compete with men in the field of industry. Insisting that woman's role in reproduction demanded far more energy than it did of man, scientists decried any attempts by women to compete with men, on the grounds that doing so would permanently damage their physical constitutions.

Azel Ames (1845–1908), for example, accepted Edward Clarke's warnings about the dangers of advanced education for woman, but argued that woman's participation in industry posed an equally grave risk to her health. He explained that the "monotony, depression, bodily fatigue, and 'constrained position,'" of industrial work had an extremely deleterious effect on woman, causing her to "become both physically and morally unsound."[60]

Nineteenth-century scientist unleashed a storm of protest against women's attempts to compete with men in the public realm, insisting that doing so would "unsex" woman. The flavor of these attacks is well represented in James McGrigor Allan's essay "On the Real Differences in the Minds of Men and Women," published in 1869 in the *Anthropological Review*. Allan's images speak for themselves:

Compare the true woman, who recognizes the value and importance of the natural functions in their influence on future generations, with the little creature who "shunts" the conjugal and maternal duties; who rebels against the very instincts of Nature; who is, forsooth, ashamed of being a woman, and in aping man, becomes a nondescript—a monster more horrible than that created by Frankenstein. Is it possible to conceive a more contemptible and deplorable spectacle than that of the female (I will not profane the beautiful name of *woman*) who, having undertaken, and having appointed to her, by nature, those functions, in the proper fulfillment of which consist the charm and glory of the sex, deliberately neglects and abdicates the sacred duties and privileges of wife and mother, to make herself ridiculous by meddling in and muddling men's work? Let the being who has thus morally, mentally, and physically, as far as possible, unsexed herself, be consistent, and imitate the example of American ladies, who, in laying aside womanly grace and modesty, have also laid aside the garb of woman.[61]

Numerous scientists generalized the negative effects of any attempt to equalize female and male social roles by insisting that such efforts would result in the devolution of the race itself. Relying on studies of "primitive" societies in which the roles of woman and man were more similar, scientists insisted that a "hermaphroditic" form of government or society was evidence of a lower evolutionary level. In other words, they claimed that the sexual division of labor among the nineteenth-century European middle class was the result of centuries of evolutionary development. Civilization demanded the rule of man in the public realm and the focusing of woman's energies around home and family.

Some scientists thus discounted the attempts of women's rights activists by arguing that the demands for women's equality in the public realm could be realized only at the cost of the race itself. "Whether women turn traitors to their cause or not, no outcries from unemployed spinsters or tormented wives should tempt us to meddle with what revelation, science, and experience declare to be a necessary condition of the prosperity of mankind. To discourage subordination in women, to countenance their competition in masculine careers by way of their enfranchisement, is probably among the shortest methods of barbarizing our race."[62]

Others argued even more vehemently that such efforts could result in the extinction of the entire human species. "I cannot conclude this discussion of the more abstract aspect of the subject without an acknowledgment of the fact that the rejection of maternal functions by modern women may be Nature's plan for securing the disappearance of Man to ensure further evolution."[63] The steps of the woman who ventures outside of the private realm of the family lead backward on the path of evolution.

A DANGER TO SOCIETY

The fear of the untamed woman clearly was not limited to the damage she could cause to herself or to her family. Although theorists were careful to depict the horrors such a woman could bring to her unfortunate husband, they also stressed that an undomesticated woman was a threat to society in general. However, those who argued that woman had the potential to destroy the social order changed their emphasis from the effects of woman's sexuality on man to the ways in which her biological function made her unfit for the public realm.

Scientists and philosophers, from the classical period well into the nineteenth century, argued that woman's role in reproduction made her particularly fit for the care and early training of children. Being more attuned to her emotions, she was more capable than man of the empathy and love believed necessary for the proper care of a child. Scientists also argued that her mental development, being at a more arrested state, made her more successful in the education of children. "In truth, the minds of females, as well as their persons, are formed for the most important offices of humanity—the charge of infancy, and the sustaining with patience, that trouble in their own person, which is annexed to their bringing infants into life. Therefore all their feelings are softer and finer; all their passions are more delicate and more exquisitely tempered with sentiment."[64]

The other side of this argument is that woman is not fit for the governing of society or the workings of the state. In fact, she was seen as a threat because her thoughts and desires were tied to the realm of the particular, the realm of the family. Since the public realm of government and business was believed to be founded on notions of rights and justice, woman's inability to comprehend such abstract principles precluded her participation. Any attempt by her to enter into the public realm would only pervert the aims of the state from the universal to the particular. In the words of Hegel, "womankind—the everlasting irony [in the life] of the community—changes by intrigue the universal end of the government into a private end, transforms its universal activity into a work of some particular individual, and perverts the universal property of the state into a possession and ornament for the Family."[65]

The relegation of woman to the private realm of the family was reinforced by the belief that her influence on the workings of the state would result in disruption of its order. Aristotle, for example, blamed the fall of the state of Sparta on its women, who were ungoverned and lived "in every sort of intemperance and luxury."[66] Over twenty centuries later, Arthur Schopenhauer (1788–1860) echoed Aristotle's attack by insisting that it was the "ever-growing influence of the women in France, from the time of Louis XIII," that was responsible for the French Revolution.[67]

Rousseau, contradicting the facts but not the spirit of Aristotle's position, cited approvingly what he thought was the Spartan practice of shutting up married women in their houses and thereby limiting "all their cares to their households and their families."[68] He insisted that these women not only gave birth to "the healthiest, the most robust, the most well-built men in the world," but that they were the purest and most lovable of all women.[69] A woman who stepped outside of the boundaries of the home endangered the fiber of society and the well-being of her children. "Never has a people perished from an excess of wine; all perish from the disorder of women."[70]

The belief that woman was by nature a danger to society remained influential through the nineteenth century and well into the twentieth. Weininger insisted that just as "children, imbeciles and criminals would be justly prevented from taking any part in public affairs even if they were numerically equal or in the majority; woman must in the same way be kept from having a share in anything which concerns the public welfare, as it is much to be feared that the mere effect of female influence would be harmful."[71] Freud, attempting to justify the exclusion of woman from the public realm, explained that woman's psychology results in her being in "opposition to civilization." Woman, he said, is a "retarding and restraining influence" on the development of the social order.[72]

According to Freud, a precondition for the development of civilization is the ability to sublimate one's instincts. He claimed that woman, due to her psychological inability to emerge completely from the Oedipal stage, cannot control her instincts or the subjectivity of her feelings. "The work of civilization has become increasingly the business of men, it confronts them with ever more difficult tasks and compels them to carry out instinctual sublimations of which women are little capable."[73] Because woman is less likely than man to develop an objective super-ego, she is less able to develop the social capacities and interests the superego makes possible. In Freud's system, it is woman's psychology that renders her incapable of the objectivity needed for participation in the public realm.

The containment of woman in the private domain has long been seen as necessary for controlling the destructive effects of her passions on society. By limiting woman to the private realm and channeling her passions and emotions into the nurturance of the family, her passions were contained and thereby rendered harmless to the public order. A good wife devoted herself to her family and, by providing a supportive home life and a place of love and tranquility for her husband, served to assist man in his public role. But woman must always remain within the control of man lest she give voice to her own power and, like Lilith before her, fly over the walls of her confinement.

Postscript

> In college, educated women (I found out) were
> frigid; active women (I knew) were neurotic; women
> (we all knew) were timid, incapable, dependent,
> nurturing, passive, intuitive, emotional, unintelli-
> gent, obedient, and beautiful. You can always get
> dressed up and go to a party.
>
> Joanna Russ, *The Female Man*

Should we breathe a sigh of relief that we live at the end of the twentieth century, when science has progressed so far that we have rejected these erroneous
concepts of woman? Such a reaction would be premature. Although belief in woman's inherent inferiority is not expressed as explicitly today as it was in earlier
centuries, it remains a part of the fabric of Western culture. The fact that feminists have devoted much time and energy over the last two decades to exposing
the systematic bias against woman in contemporary social, cultural, economic, and
political institutions testifies to the strength of the centuries-old traditional view.

The patterns of the gender system found in twentieth-century science, religion, and philosophy, though often varying in detail, remain grounded in the tradition discussed in the preceding chapters. The definition of woman in terms of
lack, and her role in reproduction continue to be seen as the fundamental sources
of her "difference."

A brief illustration of my point is provided by a revealing glance at recent embryological theory. You will remember that until the sixteenth century a central
tenet of such theory was Aristotle's belief that woman resulted from a lack of heat
in the generative process. To this was added Galen's view that the female embryo was at a lower stage of development than the male. Even after this Aristotelian perspective was overturned by a preformationist position, theorists
continued to insist on the passivity of the female role in reproduction. Such
themes remain surprisingly pervasive today. Theories of primary sex differentiation, for example, continue to perpetuate the notion that female development is
due to a lack or absence of certain factors, and accounts of fertilization emphasize
the passivity of the female role.

According to generally accepted developmental theories, all mammalian embryos initially develop a single pair of gonads. This is the "indifferent period," in
which XX and XY embryos evince no sex differences. The organism will then
take either a female or a male path of development, and the gonad evolves into
either the ovaries or the testes.

Although the developmental process is analogous for females and males, current embryological theory has cast the female role as one of absence. In either case, the path of gonadal development is determined by the sex chromosomes and hormones. But in contemporary accounts of this process, the male path is depicted as resulting from an addition, not of heat, but of the H-Y antigen. The female path is viewed as resulting from a lack of this antigen. An example of this thinking can be found in a widely used undergraduate embryology text, Bruce Carlson's *Patten's Foundations of Embryology:*

> The sex-determining function of the Y chromosome is intimately bound with the activity of the H-Y antigen . . . its major function is to cause the organization of the primitive gonad into the testis. In the absence of the H-Y antigen the gonad later becomes transformed into the ovary.[1]

Notice that male development is portrayed as the result of an infusion of the H-Y antigen, while female development is depicted as the passive result of its *absence*. This absence metaphor is quickly picked up by those writing popularized texts, particularly those desiring to document significant "innate" differences between the sexes. As one example of this genre, consider the following quote from philosopher Michael Levin's attack on feminism: "The male XY chromosomal pair in a newly formed zygote signals the embryonic gonads to produce testosterone, which in turn "virilizes" the developing brain. The mammalian fetal brain unexposed to male hormones remains that of the homogametic sex, which in humans is the female."[2] Again, woman is seen as the result of a lack, this time the lack of exposure to male hormones, which causes the lack of a virile brain. Although this is an account far removed from the Aristotelian and Galenic theories of impure blood and deficiencies in heat, the underlying metaphor remains the same.[3]

And, as one might expect, scientists and philosophers do not hesitate to spell out the implications of these differences. In the words of reproductive biologist R. V. Short, "In all systems that we have considered, maleness means mastery; the Y chromosome over the X, the medulla [of the gonad] over the cortex, androgen over oestrogen. So physiologically speaking, there is not justification for believing in the equality of the sexes; *vive la différence!*"[4] And Levin concluded that the "unvirilized" mind causes woman to be less aggressive and possess less of a tendency toward dominance than man. "Women have preferences just as firm as men about how other people should behave, but a woman proverbially seeks to shape the behavior of others by indirection, getting them to want to do of their own accord what she wants them to do. Dominance-aggression is willingness to *make* others do what one wants them to do."[5] In other words, woman is passive and manipulative.

Female passivity is also seen in theories of conception. Theorists continue to perpetuate a view of the active sperm and the passive ovum awaiting penetration.[6] Comparing contemporary embryological theory to Aristotle's account, the philosopher Michael Boylan claimed that in modern biological theory "the sperm is the active agent that must move and penetrate the ovum. The egg passively awaits the sperm."[7] And theorists chart this active-passive polarity onto the characters of woman and man. The psychologist Karl Stern, for example, argued that "just as in the function of the spermatozoon in its relation to the ovum, man's attitude toward nature is that of attack and penetration. He removes rocks and uproots forests to make space for agriculture. He dams rivers and harnesses the power of water." Woman's response is the opposite. "Just as in sexual physiology the female principle is one of receiving, keeping and nourishing—woman's *specific* form of creativeness, that of motherhood, is tied up with the life of nature, with a *non-reflective bios.*"[8]

The "difference" we are encouraged to celebrate continues to be grounded in woman's role in reproduction and reproductive labor. Turning from science to religion, consider the following excerpt from an address by Pope Pius XII: "Now a woman's function, a woman's way, a woman's natural bent is motherhood. Every woman is called to be a mother. . . . To this end the Creator has fashioned the whole of woman's nature: not only her organism, but also and still more her spirit, and most of all her exquisite sensibility."[9] And the theologian Emil Brunner contended that reproductive differences between woman and man have their counterpart in what he refers to as "the mental and spiritual nature" of the sexes. In a passage that by now should sound hauntingly familiar, he claims that

> . . . man is the one who produces, he is the leader; the woman is receptive, and she preserves life; it is the man's duty to shape the new; it is the woman's duty to unite it and adapt it to that which already exists. The man has to go forth and make the earth subject to him, the woman looks within and guards the hidden unity. The man must be objective and generalize, the woman must be subjective and individualize; the man must build, the woman adorns; the man must conquer, the woman must tend; the man must comprehend all with his mind, the woman must impregnate all with the life of her soul.[10]

Despite the vast differences in the lives of a fourth-century BCE woman, a twelfth-century woman, and a twentieth-century woman, there remains profound continuity in the conceptions of her generic nature.

The perpetuation of this continuity goes deeper than our contemporary practice of science or our beliefs about the nature of the scientific method. It is rooted in our ways of thinking and talking about the world. The notion of difference has, for centuries, been understood as involving absence. If two people are different from one another, whether that difference is grounded in gender or in race, one of them is perceived as less developed, less perfect than the other—as falling short of the ideal. We understand difference in terms of opposition and negation—not active, not rational, not aggressive. And such opposition carries with it a hierarchization of certain traits. Reason, for example, is privileged over emotion, and emotion is characterized as resulting from the lack of rational control of the passions. The "difference" we are asked to accept, even celebrate, between woman and man perpetuates the conception of woman as lacking, for we continue to privilege the male as the true form, the "ideal" against which woman is to be measured, and to be found lacking.

We must reject such a notion of difference. Failure to do so leaves those who would deny the centuries-old tradition of seeing woman as inferior, the tradition on which I have focused in this book, with only two options: to deny any differences between woman and man, or to argue for the superiority of traits ascribed to woman over those attributed to man. The first option of denying difference was adopted by many feminists during contemporary struggles to ensure women's rights; they maintained that women were as capable of being business leaders, or soldiers, or politicians as men, for without societal or cultural barriers, women could also be analytic, aggressive, and courageous. In other words, women are capable of being men. But to argue in this fashion simply continues to treat man as the true measure of humanity, and perpetuates the tradition of privileging those traits perceived as masculine.

The second option, reversing the logic and privileging female traits over male, fares no better, for to do so maintains the same logic of exclusion, now simply in reverse. This approach does not question the division of the world into simple binary categories, and thus does not allow for the existence of real difference. Difference continues to be defined in terms of lack.

Breaking the cycle of denigration of the feminine, and of viewing woman as inferior, involves two processes. First, we must be aware of the ways in which these concepts are woven into the very fabric of our ways of thinking. Second, we must reject the idea of difference as lack, and replace it with an understanding of difference that allows for "otherness" without hierarchization—that is, that one group of people can be different without that difference entailing superiority or inferiority. My analysis in this book is designed as a contribution to the first part of this process. An awareness of the patterns I have identified will enable us to recognize and reject them in contemporary conceptions of woman.

However, recognition alone is not sufficient. These conceptions must be replaced, and this requires us to expand our notion of difference in a way that goes beyond the dichotomies.[11] We must work together to create new ways of speaking, a new metaphysic. In the words of Luce Irigaray, "If we continue to speak this sameness, if we speak to each other as men have spoken for centuries, as they have taught us to speak, we will fail each other. Again . . . words will pass through our bodies, above our heads, disappear, make us disappear."[12]

Notes

PREFACE

1. I concur with Thomas Laqueur's thesis that a one-sex model that "construed the male and female bodies as hierarchically, vertically, ordered versions of one sex" was the dominant discourse of science until the late eighteenth century (*Making Sex*, p. 10). Laqueur argues that by the nineteenth century a new model of radical dimorphism in which female and male bodies were perceived as opposites began to replace the one-sex model. I would suggest, as does Laqueur himself, that the one-sex model continued to have a significant influence on conceptions of female and male bodies well into the twentieth century. See, for example, his chapter on Freud.

2. For a more detailed discussion of the sources of the Greek view of the male as the true form see Tuana, "Aristotle and the Politics of Reproduction."

3. See, for example, Haraway, *Primate Visions;* Harding, *The Science Question in Science* and *Whose Science? Whose Knowledge?;* Keller, *Reflections on Gender and Science;* Longino, *Science as Social Knowledge;* Nelson, *Who Knows;* Tuana, *Feminism and Science.*

4. Longino and Doell, "Body, Bias, and Behavior," p. 182 n. 29.

5. Nelson, *Who Knows,* p. 99.

6. Haraway, "Animal Sociology," part I, p. 25.

7. Keller, *Reflections on Gender and Science,* p. 7.

8. For a further clarification of this distinction between good and bad science and a developed explanation of the ways in which values permeate the practice of science, see Longino, *Science as Social Knowledge* and Nelson, *Who Knows.*

9. Harding, *Whose Science? Whose Knowledge?,* p. 149.

10. Nelson, *Who Knows,* p. 15.

11. In my analysis I will focus on theorists' claims concerning women as a group, and will not comment on the ways in which their positions might also have been affected by class or race biases. There were, indeed, many theorists who held that women of certain races or classes were even more lacking than women of what they perceived as privileged classes. Although I do not want to discount the importance of these additional prejudices, they did not result in different theoretical stances. Women of classes or races that were not perceived as privileged were not seen as possessing characteristics or traits different than those of other women. Rather, they were seen as being even more misbegotten, that is, more lacking in desirable traits, than those women who were perceived as privileged—a difference in degree, not in kind. For studies on the intersections of gender, race, and class in science, see Brace, "The Roots of the Race Concept in American Physical Anthropology"; Gilman, "Black Bodies, White Bodies"; Gould, *The Mismeasure of Man;* Haller, *Outcasts from Evolution;* Hammonds, "Race, Sex, and AIDS"; Haraway, *Primate Visions;* and Stepan, *The Idea of Race in Science.*

12. For feminist critiques of contemporary science, see: Bleier, *Science and Gender;* Fausto-Sterling, *Myths and Gender;* Haraway, *Primate Visions;* Harding and O'Barr, *Sex and Scientific Inquiry;* Keller, *A Feeling for the Organism* and *Reflections on Gender and Science;* and Longino, *Science as Social Knowledge.* For critiques of the practice of philosophy, see: Bordo, *The Flight to Objectivity;* Code et al., *Feminist Perspectives;* Griffiths and Whitford, *Feminist Perspectives in Philosophy;* and Harding, *Feminism and Methodology.* For critiques of theology see Christ and Plaskow, *Womanspirit Rising;* Hayter, *The New Eve in Christ;* Hageman, *Sexist Religion and Women in the Church;* and Ruether, *Women-Church.*

13. To assist the reader in this task, I offer an extensive bibliography.

1. IN THE BEGINNING

1. Lovejoy, *The Great Chain of Being.*

2. I have actually stated this too simply here. Race as well as class is a factor in this hierarchy. Women of "civilized" races were often viewed as being superior to men of "primitive" races. Nevertheless, it remained true that within each race, woman was seen as man's inferior.

3. Hesiod, *Theogony,* lines 571–95.

4. Hesiod, *Works and Days,* line 80. Hesiod augments his account of the creation of woman in his *Works and Days,* a manual of instruction written somewhat later than the *Theogony.*

5. Ibid., line 83.

6. Ibid., line 69.

7. Ibid., lines 276–79.

8. Although I adopt the conventional juxtaposition of man and animal, I realize that this contrast is doubly exclusive. I will focus on the exclusion of woman from the supposedly generic "man." The second exclusion, which will not be a topic of my analysis, is the exclusion of human from the supposedly generic term "animal." For a feminist analysis of this latter exclusion, see Adams, *The Sexual Politics of Meat.*

9. The use of the gender specific term here is intentional since Plato claims that humans were originally created as male. Woman is, as we will see, a later stage.

10. Plato envisioned this creator god as male, a position consistent with his depiction of the female form as a sign of degeneration from a more perfect and male stage of existence.

11. Plato, *Timaeus,* 41d.

12. Ibid., 42d.

13. Ibid., 42b-c.

14. Krell, in his article "Female Parts in the *Timaeus,*" discusses the general denigration of all things female in the *Timaeus.* See Allen's "Plato on Women" for a comparison of Plato's *Timaeus* with his *Republic.* Allen argues that the two dialogues are not inconsistent, but rather that the spirit of the *Timaeus* is carried through in Plato's other works, including the *Republic.*

15. For an excellent discussion of the gender and race implications of Plato's distinction between the body and the soul, see Spelman's *Inessential Woman.*

16. Plato, *Timaeus,* 90e.

17. All Biblical citations are from *The Oxford Annotated Bible with the Apocrypha.*

18. Bal, "Sexuality, Sin, and Sorrow."

19. Ibid., p. 326.

20. Ibid., p. 324.

21. The interpretation of woman's metaphysical equality to man has received some support from the Jewish tradition that focuses on woman's role as a helper and involves the conclusion that only a being equal in all ways to a man would be a suitable helper. For example, Elie Munk in *The Call of the Torah* argues that the statement, "Make him a helpmeet," "clearly indicates that woman is created to give man the physical, moral, and spiritual completion which he requires. Man's task on earth is too great for one alone to bear. He needs a helpmeet at his side. . . . Consequently the role reserved for woman appears here as being invested with the highest nobility. A helpmeet means moreover that the wife is not the shadow or the slave of her husband, she is not the scorned object of a tyrannical husband as witnessed in the pagan antiquity. She is her husband's cherished and indispensable partner, a partner which no other creature in the world could have replaced" (p. 66). The interpretation of woman's metaphysical superiority has been adopted by no major religious tradition, although it has been advanced by some feminist theorists. See, for example, Stone's *When God Was a Woman.*

22. Philo, *On the Virtues,* III, LXXXIX, p. 453.

23. Philo, *On the Account of the World's Creation,* LIX, p. 131.
24. Philo, *Questions and Answers on Genesis,* #27, p. 16.
25. Philo, *Allegorical Interpretation of Genesis,* XVIII, p. 271.
26. Aquinas, *Summa Theologica,* I.98.2.
27. Ibid., I.92.1.
28. Ibid., I.92.1.
29. Ibid., II.2.156.
30. Augustine, *Confessions of St. Augustine,* XIII, Ch. 32.
31. Luther, *Lectures on Genesis,* I.27, p. 69.
32. Ibid., I.27, pp. 68–69, my emphasis.
33. Ibid., I.27, p. 68.
34. Ibid., I.27, p. 69.
35. Ibid, 2.18, p. 115.
36. Ibid.
37. Ibid., 3.1, p. 151.
38. Ibid., 2.18, p. 115.
39. In *Meditations on Modern Political Thought* Elshtain argues that, at a symbolic level, Luther's theology undercut the authority of the female. Noting that the very institution that Luther attacks—the church—was construed as female, specifically as a mother or bride of Christ, Elshtain delineates the demotion of female symbolism in what she terms Luther's "masculinization of theology" (p. 16).
40. Calvin, *Commentaries on Genesis,* II:21, p. 133.
41. Ibid. Calvin disagreed with earlier Christian theologians who had argued that married life was inferior to celibate life. Through his interpretation of woman's creation, Calvin was able to conclude that "the children of God may embrace a conjugal life with a good and tranquil conscience, and husbands and wives may live together in chastity and honour" (II:22, p. 134).
42. Ibid., II:18, p. 129.
43. Ibid., III:16, p. 172.
44. The use of the gender specific "man" is intentional here, for as we will see, woman's relation to the macrocosm is different than that of man.
45. Mirnefindo, "Tractatus Micreris," p. 109, as quoted in Carl Jung, *Mysterium Coniunctionis,* p. 11.
46. Philo, *On the Account of the World's Creation,* LI, p. 115.
47. Aquinas, *Summa Theologica,* I.91.1.
48. Although there are records of women who were alchemists, it is clear that an alchemical tradition that includes the premise that the male form is superior to the female precludes the ability of women to accomplish the final stages of the transmutation process, relegating women alchemists to a position of assistant to a male alchemist. I will demonstrate in chapter eight that the alchemical science of thinkers such as Paracelsus and Michael Maier contained such a premise.
49. Modern science retains, in a modified form, the belief that an experiment conducted on the microcosm can be seen as an experiment on the macrocosm.
50. Paracelsus, *The Hermetic and Alchemical Writings,* vol. 2, p. 289.
51. Ibid.
52. Paracelsus, *Four Treatises of Paracelsus,* p. 33.

2. THE MISBEGOTTEN MAN

1. Aristotle, *Generation of Animals,* 726.b.33.
2. Aristotle, *History of Animals,* 538.a.23–b.8.
3. Ibid., 608.b.10–12.
4. Aristotle, *Generation of Animals,* 727.a.3–4.
5. Ibid., 727.a.5–10.

6. Ibid., 726.b.30–31.

7. Ibid., 766.a.18–20.

8. It is accurate to interpret Aristotle as claiming that *only* males are fully human, but it would be an error to infer that he also supported the position that *all* males are fully human. He viewed male slaves as possessing no deliberative faculty and thus falling far short of full humanity. See *Politics* 1260.a.12–14.

9. Aristotle, *Generation of Animals*, 767.b.8–9.

10. In her article "Aristotle and Women" Horowitz suggests that Aristotle's view of women as monstrosities may have tied in with euthanasia practices in which defective children were often left out in the open to die, and rates of female infants so treated were much higher than male.

11. Aristotle, *Generation of Animals*, 766.b.28–33.

12. Aristotle, *History of Animals*, 583.b.3–5.

13. Boylan, *Method and Practice in Aristotle's Biology*, p. 157.

14. Aristotle, *Generation of Animals*, 737.a.27–28.

15. Ibid., 775.a.6–7.

16. Ibid., 775.a.14–21.

17. Ibid., 737.a.27–28.

18. Galen, *On the Usefulness of the Parts of the Body*, 14.II.296.

19. Ibid.

20. Ibid., 14.II.297.

21. Laqueur, in his "Orgasm, Generation, and the Politics of Reproductive Biology," offers an excellent discussion of how the change in biology from a hierarchical model of sexual differences to a model of the sexes as being different in kind was not the consequence of increased scientific knowledge, but rather the result of new ways of representing and constituting social and political realities.

22. Galen, *On the Usefulness of the Parts of the Body*, 14.II.299.

23. Aquinas, *Summa Theologica*, I.92.1. I will discuss in detail the nature of this "nobler" function in section three.

24. Ibid.

25. Ibid.

26. Ibid., I.99.2, my emphasis.

27. Geddes and Thomson, *The Evolution of Sex*, p. 26.

28. Gratian, *Decretum*, 2.32.2.8, as cited in Williams, "Religious Residues and Presuppositions in the American Debate on Abortion," p. 28.

29. Paré, *Collected Works*, p. 895.

30. For an excellent discussion of the history of abortion in America see Mohr, *Abortion in America*.

31. Paré, *Collected Works*, p. 128.

32. Freud, "Femininity," p. 114.

33. Laycock, *An Essay on Hysteria*, p. 63.

34. To those interested in further study of the alchemical tradition I suggest the following secondary texts as a beginning: Dobbs, *The Foundations of Newton's Alchemy;* Eliade, *The Forge and the Crucible;* von Franz, *Alchemy: An Introduction;* Gilchrist, *Alchemy: The Great Work;* Jung, *Alchemical Studies;* Waite, *The Hermetic Museum Restored and Enlarged;* and Yates, *Giordano Bruno and the Hermetic Tradition*.

35. Flammel, *Alchemical Hieroglyphics*, pp. 43–44, spelling modernized.

36. Vaughan, *The Works of Thomas Vaughan*, pp. 33–34.

37. Burckhardt, *Alchemy: Science of the Cosmos*, p. 151.

38. Bacon, *The Mirror of Alchimy*, p. 6n.97.

39. Norton, *The Ordinall of Alchimy*, p. 90.

40. In fact, women principally played a "helpmate" role in the practice of alchemy. Some alchemists believed that the presence of a woman would augment the transformative processes when the substance was in its female forms. But the presence of women would only

impede the final and perfecting stages when the substance, as well as the soul of the alchemist, was to be transformed into its perfect masculine form.

41. Maier, *Michael Maier's Atalanta Fugiens*, p. 316. An excellent discussion of Maier's theory can be found in Allen and Hubbs, "Outrunning Atalanta."

42. Maier, *Atalanta Fugiens*, p. 231.

43. Ibid., p. 166.

44. Ibid., p. 174.

45. Addison, *The Spectator*, No. 519, as quoted in Eisley, *Darwin's Century*, p. 259.

46. Pouchet, *The Plurality of the Human Race*, p. 16.

47. Darwin, *On the Origin of Species*, p. 108.

48. Darwin, *Descent of Man*, p. 276.

49. Ibid., p. 279.

50. Ibid., p. 283.

51. Ibid., p. 291.

52. Ibid., pp. 716–17.

53. Ibid., p. 717.

54. Ibid., pp. 725–26.

55. This, in fact, is still the argument of contemporary sociobiologists. See, for example, the writings of Wilson, *Sociobiology: The New Synthesis;* Barash, *The Whisperings Within;* and Dawkins, *The Selfish Gene.* For a sampling of the debates that have arisen around the science of sociobiology, see Caplan, *The Sociobiology Debate;* Ruse, *Sociobiology: Sense or Nonsense?;* and Lewontin et al., *Not In Our Genes.*

56. Darwin, *Descent of Man*, pp. 295–96.

57. Ibid., p. 717.

58. "The Probable Retrogression of Women," p. 11.

59. For an excellent discussion of such arguments see Gould's "Women's Brains."

60. Allan, "On the Real Differences," p. cciv.

61. Delauney, "Equality and Inequality in Sex," p. 184.

62. For a discussion of these theories, see Fee, "The Sexual Politics of Victorian Social Anthropology."

63. Allan, "On the Real Differences," p. ccxiii.

64. Hall, *Adolescence*, vol. 2, p. 567.

65. Ibid., vol. 2, p. 562.

66. Haeckel, *The History of Creation*, p. 310. Although transformed by evolutionary theory, the image of recapitulation was not a new one. Earlier notions of man as a microcosm in which the rest of the universe was reflected often contained the belief that animals were fetal stages of man.

67. For an excellent discussion of the use and abuse of recapitulation theory for justifying racism see Gould, *The Mismeasure of Man.*

68. "Thoughts and Facts Contributing to the History of Man," p. 179.

69. Le Bon, "Recherches anatomiques et mathématiques sur les lois de variations du volume du cerveau," pp. 63–64, my translation.

70. Cope, *The Origin of the Fittest*, p. 154.

71. Ibid.

72. Ibid., p. 159.

73. Ibid.

74. In fact, the phrase "undeveloped man" was a common appellation for woman in the nineteenth century. The British psychiatrist Harry Campbell, for example, referred to woman as the undeveloped man in his book *Differences in the Nervous Organization of Man and Woman.*

75. Cope, *The Origin of the Fittest*, p. 290.

76. Albrecht, "Address Delivered at the Anthropological Congress in Breslau, 1884," p. 50.

77. Hall, *Adolescence*, vol. 2, p. 194.

78. Geddes and Thomson, *The Evolution of Sex,* p. 39.

79. Physical anthropology was influenced by the earlier science of phrenology and the belief that psychical characteristics, such as intelligence, would affect external appearance, so that one could, so to speak, read backward from body to "mind." For a discussion of the influence of phrenology on physical anthropology, see Russett, *Sexual Science.*

80. An excellent account of these problems can be found in Fee, "Nineteenth-Century Craniology: The Study of the Female Skull."

81. Shaaffhausen, "On the Primitive Form of the Human Skull," p. 425.

82. Ecker, "On a Characteristic Peculiarity in the Form of the Female Skull," p. 355.

83. Cleland, *The Relation of Brain to Mind.*

84. Spencer, "Psychology of the Sexes," p. 32.

85. Spencer, *The Study of Sociology,* p. 63.

86. Weismann, *The Evolution Theory,* p. 353.

87. Ibid., p. 345.

88. In "Stereotypes of Femininity in a Theory of Sexual Evolution" Conway analyzes the social theory Geddes derived from his biological tenets and the popularization of his views in the United States by Jane Addams.

89. Geddes and Thomson, *Evolution of Sex,* p. 54.

90. Ibid., pp. 51–52.

91. Ibid., p. 260.

92. Ibid., p. 289.

93. Ibid., p. 17.

94. Ibid., my emphasis.

95. Ibid., p. 18.

96. Ibid., p. 289.

97. Ibid., p. 27.

98. Ibid., pp. 18, 27, 290.

99. Recent feminist critiques of science are, in part, dedicated to documenting this claim. See Harding, *The Science Question in Feminism* and *Whose Science? Whose Knowledge?'* Hubbard, *The Politics of Women's Biology;* Keller, *Reflections on Gender and Science;* Longino, *Science as Social Knowledge;* Nelson, *Who Knows;* and Tuana, *Feminism and Science.*

3. NOT IN GOD'S IMAGE

1. Plato, *Timaeus,* 73a.

2. Ibid., 42a.

3. Plato, *Republic,* 454d–e.

4. Plato, *Phaedo,* 80b.

5. Plato, *Republic,* 455b–c.

6. Plato, *Apology,* 35b.

7. Plato, *Republic,* 395c–396d.

8. Plato, *Laws,* 944d–945a.

9. For a recent example, see Vlastos, "Was Plato a Feminist?" An overview of the controversy as to whether Plato's views about women are consistent with feminist principles can be found in Tuana and Cowling, "Plato and Feminism."

10. Actually, this is true of most theorists. As we have seen, many scientists made clear distinctions between "primitive" and "civilized" women. To treat the concept of woman as generic would suppress the ways in which racism often accompanies sexism. For a full discussion of the problems resulting from the treatment of woman as a group without reference to class or race differences see Spelman's *Inessential Woman.*

11. Plato, *Republic,* 456a.

12. Ibid., 457a–b

13. Aristotle, *Generation of Animals,* 731.b.25–30.

14. Ibid., 744.a.25–30.

15. Aristotle, *History of Animals* 653.a.37–653.b.3.

16. Aristotle, *Generation of Animals,* 732.a.4.

17. Gratian, *Decretum,* vol. 1, col. 1256. All quotes from Gratian's *Decretum* are cited in Raming, *The Exclusion of Women from the Priesthood,* p. 35.

18. Gratian, *Decretum,* vol. 1, col. 1254 (p. 34), my emphasis.

19. Ibid.

20. Ibid., vol. 1, cols. 1255–1256 (p. 38).

21. Gratian did not acknowledge that it is *homo,* not *vir,* that is the Latin equivalent of *mulier.*

22. *Gospel of Thomas,* p. 57.

23. See Buckley, *Female Fault and Fulfillment in Gnosticism,* for a fuller development of this theme.

24. Philo, *Special Laws,* I, XXXVII, pp. 200–201.

25. Lloyd's *The Man of Reason* contains an excellent discussion of Philo's equation of reason and maleness.

26. Philo, *Questions and Answers on Genesis,* Bk. 1, #33, p. 20.

27. Philo, *Questions and Answers on Exodus,* Bk. 1, #8, pp. 15–16.

28. Philo, *On the Cherubim,* XIV, p. 39.

29. Philo, *Special Laws,* I, XXXVII, pp. 200–201.

30. Augustine, *On the Holy Trinity,* XII.7.12.

31. Ibid., XII.7.10.

32. Ibid.

33. Ibid.

34. Although the unmarried woman cannot attain this perfection, those who pledged a life of religious virginity were not seen as unmarried. They became the brides of Jesus, and thus achieved the *imago dei* through their connection to him.

35. Augustine, *On the Holy Trinity,* XII.7.10.

36. Augustine, *Of the Work of Monks,* 40, p. 524.

37. Augustine, *On the Holy Trinity,* XII.7.10.

38. For a discussion of the witch persecutions and the types of individuals most likely to be accused of witchcraft, see the works of Monter.

39. The *Malleus* was compiled in response to a papal bull issued by Pope Innocent VIII. It became the official and authoritative text on the identification and prosecution of witches for the entire Catholic church. It went through fourteen editions between 1487 and 1520, and at least sixteen more by the end of the seventeenth century.

40. Sprenger and Kramer, *Malleus Maleficarium,* I.6, p. 44.

41. Ibid.

42. Ibid., I.6, p. 45.

43. A version of this discussion of Descartes was originally published in Tuana, *Woman and the History of Philosophy.*

44. Descartes, *Rules for the Direction of the Mind,* Rule XII, p. 46.

45. Ibid., Rule XII, p. 47.

46. Ibid., Rule IV, p. 9.

47. Ibid., Rule III, p. 7.

48. Descartes, *Meditations on the First Philosophy,* p. 157.

49. Descartes, *Passions of the Soul,* Article XXVII, p. 344.

50. Ibid., Article XXXIII, p. 347.

51. Descartes, *Meditations on the First Philosophy,* VI, p. 193.

52. Descartes, *Passions of the Soul,* Article L, p. 356.

53. Descartes, *Discourse on Method,* p. 81.

54. Descartes, Letter to Vatier, February 22, 1638, cited in Lloyd, *The Man of Reason.* As Lloyd points out, Descartes's insistence here was due in large part to his attempt to

reject scholastic training as necessary to the acquisition of truth, and to replace it with individual reasoning.

55. Princess Elizabeth to Descartes, June 10/20, 1643, cited in Lloyd, *The Man of Reason*, pp. 48–49.

56. Although my focus here has been on gender, it is also important to remember that the man of reason is also not race or class neutral.

57. For an excellent critique of the view that running a household and raising children does not involve rationality, see Ruddick's *Maternal Thinking*.

58. An important lesson to be learned from this examination of gender in Descartes's theory is that an attempt to offer a nonsexist model of rationality of which both woman and man are equally capable will be unsuccessful if the abilities and faculties constituting rationality stress traits perceived as masculine and exclude traits accepted as feminine. Nor will it do to simply reverse this ordering and stress traits perceived as feminine and exclude traits accepted as masculine. Similar lessons can be inferred from this analysis concerning nonracist and nonclassist models of rationality. That is, a model of rationality must not privilege traits associated with one race or class over those associated with another. A truly nonsexist model of rationality must either include a mixture of feminine and masculine traits with no privileging of either gender, or must occur in a social context in which the concepts of masculine and feminine do not exist.

59. Weininger, *Sex and Character*, p. 54.

60. Ibid., p. 92.

61. Ibid., pp. 88–89.

62. Ibid., p. 145.

63. Ibid.

64. Ibid., p. 148.

65. Ibid., pp. 192–94.

66. Ibid., p. 286.

67. Ibid., pp. 298, 252.

68. Darwin, *Descent of Man*, p. 726.

69. Ibid., p. 728.

70. Ibid., p. 778.

71. Ibid., p. 725.

72. Spencer, "Psychology of the Sexes," p. 32.

73. Ibid.

74. Ibid.

75. Ibid.

76. Cope, *The Origin of the Fittest*, pp. 160–61.

77. Ibid., p. 159.

78. Geddes and Thomson, *The Evolution of Sex*, p. 291.

79. Ibid., p. 290.

80. Ibid.

81. Ibid.

82. Malebranche, *The Search after Truth*, p. 130.

83. For a history of racial anthropology see: Gould, *The Mismeasure of Man;* Haller, *Outcasts from Evolution;* Harris, *Rise of Anthropological Theory;* and Stocking, *Race, Culture and Evolution*.

84. Broca, "Sur le volume" and "Sur la capacité des cranes." Boyd, "Tables of Weights." Vierordt, *Anatomische*.

85. Jerison, *Evolution of the Brain and Intelligence*, p. 393.

86. Davis, "Contributions," p. 505.

87. In his *The Mismeasure of Man*, Gould argues that racial prejudices similarly biased the work of craniologists. See, for example, his study of the weighing techniques of Samuel George Morton. Gould's reanalysis of Morton's studies led him to conclude that "Morton's

summaries are a patchwork of fudging and finagling in the clear interest of controlling a priori convictions" concerning the superiority of the Caucasian race over all others (p. 54).

88. Birkby, "Sex-Identification from Cranial Measurements," p. 21.

89. McDonnell, "A Study of the Human Skull," p. 203.

90. Davis, "Contributions," p. 523fn.

91. Sutherland, "Woman's Brain," p. 803.

92. Tiedemann, *A Systematic Treatise*, pp. 60ff.

93. Sutherland, "Woman's Brain," p. 802–810.

94. Broca, "Sur le volume," p. 153.

95. Manouvrier, "Conclusions générales."

96. Blakeman, "A Study of Biometric Constants."

97. Sutherland, "Woman's Brain," pp. 802–810.

98. Broca, "Sur le volume." Buchner, "The Brain of Women." Huschke, *Schadel.*

99. Dunn, "Civilization and Cerebral Development."

100. Buchner, "The Brain of Women," pp. 170–71.

101. Schaaffhausen, "On the Primitive Form of the Human Skull."

102. Gratiolet and Leuret, *Anatomie.*

103. Retzius, *Cerebra simiarum illustrata.* Quotation cited in Allan, "On the Real Differences," p. cciv.

104. For a detailed discussion of these points see Lloyd's *The Man of Reason* and Tuana's *Woman and the History of Philosophy.*

105. Romanes, "Mental Differences Between Men and Women," pp. 654–55.

106. Ibid., p. 655.

107. Ibid.

108. Ibid., p. 656.

109. Allan, "On the Real Differences," p. ccx.

110. Harris, "On the Distinctions," p. cxcv.

111. Spencer, *Study of Sociology.*

112. Meigs, *Females and their Diseases,* p. 350.

113. Allan, "On the Real Differences," p. cxcix.

114. Allan, "On the Real Differences," pp. cxcviii–cxcix.

115. Clarke, *Sex in Education,* p. 33.

116. Ibid., pp. 41–42.

117. Ibid., pp. 86–87.

118. For further discussion of this topic, see Showalter, *The Female Malady* and Smith-Rosenberg, "The Hysterical Woman."

119. Clarke, *Sex in Education,* p. 91.

120. Ibid., p. 127. For historical studies of ideological responses to woman's changing role in the nineteenth century, see Barker-Benfield, *The Horrors of the Half-Known Life;* Smith-Rosenberg, *Disorderly Conduct;* and Vicinus, *Independent Women.*

4. THE LESS NOBLE SEX

1. Hesiod, *Works and Days,* line 69.

2. Ibid., line 375.

3. Ibid., lines 58–59.

4. Plato, *Timaeus,* 86d.

5. Aristotle, *History of Animals,* 608.b.1–3.

6. Ibid.

7. Aristotle, *Politics,* 1253.a.15–17.

8. Ibid., 1254.a.33–1254.b.9.

9. Philo, *Questions and Answers on Genesis,* Bk. 1, #33, p. 20.

10. Rubin, *Testament of Rubin,* v. 1–6, p. 519.

11. Hesiod, *Works and Days,* lines 67, 704–705.
12. Sprenger and Kramer, *Malleus Maleficarum,* I.6, p. 47.
13. Ibid.
14. Kant, *Grounding for the Metaphysics of Morals,* p. 14 (402).
15. Ibid., p. 11 (398).
16. Ibid., p. 13 (400).
17. Kant, *Observations,* p. 76.
18. Kant viewed all non-European races as inferior and "primitive." He claimed that one mark of this inferiority was a lack of either type of understanding.
19. Kant, *Observations,* p. 81.
20. Rousseau, *Emile,* Book V, p. 386.
21. Ibid., Book IV, p. 341.
22. Ibid., Book V, p. 359.
23. Ibid., Book V, p. 370.
24. Ibid., Book V, p. 371.
25. Ibid., Book V, p. 358.
26. Ibid., Book V, p. 360.
27. Ibid., Book V, p. 358.
28. Ibid., Book V, p. 359.
29. Ibid., Book V, p. 361.
30. Ibid.
31. Kant, *Anthropology,* p. 140.
32. Ibid.
33. Kant, *Observations,* pp. 78, 87.
34. Ibid., pp. 87–88.
35. Kant, *Anthropology,* p. 169.
36. Ibid.
37. Kant, *Observations,* p. 95.
38. Kant, *Anthropology,* p. 168.
39. Ibid., my emphasis.
40. Meigs, *Females and their Diseases,* p. 43.
41. Spencer, "Psychology of the Sexes," p. 32.
42. Spencer, "Psychology of the Sexes," pp. 36–37.
43. Meigs, *Females and their Diseases,* p. 46, my emphasis.
44. For studies of the nineteenth-century debates concerning woman's moral superiority, see: Paula Baker, *The Moral Framework of Public Life;* Nancy Cott, *The Bonds of Womanhood;* Sheila M. Rothman, *Woman's Proper Place;* and Mary Ryan, *Women in Public.*
45. Weininger, *Sex and Character,* p. 186.
46. Ibid., p. 197.
47. Ibid., p. 204.
48. Ibid., p. 207.
49. Ibid., p. 345.
50. Freud, "Femininity," p. 129.
51. Freud, "Some Psychical Consequences," p. 252.
52. Freud, "Femininity," p. 125.
53. Ibid., p. 128.
54. Freud, "Female Sexuality," p. 229.
55. Freud, "Femininity," p. 129.
56. Ibid., p. 132.
57. Ibid., p. 125.
58. Freud, "Some Psychical Consequences," pp. 257–58.
59. Freud, *Civilization and Its Discontents,* p. 103.
60. Freud, "Femininity," p. 118.

61. Ibid.

62. Freud, *Civilization and Its Discontents,* p. 103.

63. Freud, " 'Civilized' Sexual Morality," pp. 198–99.

64. Ibid., p. 199.

5. THE HYSTERIA OF WOMAN

1. In "Female Parts in *Timaeus,*" Krell suggests that "hysteria" may also be etymologically related to "swine," and thereby to the stupidity and filthiness, but also the fertility, of the sow, who is both a tabooed and a sacred object.

2. Hippocrates, *Diseases of Women, #2,* p. 573.

3. Ibid., #7, p. 576.

4. Aristotle, *History of Animals,* 582.b.23–26.

5. Lefkowitz in "The Wandering Womb" argues that in maintaining that the womb could wander, classical physicians were less concerned with healing than with upholding the established values of society.

6. Plato, *Timaeus,* 91c. Krell argues that the *Timaeus* contains a negative image of the uterus, seeing female parts as animal parts that are fundamentally diseased and prone to disorder.

7. Aretaeus, *Extant Works,* pp. 285–86.

8. Aretaeus, *Extant Works,* p. 451.

9. Aretaeus, *Extant Works,* p. 286.

10. Aretaeus, *Extant Works,* pp. 286–87.

11. For a detailed discussion of the impact of values on the practice of science and an analysis of the complexity of this empirical relationship, see Longino, *Science as Social Knowledge* and Nelson, *Who Knows.*

12. Soranus, *Gynecology,* p. 153.

13. Ibid.

14. Ibid., p. 171.

15. Celsus, *Diseases of the Womb,* I.IV.20, p. 307.

16. Trotula, *Diseases of Women,* p. 2.

17. Ibid., pp. 10–11.

18. Guainerius, *Tractatus,* f. w6rb. English translations are from Lemay, "Anthonius Guainerius and Medical Gynecology," p. 350.

19. Paracelsus, *Diseases,* p. 163.

20. Paracelsus, *Diseases,* p. 164.

21. Scott, *Discoverie of Witchcraft,* p. 65.

22. Paré, *Collected Works,* p. 939, spelling modernized.

23. Ibid., spelling modernized. Paré's claim that women who are "destitute of husbands," meaning they are not having sex, are prone to hysteria gained attention in the seventeenth century, but, as I will discuss later, it was not until the nineteenth century that the association between sex and insanity was reified. Notice, however, that with this connection the emphasis shifted from a lack of sex to too much sex!

24. Sydenham, *Compleat Method,* p. 410.

25. Sydenham, *Compleat Method,* pp. 410–14.

26. Arnold, *Observations of Insanity,* v. 2, p. 145.

27. Wiltbank, *Introductory Lecture,* p. 7.

28. Laycock, *An Essay on Hysteria,* p. 63.

29. Laycock, *A Treatise on the Nervous Diseases of Woman,* p. 150.

30. Ray, "Insanity Produced by Seduction," quoted in Barker-Benfield, *The Horrors of the Half-Known Life,* p. 83.

31. Laycock, *Essay on Hysteria,* pp. 60–61.

32. Hollick, *Diseases of Woman,* p. 205.

33. Storer, *Reflex Insanity in Women,* p. 150.

34. Laycock, *Essay on Hysteria,* p. 64.

35. Tate, *Treatise on Hysteria,* p. 14.

36. Storer, *Reflex Insanity,* p. 78.

37. Kellogg, *Reciprocal Influence,* p. 307.

38. Walker, *Women Physiologically Considered,* p. 245.

39. Johnson, *Morbid Emotions of Women,* p. 4.

40. Ibid., pp. 182–200.

41. See chapter four.

42. Johnson, *Morbid Emotions of Women,* pp. 232–33.

43. Meigs, *Females and their Diseases,* p. 467.

44. Meigs, *Woman,* p. 47.

45. Meigs, *Females and their Diseases,* pp. 351–52.

46. Ibid., p. 352.

47. Burrows, *Commentaries on Insanity,* p. 146.

48. Blandford, *Insanity and Its Treatment,* p. 69.

49. Storer, *Reflex Insanity in Women,* p. 78.

50. Showalter in *The Female Malady* and Bassuk in "The Rest Cure" discuss the connections between the rest cure for neurasthenia prescribed by Silas Weir Mitchell and social views of woman as childlike, passive, emotional, and dependent.

51. Carter, *Treatment of Hysteria,* pp. 33–34.

52. Ibid., p. 31.

53. Ibid., p. 67.

54. Ibid., p. 69.

55. Gardner, *Conjugal Sins,* p. 70.

56. Ibid., p. 82. Gardner is here quoting from the work of M. Lallemand, *A Practical Treatise on the Causes, Symptoms and Treatment of Spermatorrhoea.*

57. Gardner, *Conjugal Sins,* p. 83.

58. Laycock, *Essay on Hysteria,* p. 113.

59. Brown, *The Curability of Hysteria,* p. 7.

60. For an account of the introduction of Brown's surgery and the reasons for its subsequent demise in England, see Skull and Favreau, "The Clitoridectomy Craze."

61. In *The Female Malady,* Showalter argues that clitoridectomy constituted "the surgical enforcement of an ideology that restricted female sexuality to reproduction" (p. 77).

62. Battey, "Castration," p. 484.

63. Bliss, *Woman,* p. 96.

64. Maudsley, *Body and Mind,* pp. 87–88.

65. Sims, "Remarks on Battey's Operation."

66. van de Warker, "The Fetish of the Ovary," p. 371. Longo in "The Rise and Fall of Battey's Operation" argues that this estimate appears inflated and calculates the total to be closer to 15,000.

67. Although some theorists were consistent in prescribing male castration as a cure of satyriasis, it was only infrequently performed.

68. Palmer, *Mary in the Documents of the Church,* p. 188.

69. Kitto, "Ovariotomy," p. 517.

70. Goodell, "Oophorectomy," p. 295. See also Gilliam's essay "Oophorectomy: A Plea For its More General Adoption."

71. Bell, *The Sex Complex,* p. 201.

6. CHILDREN OF THE GODS

1. In fact, it is reasonable to postulate a period in the prehistory of the human race, prior to the discovery of the male role in reproduction, when the female was considered the sole creative force. This postulate is supported by the existence of cultures, such as

the Trobriand Islanders, in which people were not aware of the connection between conception and the sex act and thus identified the female with the life-producing forces in the universe. See the work of Bronislaw Malinowski for a detailed discussion of the Trobriand Islanders, especially *The Sexual Lives of Savages.*

2. In chapters six and seven, I will employ the term "creativity" to refer to generative and procreative powers. I will not discuss artistic, literary, or scientific creativity. Although I believe a culture's views on woman's abilities in these other creative areas are directly related to beliefs concerning the female generative principles, I will not be able to make those connections at this time. For a discussion of these points, see Battersby, *Gender and Genius* and Merchant, *The Death of Nature.*

3. This is particularly true in Genesis 2 when the term for create/creation switches from *"barah,"* a term used only in relation to divine activity, to *"yastar,"* a term used to refer to the work of artists or craftspersons. In "Sexuality, Sin, and Sorrow," Bal notes that the verb used for God's creation of the original human in Genesis 2.7 was the specific verb for pottery, while the verb used in 2.22 refers specifically to architecture and the construction of buildings. On the basis of this, she argues that the creation of female and male from the original being was an action more difficult and sophisticated, and thus indicates a higher level of creation. For further discussion of such craftsperson imagery, see Cassuto, *Commentary on Genesis.*

4. Oppenheim, *Ancient Mesopotamia,* and Phillips, *Eve.*

5. Although there is some exegetical controversy over this point, the belief in conception *ex nihilio* has been a common theological tenet. Tertullian, for example, in his *Treatise Against Hermogenes* stated that God " . . . is the One-only God for the only reason that He is the sole God, and the sole God for the only reason that nothing existed with him" (chapter 17, p. 48).

6. Tertullian, *Apology,* XXI. 10.

7. Gottwald in *The Hebrew Bible* illustrates the ways in which the Genesis description of creation interweaves two ways of depicting creation: fiat, God speaking the world into being, and craft, God crafting the world into being.

8. Hesiod, *Theogony,* lines 116–36.

9. Ibid., line 116.

10. Ibid., lines 133–49.

11. Ibid., lines 237–39.

12. Ibid., lines 821–22.

13. Ibid., lines 211–32.

14. Ibid., lines 123, 124–25, 223, 226, 237, 306–308.

15. *Enuma Elis,* I:1.

16. Ibid., IV:98–102.

17. Ibid., IV:135–38; V (additions):47–62.

18. Ibid., VI:9.

19. Ibid., VI:33.

20. Ibid., I:83–85.

21. Ibid., I:82.

22. Ibid., I:1–2.

23. Ibid., IV:15–28.23.

24. Interestingly, this image of creation in the *Enuma Elis* resembles alchemical beliefs about creation. In the alchemical tradition the female principle is a necessary component of the transmutation process, but one that must ultimately be destroyed for the process to reach completion.

25. Even the creation of woman is depicted as an imposition of form upon matter. In this case, rather than dust, God uses man's rib as the matter upon which he forms woman: "and the rib which the Lord God had taken from the man he made into a woman" (Genesis 3.22). There is no hint, even here, of birth imagery.

26. In *Feminist Interpretation of the Bible,* Russell notes that throughout the Hebrew Bible it is clear that the power of life and death is God's power. She claims, however, that the fact that women are rendered taboo by menstruating or giving birth—the lifebearing functions of the reproductive cycle—can be interpreted as a recognition of women's participation in divine power. She argues that this system of ritual purity also served an opposite function, that is, to diminish or negate the power of female human beings in the life process. Given this she suggests that such taboos may also be seen as a means of male (priestly) control over female power (p. 88).

27. Even though Christian theologians have viewed humans as made in God's image, the metaphor here is interpreted in terms of resemblance rather than in terms of being a part of God or being created out of the body of the divine.

28. Berger, *The Goddess Obscured;* Campbell, *The Masks of God;* Gimbutas, *The Goddesses and Gods of Old Europe;* Goldenberg, *The Changing of the Gods;* Graves, *The White Goddess;* O'Brien, "Nammu, Nami, Eve and Pandora"; Ruether, *New Woman, New Earth;* Stone, *When God Was a Woman.*

29. Athanassakis, "Introduction," in Hesiod, *Theogony,* p. 7.

30. Hesiod, *Theogony,* lines 155–58.

31. Ibid., lines 159–60.

32. Ibid., lines 167–75.

33. Ibid., lines 176–81. The castrated Ouranos does not die. He is an agent throughout the *Theogony.* However, after the castration he is less powerful and plays a far less significant role.

34. Ibid., lines 211–12.

35. Ibid., lines 453–57.

36. Ibid., lines 486–87.

37. Ibid., lines 493–96.

38. Ibid., lines 226–32.

39. Ibid., line 887.

40. Ibid., line 896.

41. Ibid., lines 890–91.

42. Ibid., line 900.

43. Ibid., line 924.

44. The brain was associated with intellect in the classical period. Hippocrates in *On the Sacred Disease* and Plato in the *Timaeus* located the seat of thought and feeling as the brain. Even Aristotle, who deviated from this tradition in locating the source of sensation in the heart, did not completely deny the association of the brain and the intellect. Man's "brain is the most fluid and largest. This again is because the heat in man's heart is purest. His intellect shows how well he is tempered, for man is the wisest of animals" (*Generation of Animals* 744.a.26–30). The womb, you will remember, is the cause of hysteria and the source of woman's greater passions.

45. Orpheus, *Hymns,* XXXI, line 17.

46. Pindar, *Odes,* "The Olympian Ode," 7, lines 35–37.

47. Aeschylus, *Oresteia,* "The Eumenides," lines 667–68.

48. For an excellent discussion and analysis of ancient and classical birth metaphors, see duBois, *Sowing the Body.*

49. For the story of Erichthonius, see Apollodorus, *Library* III.xiv.6, Pausanias, *Guide to Greece,* book I.2.6, and Hyginus, *"Fabulae,"* CLXVI.

50. Hesiod, *Theogony,* lines 188–89.

51. Ibid., lines 191–92.

52. Ibid., lines 200–201.

53. Plato, in the *Symposium,* refers to two Aphrodites: the heavenly Aphrodite and the earthly Aphrodite. The heavenly Aphrodite is the child of a male parent only— "sprung from no mother's womb," daughter of Uranos (180d). The earthly Aphrodite is born of the union of female and male—daughter of Zeus and Dione. Plato's view of

the earthly Aphrodite is quite negative. "The earthly Aphrodite's Love is a very earthly Love indeed, and does his work entirely at random . . . their desires are of the body rather than the soul; and, finally, they make a point of courting the shallowest people they can find. . . . For this is the Love of the younger Aphrodite, whose nature partakes of both male and female" (181b–c). The heavenly love, on the other hand, "springs from a goddess whose attributes have nothing of the female," is "innocent of any hint of lewdness," and prefers those with a "vigorous and intellectual bent" (181c–d). The association of lust with the female and the consequences of this association are discussed in depth in chapter nine.

54. Ovid, *Metamorphoses*, IV. 796–803. Notice that only Medusa is punished for the "desecration." The implications here are twofold. First, sex is viewed as a profane act. There are versions of the Medusa myth where she is punished by Athena for simply having sex with Poseidon in the temple. If sex were seen as sacred, no notion of desecration would be possible. Second, the female is seen as responsible for sexuality *even when she is raped.* Poseidon is not punished by Athena. Medusa alone is held responsible: an early case of blaming the victim.

55. See Apollodorus, *Library,* II.4.2 and Ovid, *Metamorphoses,* IV.792–802.

56. Apollonius, *The Voyage of Argo,* IV.1513–1517.

57. Hesiod, *Theogony,* lines 185–87.

58. Homer, *The Homeric Hymns,* "Hymn to Pythian Apollo," lines 314–18.

59. Homer, *Iliad,* I.597–600; *Odyssey,* VIII.266–367.

60. Homer, *The Homeric Hymns,* "Hymn to Pythian Apollo," lines 326–30.

61. Ibid., lines 340–55.

62. Hesiod, *Works and Days,* lines 61–63. In *Hesiod and the Language of Poetry,* Pucci argues that the nature of woman's creation introduces a distinction between what is original—men and gods—and what comes later and is no longer original. Pandora is a copy, an imitation. She is a patchwork of various traits and characteristics. Woman, then, is artificial.

63. Hesiod, *Works and Days,* lines 69, 79–80.

64. Ibid., line 65.

65. Ibid., line 77.

66. Ibid., lines 66–67.

67. Ibid., lines 74–76.

68. Pope Leo I, cited in Miegge, *The Virgin Mary,* p. 63.

69. St. Ephrem, *Hymn 3,* cited in Palmer, *Mary in the Documents of the Church,* p. 20.

70. Ibid., p. 21.

71. John, *Apocryphon,* 4.25–30.

72. Ibid., 4.30.

73. Ibid.

74. Ibid., 4.30–5.10.

75. Ibid., 5.10–35.

76. Ibid., 6.10–15.

77. Ibid., 6.20.

78. Ibid, 9.25–35.

79. Ibid., 10.1–5.

80. Ibid., 10.9. Buckley in *Female Fault and Fulfillment in Gnosticism* argues that the appearance of Sophia's offspring, his serpent shape, expresses the phallic threat to the male of the female capable of parthenogenetic creation. "His shape displays his mother's illegitimate phallic capacity. She creates an objectified male power that by its very form manifests Sophia's 'lack.' . . . Sophia's condition is one of simultaneous deficiency and excess of power" (132).

81. John, *Apocryphon,* 10.10–15.

82. Interestingly, the Apocryphon of John also depicts the creation of man as prior to the creation of woman. In this account, all humans were originally male. Woman was

created later, and the evil powers planted sexual desire in her in order to make salvation for man more difficult (24.29).

7. THE WEAKER SEED

1. Aristotle, *The Generation of Animals,* 716.a.5.
2. Ibid., 715.a.5.
3. Ibid., 729.a.10.
4. Ibid., 727.a.1.
5. Ibid., 727.a.5.
6. Ibid., 727.a.25–30.
7. Ibid., 727.b.35.
8. Ibid., 728.a.1.
9. Ibid., 728.a.30.
10. Ibid., 727.b.5–10.
11. Ibid., 716.a.20, my emphasis.
12. Ibid., 729.b.15–730.b.25.
13. Ibid., 732.a.1–10.
14. Ibid., 738.b.25.
15. Ibid., 737.a.25.
16. Aeschylus, *Oresteia,* "The Eumenides," lines 666–669.
17. The Hippocratic writings were not all written by one individual named Hippocrates. However, for the sake of convenience, I will refer to the ideas contained within these writings as Hippocrates's.
18. Hippocrates, *Regimen,* XXVIII, XXIX.
19. Galen, *Usefulness of the Body,* 14.II.301.
20. Galen, *Usefulness of the Body,* 14.II.306.
21. St. Gregory of Nyssa, *Against Eunomius.*
22. Aquinas, *Summa Theologica,* I.118.1.
23. *Lev. Rabbah,* 14, 9; *Yalkut* to Job 10, 10, cited in Feldman, *Marital Relations, Birth Control and Abortion.*
24. R. Moses ben Nahman, cited in Feldman, *Marital Relations, Birth Control and Abortion.*
25. Talmud, *Niddah* 31a, cited in Feldman, *Marital Relations, Birth Control and Abortion.*
26. Anglici, *Anatomia Vivorum,* p. 88.
27. Ibid., p. 105.
28. Albertus, *De Animalibus,* xvi tr.1, c. 16, cited in Weisheipl, *Albertus Magnus.*
29. Albertus, *De Homine,* q. 17, art. 2, cited in Weisheipl, *Albertus Magnus.*
30. Albertus, *De Animalibus,* xv tr. 2, c.11, cited in Weisheipl, *Albertus Magnus.*
31. Ibid., xvi tr. 1, c. 10, cited in Weisheipl, *Albertus Magnus.*
32. See Hewson, *Giles of Rome.*
33. *Aristotle's Masterpiece,* p. 19.
34. Achillini, *Anatomical Notes,* p. 49.
35. Benedetti, *History of the Human Body,* p. 99.
36. de Laguna, *Anatomical Procedure,* p. 278.
37. Massa, *Introductory Book of Anatomy,* p. 204.
38. Ibid., p. 207.
39. Boerhaave, *Academical Lectures,* p. 42n.
40. My position here is in agreement with the insights of Thomas Laqueur in "Orgasm, Generation, and the Politics of Reproductive Biology." He argues that the prevalence of the view of woman as an imperfect man until the 1800s and its subsequent revision to a model of biological difference or divergence were not the result primarily of scientific advances, but were due to new ways of representing and constituting social relations.

41. Norton, *Ordinall of Alchimy,* p. 90.

42. Maier, *Atalanta Fugiens,* p. 304.

43. Graves, *The Greek Myths,* vol. 1, pp. 151–54.

44. Maier, *Atalanta Fugiens,* pp. 305–306.

45. Paracelsus, *The Prophecies of Paracelsus,* pp. 63–64.

46. Paracelsus, *The Prophecies of Paracelsus,* pp. 64–65.

47. Paracelsus, *The Prophecies of Paracelsus,* p. 174.

48. Basilius, "Rosinus ad Sarratantam," p. 318.

49. Paracelsus, "Liber Azoth," cited in Jung, *Alchemical Studies,* p. 139.

50. Paracelsus, *The Prophecies of Paracelsus,* p. 124.

51. Ibid., p. 168.

52. Swammerdam, *Miraculum Naturae,* cited in Glass et al., *Forerunners of Darwin.*

53. Malpighi, *Dissertatio epistolica de formatione pulli in ovo.*

54. Leeuwenhoek, "Correspondence," pp. 1120–34.

55. Cited in Cole, *Early Theories of Sexual Generation,* p. 69. It is now thought that this account was a hoax. However, it appears to have been taken seriously by numerous scientists of the time.

56. See Cole, *Early Theories of Sexual Generation,* for further details on the animalculism/ovism debates.

57. An excellent discussion of this transition period in the history of embryology can be found in Roe, *Matter, Life, and Generation.*

58. Garden, "A Discourse Concerning Generation," pp. 474–83.

59. Boerhaave, *Academical Lecturers,* p. 138.

60. Cited in Cole, *Early Theories of Sexual Generation,* p. 108.

61. Cooke, *The New Theory of Generation,* pp. 63–64.

62. Ibid., pp. 15–16.

63. Darwin, *Zoonomia,* p. 484.

64. Good, *The Nature of Things,* p. 122.

65. Holcombe, *The Sexes,* p. 172.

66. Astruc, *A Treatise on the Diseases of Women,* vol. III, pp. 47–48.

67. For a discussion of the effects of such biases on contemporary embryological theories, see the Biology and Gender Study Group, "The Importance of Feminist Critique for Contemporary Cell Biology."

8. IN MAN'S CONTROL

1. Salimbene. Translated in G. G. Coulton, *From St. Francis to Dante,* pp. 91–92.

2. Euripides, *Medea,* lines 573–75.

3. Euripides, *Hippolytos,* lines 957–59.

4. Aristotle, *Politics,* 1254.b.10.

5. Ibid., 1259.b.3.

6. Xenophon, *Oeconomicus,* VII.5.

7. Plato, *Laws,* 785b.

8. Hesiod, *Works and Days,* lines 695–98.

9. Ibid., line 699.

10. Xenophon, *Oeconomicus,* VII.5.

11. Ibid., VII.19–21.

12. Ibid., VII.22–25.

13. Ibid., VII.23.

14. Ibid., VII.35–38.

15. Livy, *The History of Rome,* XXXIV.2–3.

16. Philo, *Questions and Answers on Genesis,* Bk. I. #27, p. 16.

17. Ibid., #29, p. 18.

18. Ibid., #27, p. 16.

19. Ibid., #26, pp. 15–16.
20. Chrysostom, *Homilies on Timothy*, IX.435.
21. Chrysostom, *Exhortation to Theodore*, p. 112.
22. Augustine, *City of God*, XIV, 11, p. 459.
23. Augustine, *Confessions*, XIII.13.32. p. 347.
34. Aquinas, *Summa Theologica*, I.92.1.
25. Gratian, *Apostolic Constitution*, III.ix, p. 429, cited in Raming, *The Exclusion of Women from the Priesthood*.
26. Luther, *Lectures on Genesis*, p. 115.
27. Ibid., p. 203.
28. Locke, *Two Treatises*, I.47–48, pp. 191–92.
29. Filmer presented this position in 1680 in his book *Patriarcha; or the Natural Power of Kings*. His primary thesis was that God, not people, determined the political structure of society, thus the people could not limit monarchy. He applied a similar argument to the power of man over woman.
30. Locke, *Two Treatises*, I.47, p. 191.
31. Ibid.
32. Clark argued in "Women and Locke" that one of Locke's major concerns was to justify patrilineal inheritance, and this right could be established and maintained only by positing an inherent inequality in the marriage relationship.
33. Locke , *Two Treatises*, II.82, p. 339.
34. Locke acknowledged that there could be certain rare occasions in which a woman's natural limitations are counteracted by other forces, such as financial wealth or noble birth. In other words, Locke wished to allow for the rule of queens.
35. For a further discussion of this point see Tuana, *Woman and the History of Philosophy*.
36. Locke, *Two Treatises*, II.4, p. 309.
37. In "Women and Locke," Clark also argues that Locke accepted the presupposition that reproduction constitutes a natural liability, that is, that woman's role in reproduction is the cause of her inferiority to man. Her essay documents the centrality and necessity of this assumption in Locke's theoretical perspective.
38. Rousseau, *Emile*, book V, pp. 358–59.
39. Ibid., p. 359.
40. Ibid., p. 369.
41. Ibid., p. 370.
42. Rousseau, *Discourse on Political Economy*, p. 210.
43. Ibid.
44. Ibid.
45. Rousseau, *Social Contract*, p. 47.
46. Ibid., p. 50.
47. Ibid., p. 46, my emphasis.
48. Rousseau, *Origin of Inequality*, p. 70, my emphasis.
49. Rousseau, *Social Contract*, II, p. 47.
50. Kant, *Anthropology*, p. 79.
51. Ibid., p. 169.
52. Ibid.
53. Ibid., p. 167.
54. Ibid.
55. Ibid., p. 172.
56. Ibid.
57. Ibid., p. 173.
58. Ibid.
59. Meigs, *Females and their Diseases*, p. 364.
60. Ames, *Sex in Industry*, pp. 16, 56.

61. Allan, "On the Real Differences," pp. ccxii–ccxiii.
62. "The Probable Retrogression of Women," p. 11.
63. Bell, *The Sex Complex,* p. 108.
64. Wilson, *Medical Researches,* pp. 57–58.
65. Hegel, *Phenomenology,* p. 475.
66. Aristotle, *Politics,* 1269.b.20.
67. Schopenhauer, "On Women," p. 352.
68. Rousseau, *Emile,* book V, p. 366.
69. Ibid.
70. Rousseau, "Letter to D'Alembert," VIII, p. 109.
71. Weininger, *Sex and Character,* p. 339.
72. Freud, *Civilization and its Discontents,* pp. 103.
73. Ibid.

POSTSCRIPT

1. Carlson, *Patten's Foundations of Embryology,* p. 459.
2. Levin, *Feminism and Freedom,* p. 79.
3. The Aristotelian and Galenic theories were maintained for centuries in spite of the fact that they were grounded on an anatomical error. What of current theories of sex determination? Is there evidence that runs contrary to this view of female development as due to an absence of certain factors? The answer is yes. There has been research that indicates that there is a parallel process in which "female" hormones actively induce female development. For example, the addition of estrogen to the water of tadpoles results in the exposed larva becoming females. But perhaps even more revealing is the general absence of careful study of the genes involved in the development of ovaries from the undifferentiated gonad. The perhaps unconscious acceptance of the belief in the primacy of the male form has resulted in a relative lack of scientific interest in the mechanisms of female development. For further analysis of these points see Fausto-Sterling, "Society Writes Biology/Biology Constructs Gender."
4. Short, "Sex Determination and Differentiation," p. 70.
5. Levin, *Feminism and Freedom,* p. 81.
6. This view of the ovum as passive and the sperm as active is often found in scientific textbooks, and it is even more prevalent in popular literature. This is despite recent discoveries that indicate that the ovum actively capacitates the sperm and guides it. There is evidence that sperm must be activated by interacting with certain secretions of the female reproductive tract. Furthermore, it appears that the sperm does not actively penetrate the ovum. Rather, the ovum employs microvilli, projections on its surface, to hold the sperm and slowly envelop it. For further discussion of these studies and their implications, see the Biology and Gender Study Group, "The Importance of Feminist Critique for Contemporary Cell Biology."
7. Boylan, "The Galenic and Hippocratic Challenges to Aristotle's Conception Theory," p. 110.
8. Stern, *The Flight from Women,* pp. 21, 23.
9. Pope Pius XII, "Address," pp. 131–32.
10. Brunner, *Man in Revolt,* pp. 358–59.
11. Developing this new notion of difference has been a commitment of recent feminist theory, especially those feminists who emphasize the interesections of race and gender. See, for example, the writings of Gloria Anzaldúa and bell hooks. For examples of feminist critiques of traditional notions of difference, see Diana Fuss, *Essentially Speaking: Feminism, Nature and Difference* and Moria Gatens, *Feminism and Philosophy: Perspectives on Difference and Equality.*
12. Irigaray, "When Our Two Lips Speak Together," p. 69.

Bibliography

Achillini, Alessandro. *Anatomical Notes.* Trans. L. R. Lind. In *Studies in Pre-Vesalian Anatomy.* Philadelphia: The American Philosophical Society, 1975.

Adams, Carol. *The Sexual Politics of Meat: A Feminist-Vegetarian Critical Theory.* New York: Crossroad Press, 1989.

Aeschylus. *The Oresteia.* Trans. Robert Fagles. New York: Viking Press, 1975.

Alaya, F. "Victorian Science and the 'Genius' of Woman." *Journal of the History of Ideas* 38 (1977): 261–80.

Albrecht, Paul. "Address Delivered at the Anthropological Congress in Breslau, 1884."

Allan, J. McGrigor. "On the Real Differences in the Minds of Men and Women." *Anthropological Review, Supplement* 7 (1869): cxcvii-ccxix.

Allen, Christine Garside. "Plato on Women." *Feminist Studies* II, 2/3 (1975): 131–38.

Allen, Prudence, *The Concept of Woman: The Aristotelian Revolution 750 BC–AD 1250.* Montreal: Eden Press, 1985.

Allen, Sally, and Joanna Hubbs. "Outrunning Atalanta: Feminine Destiny in Alchemical Transmutation." *Signs* 6 (1980): 210–229.

Ames, Azel. *Sex in Industry: A Plea for the Working Girl.* Boston: James R. Osgood and Co., 1875. Reprint, New York: Garland Publishing, 1986.

Anglici, Ricardi. *Anatomia Vivorum.* In *Anatomical Texts of the Earlier Middle Ages.* Ed. George Corner. Washington, D.C.: Carnegie Institution, 1927.

Anglo, Sydney. *The Damned Art: Essays in the Literature of Witchcraft.* London: Routledge and Kegan Paul, 1977.

Annas, Julia. "Plato's *Republic* and Feminism." *Philosophy* 51 (1976): 307–321.

Anzaldúa, Gloria. *Borderlands/La Frontera: The New Mestiza.* San Francisco: Spinsters/Aunt Lute, 1987.

———. *Making Face, Making Soul: Haciendo Caras: Creative and Critical Perspectives by Women of Color.* San Francisco: Aunt Lute Foundation Books, 1990.

Apollodorus. *The Gods and Heroes of the Greeks: The Library of Apollodorus.* Trans. Michael Simpson. Amherst: University of Massachusetts Press, 1976.

Apollonius of Rhodes. *The Voyage of Argo.* Trans. E. V. Rieu. Baltimore: Penguin, 1959.

Aquinas, Thomas. *Summa Theologica.* Trans. Fathers of the English Dominican Province. Westminster, M.D.: Christian Classics, 1981.

Aretaeus. *The Extant Works of Aretaeus.* Trans. F. Adams. London: Sydenham Society, 1856.

Aristotle. *Generation of Animals.* Trans. A. Platt. In *The Complete Works of Aristotle.* Ed. J. Barnes. Princeton: Princeton University Press, 1984.

———. *History of Animals.* Trans. d'A. W. Thompson. In *The Complete Works of Aristotle.* Ed. J. Barnes. Princeton: Princeton University Press, 1984.

———. *Metaphysics.* Trans. W. D. Ross. In *The Complete Works of Aristotle.* Ed. J. Barnes. Princeton: Princeton University Press, 1984.

———. *Nicomachean Ethics.* Trans. W. D. Ross. In *The Complete Works of Aristotle.* Ed. J. Barnes. Princeton: Princeton University Press, 1984.

———. *Politics.* Trans. B. Jowett. In *The Complete Works of Aristotle.* Ed. J. Barnes. Princeton: Princeton University Press, 1984.

Aristotle's Masterpiece. 23rd edition. London: Booksellers, 1749. Reprint, New York: Garland Publishing, 1986.

Arnold, Thomas. *Observations of the Nature, Kinds, Causes and Prevention of Insanity.* Two volumes. London, 1806–1808.

Arthur, Chris. "Hegel as Lord and Master." *Radical Philosophy.* 50 (1988): 19–25.

Ashe, Geoffry. *The Virgin.* London: Routledge and Kegan Paul, 1976.

Ashmole, Elias. *Theatrum Chemicum Britannicum.* New York: Johnson Reprint Corporation, 1967.

Ashwell, Samuel. *A Practical Treatise on Diseases Peculiar to Women.* Philadelphia: Lea and Blanchard, 1845.

Astruc, Jean. *A Treatise on the Diseases of Women.* London: J. Nourse, 1762.

Auerbach, Nina. *Woman and the Demon: The Life of a Victorian Myth.* Cambridge: Harvard University Press, 1982.

Augustine. *The Catholic and Manichean Way of Life.* Washington, D.C.: Catholic University of America Press, 1966.

————. *City of God.* Trans. Marcus Dods. New York: Modern Library, 1950.

————. *Concerning the Nature of the Good.* Trans. John Burleigh. Philadelphia: Westminster Press, 1953.

————. *Confessions of St. Augustine.* Trans. Rex Warner. New York: New American, 1963.

————. *Of the Work of Monks. Select Library of Nicene and Post Nicene Fathers.* Ed. Philip Schaff. Buffalo, N.Y.: The Christian Literature Company, 1887.

————. *On The Holy Trinity. Select Library of Nicene and Post Nicene Fathers.* Ed. Philip Schaff. Buffalo, N.Y.: The Christian Literature Company, 1887.

Authur, Marylin. "Early Greece: The Origins of the Western Attitude Toward Women." *Aresthusa* 6 (1973): 7–58.

Bacon, Francis. *The Works of Francis Bacon.* Ed. Basil Montagu. Philadelphia: A. Hart, 1852.

Bacon, Roger. *The Mirror of Alchimy.* Lyon: Mace Bonhomme, 1557.

von Baer, Karl Ernst. *On the Genesis of the Ovum of Mammals and of Man.* Trans. C. D. O'Malley. Cambridge, England: History of Science Society, 1956.

Baker, Paula C. *The Moral Framework of Public Life: Gender, Politics, and the State in Rural New York, 1870–1930.* New York: Oxford University Press, 1991.

Bal, Mieke. "Sexuality, Sin, and Sorrow: The Emergence of Female Character (A Reading of Genesis 1-3)." In *The Female Body in Western Culture.* Ed. Susan Rubin Suleiman. Cambridge: Harvard University Press, 1986.

Baldry, H. C. *The Unity of Mankind in Greek Thought.* Cambridge: Cambridge University Press, 1965.

Banister, John. *The History of Man.* London, 1578.

Banta, Martha. *Imaging American Women.* Columbia University Press, 1987.

Barash, David P. *The Whisperings Within.* New York: Harper and Row, 1979.

Barber, Benjamin R. "Spirit's Phoenix and History's Owl or The Incoherence of Dialectics in Hegel's Account of Women." *Political Theory* 16, 1 (1988): 5–28.

Barker, Benfield, Ben. "The Spermatic Economy: A Nineteenth Century View of Sexuality." *Feminist Studies* 1 (1972): 45–74.

Barker-Benfield, G. J. *The Horrors of the Half-Known Life: Male Attitudes Toward Women and Sexuality in Nineteenth-Century America.* New York: Harper and Row, 1976.

————. "Sexual Surgery in Late-Nineteenth Century America." In *Seizing Our Bodies.* Ed. C. Dreifus. New York: Vintage, 1978.

Barojo, Caro. *The World of Witches.* Trans. O. N. V. Glendinning. Chicago: University of Chicago Press, 1965.

Bartholini, Thomas. *Anatomia Reformata.* 1651.

Basilius Valentinus. "Rosinus ad Sarratantam." *Artis Auriferae,* vol. 1. Basel, 1593.

————. *The Triumphal Chariot of Antinomy.* Ed. Lawrence Principe. Michael Principe, 1983.

Bassein, Beth Ann. *Women and Death: Linkages in Western Thought and Literature.* Westport, Conn.: Greenwood Press, 1984.

Bassuk, Ellen. "The Rest Cure: Repetition or Resolution of Victorian Women's Conflicts?" In *The Female Body in Western Culture.* Ed. Susan Rubin Suleiman. Cambridge: Harvard University Press, 1986.

Battersby, Christine. *Gender and Genius: Towards a Feminist Aesthetics.* Bloomington: Indiana University Press, 1989.

Battey, Robert. "Antisepsis in Ovariotomy and Battey's Operation—Eighteen Consecutive Cases—All Successful." *Transactions of the Medical Association of Georgia* 35 (1884): 151–65.

———. "Battey's Operation—Its Matured Results." *Transactions of the American Gynecological Society* 12 (1887): 253–74.

———. "Battey's Operation: Its Object, Results, Etc." *Transactions of the Medical Society of Virginia* 10 (1887): 188–93.

———. "Castration in Mental and Nervous Diseases. A Symposium." *American Journal of Medical Science* 184 (1886): 483–90.

———. "Extripation of the Functionally Active Ovaries for the Remedy of Otherwise Incurable Diseases." *Transactions of the American Gynecological Society* 1 (1876): 101–120.

———. "Is There a Proper Field for Battey's Operation?" *Transactions of the American Gynecological Society* 2 (1877): 279–305.

———. "Normal Ovariotomy." *Atlanta Medical and Surgical Journal* 11 (1873/4): 1–22, 65–84.

———. "Occlusion of the Entire Utero-vaginal Canal, Following Labor, With Distressing Sequelae of Unrelieved Menstrual Molimen—Battey's Operation—Cure." *Transactions of the Medical Society of Virginia* 2 (1879): 432–38.

———. "The Propriety of the Performance of Normal Ovariotomy in a Case of Absence of the Uterus With Excessive Nervous Irritation." *Journal of the Gynaecological Society of Boston* 7 (1872): 331–35, 339–40.

Bell, Linda A., and Linda Alcoff. "Lordship, Bondage and the Dialectic of Work in Traditional Male/Female Relationships." *Cogito* 2 (1984): 79–93.

Bell, Rudolph. *Holy Anorexia.* Chicago: University of Chicago Press, 1985.

Bell, W. Blair. *The Sex Complex: A Study of the Relationships of the Internal Secretions to the Female Characteristics and Functions in Health and Disease.* New York: William Wood and Co., 1916.

Benedetti, Allesandro. *History of the Human Body.* Trans. L. R. Lind. In *Studies in Pre-Vesalian Anatomy.* Philadelphia: The American Philosophical Society, 1975.

Benhabib, Seyla. "The Generalized and the Concrete Other: The Kohlberg-Gilligan Controversy and Feminist Theory." In *Feminism as Critique: On the Politics of Gender.* Eds. Seyla Benhabib and Drucilla Cornell. Minneapolis: University of Minnesota Press, 1987.

———. "On Hegel, Women and Irony." In *Feminist Interpretations and Political Theory.* Eds. Mary Lyndon Shanley and Carole Pateman. University Park: Pennsylvania State University Press, 1991.

Benhabib, Seyla, and Drucilla Cornell, eds. *Feminism as Critique: On the Politics of Gender.* Minneapolis: University of Minnesota Press, 1987.

Berger, Pamela. *The Goddess Obscured: Transformations of the Grain Protectress from Goddess to Saint.* Boston: Beacon Press, 1986.

Biology and Gender Study Group. "The Importance of Feminist Critique for Contemporary Cell Biology." *Hypatia* 3 (1988): 61–76.

Bird, H. W. "Aurelius Victor on Women and Sexual Morality." *Classical Journal* 78 (1982): 44–48.

Birkby, Walter. "An Evaluation of Race and Sex-Identification from Cranial Measurements." *American Journal of Physical Anthropology* 24 (1966): 21–28.

Blakeman, J. "A Study of the Biometric Constants of English Brain-Weights, and their Relationships to External Physical Measurements." *Biometrika* 4 (1905): 124–60.

Blandford, G. Fielding. *Insanity and Its Treatment.* Philadelphia: Henry C. Lea, 1871.

Bleier, Ruth. *Science and Gender: A Critique of Biology and Its Theories on Women.* New York: Pergamon Press, 1984.

Blinkov, S., and I. Glezer. *The Human Brain in Figures and Tables.* New York: Basic Books, 1968.

Bliss, W. W. *Woman and Her Thirty Years' Pilgrimage.* Boston: B. B. Russell, 1870.

Bloch, Maurice, and Jean Block. "Women and the Dialectics of Nature in Eighteenth Century French Thought." In *Nature, Culture, Gender.* Eds. Carol MacCormack and Marilyn Strathern. Cambridge: Cambridge University Press, 1980.

Bloom, Allan. "Rousseau on the Equality of the Sexes." In *Justice and Equality Here and Now.* Ed. Frank S. Lucash. Ithaca: Cornell University Press, 1986.

Bluestone, Natalie Harris. *Women and the Ideal Society: Plato's* Republic *and Modern Myths of Gender.* Amherst: University of Massachusetts Press, 1987.

Blum, Lawrence A. "Kant's and Hegel's Moral Rationalism: A Feminist Perspective." *Canadian Journal of Philosophy* XII, 2 (1982): 287–302.

Bodemer, Charles. "Embryological Thought in Seventeenth Century England." In *Medical Investigations in Seventeenth Century England.* Berkeley: University of California Press, 1968.

―――. "Regeneration and the Decline of Preformation in Eighteenth Century Embryology." *Bulletin of the History of Medicine* 38 (1964): 20–31.

Boerhaave, Herman. *Dr. Boerhaave's Academical Lectures on the Theory of Physic.* London: 1757.

Bordo, Susan. *The Flight to Objectivity: Essays on Cartesianism and Culture.* Albany: State University of New York Press, 1987.

Bornstein, Diane. *The Lady in the Tower: Medieval Courtesy Literature for Women.* Connecticut: Archon Books, 1983.

Boyce, Mary. *A Reader in Manichaean Middle Persian and Parthian.* Leiden: E. J. Brill, 1975.

Boyd, Robert. "Tables of the Weights of the Human Body and Internal Organs in the Sane and Insane of Both Sexes, Arranged from 2614 Post-mortem Examinations." *Philosophical Transactions of the Royal Society of London* 151 (1861): 241–62.

Boylan, Michael. "The Galenic and Hippocratic Challenges to Aristotle's Conception Theory." *Journal of the History of Biology* 17 (1984): 83–112.

―――. *Method and Practice in Aristotle's Biology.* Washington, D.C.: University Press of America, 1983.

Brace, C. Loring. "The Roots of the Race Concept in American Physical Anthropology," in *A History of American Physical Anthropology, 1930–1980.* Ed. Frank Spencer. New York: Academic Press, 1982.

Brennan, Teresa, and Carole Pateman. " 'Mere Auxiliaries to the Commonwealth': Women and the Origins of Liberalism." *Political Studies* XXVII, 2 (1979): 183–200.

Brighton Women and Science Group. *Alice Through the Microscope.* London: Virago Press, 1980.

Broca, Paul. "Sur la capacité des cranes parisiens des divers époques." *Bulletin société d'anthropologie Paris* 3 (1862): 102–116.

―――. "Sur le volume et la forme du cerveau suivant les individus et suivant les races." *Bulletin société d'Anthropologie Paris* 2 (1861): 139–207, 301–321, 441–46.

Brooks, J. G. "Castration for Hystero-epilepsy (Battey's Operation)." *Medical and Surgical Reporter* 52 (1885): 230–32.

Brown, Isaac Baker. *On the Curability of Certain Forms of Insanity, Epilepsy, Catalepsy and Hysteria in Females.* London: Robert Hardwicke, 1866.

Brown, W. Symington. *A Clinical Hand-Book on the Diseases of Women.* New York: William Wood and Co., 1882.

Brown, Wendy. *Manhood and Politics: A Feminist Reading in Political Theory.* Totowa, N.J.: Rowman & Littlefield, 1988.

Brunner, Emil. *Man in Revolt: A Christian Anthropology.* Philadelphia: Westminster Press, 1947.

Buchner, Ludwig. "The Brain of Women." *New Review* 9 (1893): 166–67.

Buckle, Henry T. "The Influence of Women on the Progress of Knowledge." *Royal Institution Proceedings* 2 (1858): 504.

Buckley, Jorunn Jacobsen. *Female Fault and Fulfillment in Gnosticism.* Chapel Hill: University of North Carolina Press, 1986.

Bullough, Vern. "Marriage in the Middle Ages: Five Medical and Scientific Views of Women." *Viator* 4 (1973): 485–501.

———. *Sexual Variance in Society and History.* New York: John Wiley and Sons, 1976.

———. *The Subordinate Sex: A History of Attitudes Toward Women.* Urbana: University of Illinois Press, 1973.

———. "Women, Menstruation, and Nineteenth Century Medicine." *Bulletin of the History of Medicine* (1973).

Burckhardt, Titus. *Alchemy: Science of the Cosmos, Science of the Soul.* Trans. William Stoddart. London: Stuart and Watkins, 1967.

Burkitt, F. C. *The Religion of the Manichees.* Cambridge: Cambridge University Press, 1925.

Burrow, J. W. *Evolution and Society: A Study in Victorian Social Theory.* Cambridge: Cambridge University Press, 1966.

Burrows, George Man. *Commentaries on the Causes, Forms, Symptoms, and Treatment, Moral and Medical, of Insanity.* London: Thomas and George Underwood, 1828.

Burstyn, Joan. "Education and Sex: The Medical Case Against Higher Education for Women." *Proceedings of the American Philosophical Society* 117 (1973): 79–80.

Butler, Melissa A. "Early Liberal Roots of Feminism: John Locke and the Attack on Patriarchy." *American Political Science Review* 72 (1978): 135–50.

Cadden, Joan. *The Medieval Philosophy and Biology of Growth.* Ph.D. dissertation, Indiana University, 1971.

Calvin, John. *Commentaries on Genesis.* Trans. John King. Grand Rapids, Mich.: Baker Book House, 1979.

Cameron, Averil, and Amelie Kuhrt. *Images of Women in Antiquity.* Detroit: Wayne State University Press, 1983.

Campbell, G. "St. Jerome's Attitude Toward Marriage and Women." *American Ecclesiastical Review* 143 (1960): 310–320; 384–94.

Campbell, Harry. *Differences in the Nervous Organization of Man and Woman.* London: H. K. Lewis, 1981.

Campbell, Joseph. *The Masks of God.* New York: Viking Press, 1959–70.

Canto, Monique. "The Politics of Women's Bodies: Reflections on Plato." In *The Female Body in Western Culture: Contemporary Perspectives.* Ed. Susan Rubin Suleiman, 339–53. Cambridge: Harvard University Press, 1986.

Cantrell, Carol H. "Analogy as Destiny: Cartesian Man and the Woman Reader." *Hypatia: A Journal of Feminist Philosophy* 5, 2 (1990): 7–19.

Cantrella, Eva. *Pandora's Daughters: The Role and Status of Women in Greek and Roman Antiquity.* Trans. Maureen B. Fant. Baltimore: Johns Hopkins University Press, 1987.

Caplan, Arthur L. *The Sociobiology Debate: Readings on the Ethical and Scientific Issues Concerning Sociobiology.* New York: Harper and Row, 1978.

Carlson, Bruce. *Patten's Foundations of Embryology.* New York: McGraw-Hill, 1981.

Carroll, Berenice A. *Liberating Women's History.* Urbana: University of Illinois Press, 1976.

Carter, Robert. *On the Pathology and Treatment of Hysteria.* London: John Churchill, 1853.

Cartwright, David. "Kant's View of the Moral Significance of Kindhearted Emotions and the Moral Insignificance of Kant's View." *The Journal of Value Inquiry* 21 (1987): 291–304.

Cassuto, Umberto. *Commentary on the Book of Genesis.* Jerusalem: Magnes Press, 1961.

Celsus. "On Diseases of the Womb." Trans. A. Lee. In *Celsus on Medicine in Eight Books.* London: E. Cox, 1831.

Chasseguet-Smirgel, Janine. *Sexuality and the Mind.* New York: New York University Press, 1986.

Chauliac, Guy de. *Gydos Questions.* 1579. Reprint, New York: DeCapo Press, 1968.

Cheselden, William. *The Anatomy of the Human Body.* Boston: Manning and Loring, 1795.

Cheyne, George. *The English Malady, or a Treatise of Nervous Diseases of All Kinds.* London, 1733.

Christ, Carol, and Judith Plaskow, eds., Womanspirit Rising: A Feminist Reader in Religion. New York: Harper and Row, 1979.

Chrysostom, St. John. *An Exhortation to Theodore after His Fall.* Vol. 9 of Select Library of Nicene and Post Nicene Fathers. Ed. Philip Schaff. Buffalo, N.Y.: The Christian Literature Company, 1889.

———. *Homilies on Ephesians 10.* Vol. 8 of *Select Library of Nicene and Post Nicene Fathers.* Ed. Philip Schaff. Buffalo, N.Y.: The Christian Literature Company, 1889.

———. *Homilies on the Statues.* Vol. 9 of *Select Library of Nicene and Post Nicene Fathers.* Ed. Philip Schaff. Buffalo, N.Y.: The Christian Literature Company, 1889.

———. *Homilies on Timothy.* Volume 8 of *Select Library of Nicene and Post Nicene Fathers.* Ed. Philip Schaff. Buffalo, N.Y.: The Christian Literature Company, 1889.

———. *On the Power of Man to Resist the Devil.* Trans. T. P. Brandram. In *A Select Library of Nicene and Post-Nicene Fathers of the Christian Church,* Vo. 9. Ed. Philip Schaff. Grand Rapids, Mich.: Wm. B. Eerdmans, 1978.

Church, F. "Sex and Salvation in Tertullian." *Harvard Theological Review* 68 (1975): 83–101.

Cicero. *Pro Caelio.* Trans. R. Gardner. Cambridge: Harvard University Press, 1958.

Clark, Anoon. *A Treatise on the Medical and Surgical Diseases of Women.* Chicago: Jansen, McClurg and Co., 1879.

Clark, Elizabeth. *Jerome, Chrysostom, and Friends.* New York: Edwin Mellen Press, 1979.

Clark, Gillian. *Women in the Ancient World.* Oxford: Oxford University Press, 1989.

Clark, Lorenne M. G. "Women and Locke: Who Owns the Apples in the Garden of Eden?" In *The Sexism of Social and Political Theory: Women and Reproduction from Plato to Nietzsche.* Eds. Lorenne M. G. Clark and Lynda Lange. Toronto: University of Toronto Press, 1979.

Clark, Lorenne M. G., and Lynda Lange, eds. *The Sexism of Social and Political Theory: Women and Reproduction from Plato to Nietzsche.* Toronto: University of Toronto Press, 1979.

Clarke, Edward H. *Sex in Education, or a Fair Chance for the Girls.* Boston: James R. Osgood, 1873. Reprint, New York: Arno Press, 1972.

Cleland, John. *The Relation of Brain to Mind.* Glasgow: James Maclehouse and Sons, 1882.

Cobbe, F. P. "Criminals, Idiots, Women and Minors: Is the Classification Sound?" *Fraser's Magazine* 78 (1868): 777–94.

Code, Lorraine, Sheila Mullet, and Christine Overall, eds. *Feminist Perspectives: Philosophical Essays on Methods and Morals.* Toronto: University of Toronto Press, 1987.

Cohen, A. *Everyman's Talmud.* New York: E. P. Dutton and Co., 1949.

Cole, F. J. *Early Theories of Sexual Generation.* London: Oxford University Press, 1930.

Coleman, William. *Biology in the Nineteenth Century.* New York: John Wiley and Sons, 1971.

Conger, George. *Theories of Macrocosm and Microcosm in the History of Philosophy.* New York: Russell and Russell, 1967.

Conway, Jill. "Stereotypes of Femininity in a Theory of Sexual Evolution." In *Suffer and Be Still: Women in the Victorian Age.* Ed. Martha Vicinus. Bloomington: Indiana University Press, 1972.

Cooke, John. *The New Theory of Generation.* London: J. Buckland, 1762.

Coole, Diana H. *Women in Political Theory: From Ancient Misogyny to Contemporary Feminism.* Sussex: Wheatsheaf Books, 1988.

Cope, Edward Drinker. *The Origin of the Fittest.* New York: D. Appleton and Co., 1887.

Corcos, Alain F. "Fontenelle and the Problem of Generation in the Eighteenth Century." *Journal of the History of Biology* 4 (1971): 363–73.

Corner, George. *Anatomical Texts of the Earlier Middle Ages.* Washington, D.C.: Carnegie Institution, 1927.

Cott, Nancy. *The Bonds of Womanhood: "Woman's Sphere" in New England, 1780–1835.* New Haven: Yale University Press, 1977.

———. "Passionlessness: An Interpretation of Victorian Sexual Ideology, 1790–1850." *Signs* 4 (1978): 219–36.

Coulton, G. G. *From Saint Francis to Dante: A Translation of All That Is of Primary Interest in the Chronicle of the Franciscan Salimbene (1221–1288).* London: David Nutt, 1906.

Curtis, E. *Manhood: The Causes of Its Premature Decline.* Philadelphia, 1870.

Cushing, C. "What are the Conditions that Justify Oophorectomy?" *Western Lancet: Journal of Medicine and Surgery* 12 (1883): 97–105.

Cushing, E. W. "Report of a Case of Melancholia; Masturbation; Cured by Removal of Both Ovaries." *Journal of the American Medical Association* 8 (1887): 441–42.

Dante. *Purgatorio.* Trans. John Sinclair. New York: Oxford University Press, 1972.

Darwin, Charles. *The Descent of Man, and Selection in Relation to Sex.* New York: Collier and Son, 1901.

———. *On the Origin of Species.* Akron, Ohio: Werner Co., 1872.

Darwin, Erasmus. *Zoonomia, or the Laws of Organic Life.* New York: AMS Press, 1974.

Davidson, Percy. *The Recapitulation Theory and Human Infancy.* New York: Columbia University Press, 1914.

Davies, Steven. *The Revolt of the Widows: The Social World of the Apocryphal Acts.* Carbondale: Southern Illinois University Press, 1980.

Davis, Joseph Barnard. *Catalogue of the Skulls of the Various Races of Man in the Collection of Joseph Barnard Davis, MD.* London, 1867.

———. "Contributions Towards Determining the Weight of the Brain in Different Races of Man." *Philosophical Transactions of the Royal Society of London* 158 (1868): 505–527.

Dawkins, Richard. *The Selfish Gene.* Oxford: Oxford University Press, 1989.

Debus, Allan. *The Chemical Philosophy: Paracelsian Science and Medicine in the Sixteenth and Seventeenth Century.*

———, ed. *Medicine in Seventeenth Century England.* Berkeley: University of California Press, 1974.

Delaney, Janice, M. J. Lupton, and E. Toth. *The Curse: A Cultural History of Menstruation.* New York: Mentor Press, 1977.

Delauney, Gaetan. "Equality and Inequality in Sex." *Popular Science Monthly* 20 (1881): 185–92.

Descartes, René, *Discourse on the Method of Rightly Conducting the Reason.* In *The Philosophical Works of Descartes.* Trans. Elizabeth S. Haldane and G. R. T. Ross. New York: Dover, 1955.

———. *Meditations on First Philosophy.* In *The Philosophical Works of Descartes.* Trans. Elizabeth S. Haldane and G. R. T. Ross. New York: Dover, 1955.

———. *The Passions of the Soul.* In *The Philosophical Works of Descartes.* Trans. Elizabeth S. Haldane and G. R. T. Ross. New York: Dover, 1955.

———. *Rules for the Direction of the Mind.* In *The Philosophical Works of Descartes.* Trans. Elizabeth S. Haldane and G. R. T. Ross. New York: Dover, 1955.

Detienne, Michael. *The Gardens of Adonis: Spices in Greek Mythology.* Trans. J. Lloyd. Sussex: Harvester Press, 1977.

Dickanson, A. "Anatomy and Destiny: The Role of Biology in Plato's Views of Women." *The Philosophical Forum* 5 (1975): 45–53.

Dijkstra, Bram. *Idols of Perversity.* Oxford University Press, 1986.

Diodorus of Sicily. *The Library of History.* Trans. C. H. Oldfather. Cambridge: Harvard University Press, 1935.

Distant, W. L. "The Mental Differences Between the Sexes." *Journal of the Anthropological Institute of Great Britain and Ireland* 4 (1874): 78–80.

Dobbs, Betty Jo Teeter. *The Foundations of Newton's Alchemy or "The Hunting of the Greene Lyon."* Cambridge: Cambridge University Press, 1975.

Dobell, Clifford. *Antony von Leeuwenhoek and His Little Animals.* Dover, 1960.

Dodds, E. *The Greeks and the Irrational.* Berkeley: University of California Press, 1951.

le Doeuff, Michele. "Ants and Women, or Philosophy without Borders." *Philosophy* (Supplement) 21 (1987): 41–54.

Donegan, Jane. *Women and Men Midwives: Medicine, Morality, and Misogyny in Early America.* Westport, Conn.: Greenwood Press, 1985.

Dover, K. J. "Classical Greek Attitudes to Sexual Behavior." *Aresthusa* 6 (1973): 59–73.

———. *Greek Popular Morality in the Time of Plato and Aristotle.* Oxford: Basil Blackwell, 1974.

duBois, Page. *Centaurs and Amazons: Women and the Pre-History of the Great Chain of Being.* Ann Arbor: University of Michigan Press, 1982.

———. "On the Invention of Hierarchy." *Aresthusa* 15 (1982): 203–220.

———. *Sowing the Body: Psychoanalysis and Ancient Representations of Women.* Chicago: University of Chicago Press, 1988.

Duering, Igemar. "Aristotle's Method in Biology." In *Aristote et les problèmes de méthode.* Louvain, 1961.

Dunn, Robert. "Civilization and Cerebral Development, Some Observations on the Influence of Civilization on the Development of the Brain in the Different Races of Man." *Transactions of the Ethnological Society* 4 (1866): 13–33.

Easlea, Brian. *Science and Sexual Oppression: Patriarchy's Confrontation with Women and Nature.* London: Weidenfeld and Nicolson, 1981.

Easton, Susan M. "Hegel and Feminism." In *Hegel and Modern Philosophy.* Ed. David Lamb. London: Croom Helm, 1987.

Eccles, Audrey. *Obstetrics and Gynaecology in Tudor and Stuart England.* Kent State University Press, 1983.

Ecker, Alexander. "On a Characteristic Peculiarity in the Form of the Female Skull, and Its Significance for Comparative Anthropology." *Anthropological Review* 6 (1868): 350–56.

Ehrenreich, Barbara, and Deirdre English. *Complaints and Disorders: The Sexual Politics of Sickness.* Old Westbury: Feminist Press, 1973.

Eisley, Loren. *Darwin's Century.* Garden City, N.Y.: Anchor Books, 1961.

Eliade, Mircea. *The Forge and the Crucible.* Trans. Stephen Corrin. London: Rider and Co., 1962.

Ellis, Havelock. *Man and Woman.* New York: Charles Scribner's Sons, 1894.

Elshtain, Jean Bethke. *Meditations on Modern Political Thought: Masculine/Feminine Themes from Luther to Arendt.* New York: Praeger, 1986.

———. *Public Man, Private Woman: Women in Social and Political Thought.* Princeton: Princeton University Press, 1981.

English, Deirdre, and Barbara Ehrenreich. *For Her Own Good: 150 Years of the Expert's Advice to Women.* New York: Doubleday, 1979.

Enoch. *I Enoch.* Trans. M. A. Knibb. In *The Apocryphal Old Testament.* Ed. H. F. D. Sparks. Oxford: Clarendon Press, 1984.

Enuma Elis. Trans. James Prichard. In *Ancient Near Eastern Texts.* Princeton: Princeton University Press, 1969.

Euripides. *Hippolytos.* Trans. Robert Bagg. New York: Oxford University Press, 1973.

———. *Medea.* Trans. Paul Roche. New York: W. W. Norton, 1974.

Evans, Judith, et al., eds. *Feminism and Political Theory.* London: Sage Publications, 1986.

Fabricius, Hieronymus. *Embryological Treatises.* Ithaca, N.Y.: Cornell University Press, 1947.

Farrington, Benjamin. *The Philosophy of Francis Bacon.* Liverpool: Liverpool University Press, 1964.

Fausto-Sterling, Anne. *Myths and Gender: Biological Theories About Men and Women.* New York: Basic Books, 1985.

―――. "Society Writes Biology/Biology Constructs Gender." *Daedalus* 116 (1987): 61–76.

Fee, Elizabeth. "Nineteenth Century Craniology: The Study of the Female Skull." *Bulletin of the History of Medicine.* 53 (1979): 415–33.

―――. "Science and the Women Problem: Historical Perspectives." In *Sex Differences: Social and Biological Perspectives.* Ed. Michael Teitelbaum. New York: Doubleday, 1976.

―――. "The Sexual Politics of Victorian Social Anthropology." In *Clio's Consciousness Raised.* Eds. M. Hartman and L. Banner. New York: Harper and Row, 1974.

Feldman, David. *Marital Relations, Birth Control and Abortion in Jewish Law.* New York: Schocken, 1974.

Ferguson, Margaret, Maureen Quilligan, Nancy Vickers, ed. *Rewriting the Renaissance: The Discourses of Sexual Difference in Early Modern Europe.* Chicago: University of Chicago Press, 1987.

Ferrero, G. "The Problem of Women, From a Bio-sociological Point of View." *The Monist* 4 (1893–94): 261–74.

Figes, Eva. *Patriarchal Attitudes.* London: Fawcett, 1970.

Filmer, Sir Robert. *Patriarcha and Other Political Writings of Sir Robert Filmer.* Ed. Peter Laslett. Oxford: Basil Blackwell, 1949.

Finot, Jean. *Problem of the Sexes.* Trans. Mary Safford. New York: Putnam's Sons, 1913.

Fisher, Elizabeth. *Woman's Creation: Sexual Evolution and the Shaping of Society.* New York: McGraw-Hill, 1979.

Flammel, Nicholas. *Alchemical Hieroglyphics.* Trans. Eirenaeus Orandus. Berkeley: Heptangle Books, 1980.

Flax, Jane. "Political Philosophy and the Patriarchal Unconscious." In *Discovering Reality.* Eds. Sandra Harding and Merill Hintikka. Dordrecht: D. Reidel, 1983.

Foley, Helene. *Reflections of Women in Antiquity.* New York: Gordon and Breach Science Publications, 1981.

Forel, August. *The Sexual Question: A Scientific, Psychological, Hygienic and Sociological Study for the Cultured Classes.* New York, 1906.

Fortenbaugh, W. W. "Aristotle on Slaves and Women." In *Articles on Aristotle,* volume 2. Eds. Jonathan Barnes, Malcolm Schofield, and Richard Sorabji. New York: St. Martin's Press, 1977, pp. 135–39.

Fox, Robin Lane. *Pagans and Christians.* New York: Alfred A. Knopf, 1987.

Frank, H. "Virginal Politics." *Frontiers* 3 (1978): 46–50.

Franz, Marie-Louise von. *Alchemy: An Introduction to the Symbolism and the Psychology.* Toronto: Inner City Books, 1980.

Fraser, Antonia. *The Weaker Vessel.* New York: Alfred A. Knopf, 1984.

Freedman, H., and M. Simon, eds. *Midrash Rabbah: Genesis I.* London: Soncino Press, 1939.

Freud, Sigmund. *Civilization and Its Discontents.* Trans. James Strachey. In *Standard Edition of the Complete Psychological Works,* vol. 21. London: Hogarth Press, 1964.

―――. " 'Civilized' Sexual Morality and Modern Nervous Illness." In *Complete Psychological Works,* vol. 9.

―――. "Female Sexuality." In *Complete Psychological Works,* vol. 21.

―――. "Femininity." In *Complete Psychological Works,* vol. 22.

―――. "Some Psychical Consequences of the Anatomical Distinction Between the Sexes." In *Complete Psychological Works,* vol. 19.

Frier, Bruce. "Bees and Lawyers." *Classical Journal* 78 (1982): 105–114.

Fries, Maureen. "Feminae Populi: Popular Images of Women in Medieval Literature." *Journal of Popular Culture* 14 (1980): 79–86.

Fromm, Erich. *The Forgotten Language*. New York: Rinehart, 1951.

Fuchs, Jo-Ann Pilardi. "On the War Path and Beyond: Hegel, Freud and Feminist Theory." *Women's Studies International Forum* 6 (1983): 565–72.

Fuss, Diana. *Essentially Speaking: Feminism, Nature and Difference*. New York: Routledge, 1989.

Galen. *On the Usefulness of the Parts of the Body*. Trans. M. T. May. Ithaca, N.Y.: Cornell University Press, 1968.

Gallagher, Catherine, and Thomas Laqueur, eds. *The Making of the Modern Body: Sexuality and Society in the Nineteenth Century*. Berkeley: University of California Press, 1987.

Galton, Francis. *Hereditary Genius*. London: MacMillian, 1914.

Garden, George. "A Discourse Concerning the Modern Theory of Generation." *Philosophical Transactions of the Royal Society* 17 (1691): 474–83.

Gardner, Augustus. *Conjugal Sins Against the Laws of Life and Health*. 1840. Reprint, New York: Arno Press, 1974.

Gasking, Elizabeth. *Investigations into Generation, 1651–1828*. Baltimore: Johns Hopkins University Press, 1967.

Gasset, Ortega y. "Landscape with a Deer in the Background." Trans. Toby Talbot. In *On Love: Aspects of a Single Theme*. New York: Meridian, 1957.

Gatens, Moria. *Feminism and Philosophy: Perspectives on Difference and Equality*. Bloomington: Indiana University Press, 1991.

————. "Rousseau and Wollstonecraft: Nature vs. Reason." *Women and Philosophy*. Bundoora: Australian Association of Philosophy, 1986.

Geddes, Patrick, and John Arthur Thomson. *The Evolution of Sex*. London: W. Scott, 1889.

————. *Sex*. London: Thornton Butterworth, 1914.

Ghougassian, Joseph. *Toward Women: A Study of the Origins of Western Attitudes Through Greco-Roman Philosophy*. San Diego: Lukas and Sons, 1977.

Gilchrist, Cherry. *Alchemy: The Great Work*. Wellingborough: Aquarian Press, 1984.

Gilliam, David. "Oophorectomy for the Insanity and Epilepsy of the Female: A Plea for its More General Adoption." *Transactions of the American Association of Obstetricians and Gynecologists* 9 (1896): 315–21.

Gilman, Sander L. "Black Bodies, White Bodies: Toward an Iconography of Female Sexuality in Late Nineteenth Century Art, Medicine, and Literature." *Critical Inquiry* 12, 1 (1985): 204–242.

Gilmore, J. T. "Normal Ovariotomy." *Atlanta Medical and Surgical Journal* 11 (1873/74): 175–76.

Gimbutas, Marya. *The Goddesses and Gods of Old Europe, 6500–3500 BC*. Berkeley: University of California Press, 1982.

Ginzberg, Louis. *The Legends of the Jews*. Philadelphia: Jewish Publication Society of America, 1909–1938.

Glanvill, Joseph. *Sadducismus Trimphatus or, Full and Plain Evidence Concerning Witches and Apparitions*. 1689. Reprint, Gainesville, Fla.: Scholar's Facsimiles and Reprints, 1966.

Glass, Hiram Bently, Owsei Temkin, and William Straus. *Forerunners of Darwin, 1745–1859*. Baltimore: Johns Hopkins University Press, 1959.

Goehring, James. "A Classical Influence on the Gnostic Sophia Myth." *Vigiliae Christianae* 35 (1981): 16–23.

Gold, Penny Schine. *The Lady and the Virgin: Image; Attitude, and Experience in Twelfth Century France*. Chicago: University of Chicago Press, 1987.

Goldenberg, Naomi. *The Changing of the Gods*. Boston: Beacon Press, 1979.

Good, J. M. *The Nature of Things: A Didactic Poem.* London: 1805.

Goodell, W. "Discussion: "Oophorectomy" by Thomas Savage." *Transactions of the International Medical Congress,* Seventh Session, vol. 4. London: J. W. Kolckmann, 1881.

Gordon, S. C. "Hysteria and its Relation to Diseases of the Uterine Appendages." *Journal of the American Medical Association* 6 (1886): 561–67.

The Gospel of Thomas. Trans. A. Guillaumont et al. New York: Harper and Brothers, 1959.

Gottfried, Robert. *Doctors and Medicine in Medieval England, 1340–1530.* Princeton: Princeton University Press, 1986.

Gottwald, Norman. *The Hebrew Bible: A Socio-Literary Introduction.* Philadelphia: Fortress Press, 1985.

Gould, Stephen Jay. *The Mismeasure of Man.* New York: W. W. Norton, 1981.

———. "Women's Brains." *New Scientist* (1978): 364–66.

Gould, Timothy. "Engendering Aesthetics: Sublimity, Sublimation and Misogyny in Burke and Kant." In *Aesthetics, Politics, and Hermeneutics.* Eds. Gerald Bruns and Stephen Watson. State University of New York Press, 1991.

———. "Intensity and Its Audiences: Notes Towards a Feminist Perspective on the Kantian Sublime." *The Journal of Aesthetics and Art Criticism* 48, 4 (1990): 305–315.

Gratian. *Apostolic Constitution.* In *The Ante-Nicene Fathers,* vol. 7. Eds. A. Roberts and J. Donaldson. New York: Scribner's Sons, 1899.

———. *Decretum Corpus Iuris Canonici.* Ed. A. Friedberg. Graz: 1955.

Gratiolet, Louis Pierre. *Mémoire sur les plis cérébaux de l'homme et des primates.* Paris: Bertrand, 1854.

Gratiolet, L., and F. Leuret. *Anatomie comparée du système nerveaux considéré dans ses rapports avec l'intelligence.* Paris: Didot, 1839–57.

Graves, Robert. *The Greek Myths.* New York: Penguin, 1955.

———. *The White Goddess: A Historical Grammar of Poetic Myth.* New York: Farrar, Straus and Cudahy, 1948.

Graves, Robert, and Raphael Patai. *Hebrew Myths: The Book of Genesis.* New York: Greenwich House, 1983.

St. Gregory of Nyssa. *Against Eunomius,* in *A Select Library of Nicene and Post-Nicene Fathers of the Christian Church,* vol. 5. Eds. Philip Schaff and Henry Wace. Grand Rapids, Mich.: Wm. B. Eerdmans, 1978.

Griesinger, Wilhelm. *Mental Pathology and Therapeutics.* 1867. Reprint, New York: Hafner Pub, 1965.

Griffin, Susan. *Woman and Nature: The Roaring Inside Her.* New York: Harper Colophon, 1978.

Griffiths, Morwenna, and Margaret Whitford, eds. *Feminist Perspectives in Philosophy.* Bloomington: Indiana University Press, 1988.

Grimshaw, Jean. *Philosophy and Feminist Thinking.* Minneapolis: University of Minnesota Press, 1986.

Guainerius, Anthonius. *Tractatus de matricibus.* In *Opera Omnia,* Pavia, 1481, f.w6rb.

Haeckel, Ernst. *The Evolution of Man.* New York: D. Appleton and Co., 1897.

———. *The History of Creation,* Vol. I, 1877.

Hageman, Alice, ed. *Sexist Religion and Women in the Church: No More Silence!* New York: Association Press, 1974.

Hall, Stanley. *Adolescence.* New York: D. Appleton and Co., 1904.

Hall, Thomas S. "Life, Death and the Radical Moisture." *Clio Medica* 6 (1971): 3–23.

Haller, John. *Outcasts from Evolution: Scientific Attitudes of Racial Inferiority, 1859–1900.* Urbana: University of Illinois Press, 1971.

Haller, John, and Robin Haller. *The Physician and Sexuality in Victorian America.* Urbana: University of Illinois Press, 1974.

Hallett, Judith. *Fathers and Daughters in Roman Society: Women and the Elite Family.* Princeton: Princeton University Press, 1984.

Hammonds, Evelyn. "Race, Sex, and AIDS: The Construction of "other." *Radical America* 20, 6 (1986): 28–38.

Hanson, Paul. "Masculine Metaphors for God and Sex-Discrimination in the Old Testament." *The Ecumenical Review* 27 (1975): 316–24.

Haraway, Donna. "Animal Sociology and a Natural Economy of the Body Politic." *Signs: Journal of Women in Culture and Society* 4, 1 (1978): 21–60.

————. "In the Beginning Was the Word: The Genesis of Biological Theory." *Signs: Journal of Women in Culture and Society* 6, 3 (1981): 469–82.

————. *Primate Visions: Gender, Race, and Nature in the World of Modern Science.* New York: Routledge, 1989.

Hardaker, M. A. "Science and the Women Question." *Popular Science Monthly* 20 (1882): 577–84.

Harding, Sandra. *Feminism and Methodology.* Bloomington: Indiana University Press, 1987.

————. *The Science Question in Feminism.* Ithaca, N.Y.: Cornell University Press, 1986.

————. *Whose Science? Whose Knowledge?* Ithaca, N.Y.: Cornell University Press, 1991.

Harding, Sandra, and Merrill B. Hintikka, eds. *Discovering Reality: Feminist Perspectives on Epistemology, Metaphysics, Methodology and Philosophy of Science.* Dordrecht: D. Reidel, 1983.

Harding, Sandra, and Jean F. O'Barr, eds. *Sex and Scientific Inquiry.* Chicago: University of Chicago Press, 1987.

Hare, E. H. "Masturbatory Insanity: The History of an Idea." *Journal of Mental Science* 108 (1962): 2–25.

Harris, George. "On the Distinctions, Mental and Moral Occasioned by the Difference of Sex." *Journal of the Anthropology Society* 7 (1869): clxxxix-cxcv.

Harris, Marvin. *The Rise of Anthropological Theory: A History of Theories of Culture.* New York: Thomas Crowell, 1968.

Hartmann, Franz. *The Life and Doctrines of Paracelsus.* New York: Macoy, 1932.

Harvey, William. *The Works of William Harvey.* Trans. Robert Willis. New York: Johnson Reprint Corporation, 1965.

Hays, H. R. *The Dangerous Sex: The Myth of Feminine Evil.* New York: Putnam's Sons, 1964.

Hayter, Mary. *The New Eve in Christ: The Use and Abuse of the Bible in the Debate about Women in the Church.* London: SPCK, 1987.

Hegar, Alfred. "Castration in Mental and Nervous Diseases. A Symposium." *American Journal of Medical Science* 184 (1886): 471–83.

Hegel, G. W. F. *Phenomenology of Spirit.* Trans. A. V. Miller. London: Oxford University Press, 1977.

————. *Philosophy of Right.* Trans. T. M. Knox. London: Oxford University Press, 1942.

Heidel, Alexander. *The Babylonian Genesis.* Chicago: University of Chicago Press, 1951.

Henderson, Katherine O., and Barbara F. McManus. *Half Humankind: Contexts and Texts of the Controversy about Women in England 1540–1640.* Urbana: University of Illinois Press, 1985.

Hesiod. *The Catalogues of Women and the Eoiae.* In *The Homeric Hymns and Homerica.* Trans. H. G. Evelyn-White. London: William Heinemann, 1920.

————. "Melampodia." In *The Homeric Hymns.*

————. *Theogony, Works and Days, and the Shield.* Trans. Apostolos Athanassakis. Baltimore: Johns Hopkins University Press, 1983.

Hewson, M. Anthony. *Giles of Rome and the Medieval Theory of Conception.* London: Athlone, 1975.

Hillman, James. *The Myth of Analysis: Three Essays in Archetypal Psychology.* Evanston: Northwestern University Press, 1972.

Hippocrates. *Airs, Waters, and Places.* Trans. J. Chadwick and W. N. Mann. In *Hippocratic Writings.* New York: Penguin Books, 1978.

————. *Diseases of Women.* Trans. A. E. Hanson. *Signs: Journal of Women in Culture and Society* 1 (1975): 567–84.

————. *On Semen and on the Development of the Child.* Trans. T. Ellinger. New York: Wolff, 1952.

————. *The Sacred Disease.* Trans. W. H. S. Jones. Cambridge: Harvard University Press, 1923.

————. *Regimen.* Trans. W. H. S. Jones. Cambridge: Harvard University Press, 1943.

Hodge, Joanna. "Women and the Hegelian State." In *Women in the Western Political Philosophy: Kant to Nietzsche.* Eds. Ellen Kennedy and Susan Mendus. New York: St. Martin's Press, 1987.

Holcombe, William. *The Sexes Here and Hereafter.* Philadelphia: J. B. Lippincott and Co., 1869.

Hollick, Frederick. *The Diseases of Woman, Their Cause and Cure Familiarly Explained.* New York: Burgess, Stringer, and Co., 1847.

————. *The Marriage Guide, or Natural History of Generation.* New York: T. W. Strong, 1850.

Homer. *The Homeric Hymns.* Trans. Apostolos Athanassakis. Baltimore: Johns Hopkins University Press, 1976.

————. *Iliad.* Trans. Robert Fitzgerald. New York: Doubleday and Co., 1961.

————. *Odyssey.* Trans. Robert Fitzgerald. New York: Doubleday and Co., 1961.

hooks, bell. *Breaking Bread: Insurgent Black Intellectual Life.* Boston: South End Press, 1991.

————. *Feminist Theory: From Margin to Center.* Boston: South End Press, 1984.

————. *Talking Back: Thinking Feminist, Thinking Black.* Boston: South End Press, 1989.

————. *Yearning: Race, Gender, and Cultural Politics.* Boston: South End Press, 1990.

Horowitz, Maryanne Cline. "Aristotle and Women." *Journal of the History of Biology* 9 (1976): 183–213.

Hubbard, Ruth. *Feminist Approaches to Science.* New York: Pergamon, 1988.

————. *The Politics of Women's Biology.* New Brunswick: Rutgers, 1990.

Hubbard, Ruth, M. S. Henifin, and B. Fried, eds. *Biological Woman: The Convenient Myth.* Cambridge: Schenkman, 1982.

Hubbard, Ruth, and Marian Lowe, eds. *Genes and Gender II.* New York: Gordian Press, 1979.

Hume, David. *A Treatise of Human Nature.* London: Oxford University Press, 1951.

Hunter, Dianne. "Hysteria, Psychoanalysis, and Feminism." *Feminist Studies* 9 (1983).

Huschke, Emil. *Schadel, Hirn und Seele des Menschen nach der Thiere nach Alter, Geschlecht und Race.* Jena, 1854.

Hyginus. "Fabulae." In *The Myths of Hyginus.* Trans. Mary Grant. Lawrence: University of Kansas Publications, 1960.

————. "Poetica Astronomica." In *The Myths of Hyginus.* Trans. Mary Grant. Lawrence: University of Kansas Publications, 1960.

Hypatia: A Journal of Feminist Philosophy. Special Issues on Feminism and Science. Vol. 2, no. 3, 1987 and vol. 3, no. 1, 1988.

Irigaray, Luce. *Speculum of the Other Woman.* Trans. Gillian Gill. Ithaca: Cornell University Press, 1985.

————. "When Our Two Lips Speak Together," *Signs: Journal of Women in Culture and Society* 6 (1987): 69–79.

Isidoris of Seville. *The Medical Writings.* Trans. William Sharpe. Philadelphia: Transactions of the American Philosophical Society, 1964.

Jacobi, Joland. *Paracelsus: Selected Writings.* Trans. Norbet Guterman. Princeton: Princeton University Press, 1973.

Jacobi, Mary Putnam. *The Question of Rest for Women During Menstruation.* New York: Putnam, 1886.

Jeffreys, Sheila. *The Spinster and Her Enemies: Feminism and Sexuality, 1880–1930.* Routledge & Kegan Paul, 1985.

Jerison, Harry. *Evolution of the Brain and Intelligence.* New York: Academic Press, 1973.

Jerome. *Letters and Select Works.* Trans. F. A. Wright. In *Select Library of Nicene and Post-Nicene Fathers.* Ed. Phillip Schaff. New York: Christian Literature Company, 1893.

———. *Select Letters.* Trans. F. A. Wright. London: William Heinemann, 1933.

John. *Apocryphon of John.* Trans. Members of the Coptic Gnostic Library Project. In *Nag Hammadi Library.* San Francisco: Harper and Row, 1977.

Johnson, Walter. *The Morbid Emotions of Women: Their Origin, Tendencies and Treatment.* London: Simpkin, Marshall and Co., 1850.

Jonas, Hans. *The Gnostic Religion.* Boston: Beacon Press, 1958.

Jordonova, L. "Natural Facts: A Historical Perspective on Science and Sexuality." In *Nature, Culture, Gender.* Eds. C. MacCormick and M. Strathem. Cambridge: Cambridge University Press, 1980.

Jung, Carl. *Alchemical Studies.* Trans. R. F. C. Hull. Princeton: Princeton University Press, 1967.

———. *Mysterium Coniunctionis.* Trans. R. F. C. Hull. Princeton: Princeton University Press, 1970.

———. *Psychology and Alchemy.* Trans. R. F. C. Hull. Princeton: Princeton University Press, 1968.

Justin Martyr. *II Apology.* In *The Ante-Nicene Fathers.* Eds. A. Roberts and J. Donaldson. New York: Scribner's Sons, 1899.

———. *Dialogue with Trypho.* In *The Ante-Nicene Fathers.* Eds. A. Roberts and J. Donaldson. New York: Scribner's Sons, 1899.

Juvenal. *Satires.* Trans. J. Mazzaro. Ann Arbor: University of Michigan Press, 1965.

Kant, Immanuel. *Anthropology From a Pragmatic Point of View.* Trans. Mary J. Gregor. Hague: Martinus Nijhoff, 1974.

———. *Grounding for the Metaphysics of Morals.* Trans. James W. Ellington. Indianapolis: Hackett, 1981.

———. *Lectures on Ethics.* Trans. Louis Infield. New York: Harper and Row, 1963.

———. *Observations on the Feeling of the Beautiful and the Sublime.* Trans. John T. Goldthwait. Berkeley: University of California Press, 1960.

Kaufman, M. "Spare Ribs: The Conception of Women in the Middle Ages and Renaissance." *Soundings* 56 (1973): 139–63.

Keller, Evelyn Fox. *A Feeling for the Organism: The Life and Times of Barbara McClintock.* San Francisco: W. H. Freeman, 1983.

———. *Reflections on Gender and Science.* New Haven: Yale University Press, 1985.

Kellogg, A. O. "Considerations on the Reciprocal Influence of the Physical Organization and Mental Manifestations." *American Journal of Insanity* 12 (1856): 305–315.

Kelly, J. N. D. *Jerome: His Life, Writings, and Controversies.* New York: Harper and Row, 1975.

Kelso, Ruth. *Doctrine for the Lady of the Renaissance.* Urbana: University of Illinois Press, 1956.

Kember, O. "Anaxagoras' Theory of Sex Differentiation and Heredity." *Phronesis* 18 (1973): 1–14.

———. "Right and Left in the Sexual Theories of Parmenides." *Journal of Hellenic Studies* 91 (1971): 70–79.

Kennedy, Ellen, and Susan Mendus, eds. *Women in Western Political Philosophy: Kant to Nietzsche.* New York: St. Martin's Press, 1987.

Kerenyi, Karl. *The Gods of the Greeks.* London: Thames and Hudson, 1951.

Keuls, Eva. *The Reign of the Phallus.* New York: Harper and Row, 1985.

Kidner, Derek. *Genesis.* London: Tyndale, 1967.

King, Helen. "Bound to Bleed: Artemis and Greek Women." In *Images of Women in Antiquity*. Eds. Averil Cameron and Amelie Kuhrt. Detroit: Wayne State University Press, 1983.

Kirschner, Julius, and Suzanne Wemple. *Women of the Medieval World*. New York: Basil Blackwell, 1985.

Kitto, Robert. "Ovariotomy as a Prophylaxis and Cure for Insanity." *Journal of the American Medical Association* 16 (1891): 516–17.

Klein, Viola. *The Feminine Character: History of an Ideology*. London: Routledge and Kegan Paul, 1946.

Klossowski, Stanislas de Rola. *The Secret Art of Alchemy*. New York: 1973.

Kneller, Jane. "Kant's Immature Imagination." In *Critical Feminist Essays in the History of Western Philosophy*. ed. Bat Ami Bar-On. State University of New York Press, 1993.

Koltun, Elizabeth, ed. *The Jewish Woman: New Perspectives*. New York: Schocken, 1977.

Korsgaard, Christine M. "Kant's Formula of Humanity." *Kantstudien* 77 (1986): 183–202.

Kraus, Henry. *The Living Theatre of Medieval Art*. Philadelphia: University of Pennsylvania Press, 1967.

Krell, David. "Female Parts in the *Timaeus*." *Arion* 2 (1975): 400–421.

Lacks, Roslyn. *Women and Judaism: Myth, History, and Struggle*. Garden City: Doubleday, 1980.

de Laguna, Andres. *Anatomical Procedure, or a Survey of the Dissections of the Human Body*. Trans. L. R. Lind. In *Studies in Pre-Vesalian Anatomy*. Philadelphia: American Philosophical Association, 1975.

Landes, Joan B. "Hegel's Conception of the Family." *Polity* 14, 1 (1981): 5–28.

———. *Women and the Public Sphere in the Age of the French Revolution*. Ithaca: Cornell University Press, 1988.

Lange, Lynda. "The Function of Equal Education in Plato's *Republic* and *Laws*." In *The Sexism of Social and Political Theory: Women and Reproduction from Plato to Nietzsche*. Eds. Lorenne M. G. Clark and Lynda Lange. Toronto: University of Toronto Press, 1979.

———. "Rousseau and Modern Feminism." *Social Theory and Practice* 7 (1981): 245–77.

———. "Rousseau: Women and the General Will." in *The Sexism of Social and Political Theory: Women and Reproduction from Plato to Nietzsche*. Eds. Lorenne M. G. Clark and Lynda Lange. Toronto: University of Toronto Press, 1979.

———. "Woman is Not a Rational Animal: On Aristotle's Biology of Reproduction." In *Discovering Reality*. Eds. S. Harding and M. Hintikka. Dordrecht: D. Reidel, 1983.

LaPlace, Jean. *Dumb Book: The Book of the Silence of Hermes*. Milano: Arche, 1979.

Laqueur, Thomas. *Making Sex: Body and Gender From the Greeks to Freud*. Cambridge: Harvard University Press, 1990.

———. "Orgasm, Generation and the Politics of Reproductive Biology." In *The Making of the Modern Body: Sexuality and the Social Body in the Nineteenth Century*. Eds. Catherine Gallagher and Thomas Laqueur. Berkeley: University of California Press, 1987.

Lattimore, Robert. *Themes in Greek and Latin Epitaphs*. Urbana: University of Illinois Press, 1942.

Laycock, Thomas. *An Essay on Hysteria*. Philadelphia: Haswell, Barrington, and Haswell, 1840.

———. *A Treatise on the Nervous Diseases of Woman: Comprising an Inquiry into the Nature, Causes and Treatment of Spinal and Hysterical Disorders*. London, 1840.

Le Bon, Gustave. "Recherches anatomiques et mathématiques sur les lois de variations du volume du cerveau et sur leurs relatios avec l'intelligence." *Revue d'Anthropologie* 2 (1879): 27–104.

Leeuwenhoek, Anton van. "Correspondence." *Philosophical Transactions of the Royal Society* 25 (1685): 1120–34.

Lefkowitz, Mary. "The Wandering Womb." In *Heroines and Hysterics.* New York: St. Martin's Press, 1981.

Lefkowitz, Mary R., and Maureen B. Fant. *Women's Life in Greece and Rome.* Baltimore: Johns Hopkins University Press, 1982.

Lemay, Helen Rodnite. "Anthonius Guainerius and Medieval Gynecology." In *Women of the Medieval World.* Eds. Julius Kirschner and Suzanne F. Wemple. New York: Basil Blackwell, 1985.

———. "Some Thirteenth and Fourteenth Century Lectures on Female Sexuality." *International Journal of Women's Studies* 1 (1978): 391–400.

Lennane, R. J. "Alleged Psychogenic Disorders in Women—A Possible Manifestation of Sexual Prejudice." *New England Journal of Medicine* (1973): 288–92.

Levin, Michael. *Feminism and Freedom.* New Brunswick, N.J.: Transaction Books, 1987.

Lewontin, R. C., Steven Rose, and Leon J. Kamin. *Not In Our Genes.* New York: Pantheon, 1984.

Life of Adam and Eve. Trans. L. S. A. Wells. In *The Apocryphal Old Testament.* Ed. H. F. D. Sparks. Oxford: Clarendon Press, 1984.

Lieu, Samuel. *The Religion of Light.* Hong Kong: University of Hong Kong, 1979.

Lind, L. R. *Studies in Pre-Vesalian Anatomy.* Philadelphia: The American Philosophical Society, 1975.

Lingo, Alison. "Medicine and the "Other" in Early Modern France." *Journal of Social History* 19 (1986): 583–604.

Livy. *The History of Rome.* Trans. Cyrus Edmonds. London: George Bell and Sons, 1891.

Lloyd, Genevieve. *The Man of Reason: "Male" and "Female" in Western Philosophy.* Minneapolis: Minnesota University Press, 1984.

———. "Rousseau on Reason, Nature and Women." *Metaphilosophy* 14, 3, 4 (1983): 308–326.

———. "Selfhood, War and Masculinity." In *Feminist Challenges.* Eds. Carol Pateman and Elizabeth Gross. Boston: Northeastern University Press, 1987.

Lloyd, Geoffrey. *Magic, Reason, and Experience: Studies in the Origin and Development of Greek Science.* Cambridge: Cambridge University Press, 1979.

———. *Polarity and Analogy.* Cambridge: Cambridge University Press, 1966.

———. *Science, Folklore, and Ideology: Studies in the Life Sciences in Ancient Greece.* Cambridge: Cambridge University Press, 1983.

Lloyd-Jones, Hugh. *Females of the Species: Semonides on Women.* London: Noyes Press, 1975.

Locke, John. *Two Treatises of Civil Government.* Cambridge: Cambridge University Press, 1967.

Longino, Helen. *Science as Social Knowledge: Values and Objectivity in Scientific Inquiry.* Princeton: Princeton University Press, 1990.

Longino, Helen, and Ruth Doell. "Body Bias and Behavior: A Comparative Analysis of Reasoning in Two Areas of Biological Science." *Signs: Journal of Women in Culture and Society* 9, 2 (1985): 206–227.

Longo, Lawrence. "The Rise and Fall of Battey's Operation: A Fashion in Surgery." *Bulletin of the History of Medicine* 53 (1979): 244–67.

Lovejoy, Arthur. *The Great Chain of Being: A Study of the History of an Idea.* Cambridge: Harvard University Press, 1936.

Lowe, Marian, and Ruth Hubbard, eds. *Woman's Nature: Rationalizations of Inequality.* New York: Pergamon Press, 1981.

Lowery, Ellen Forst. "Sublimation and Feminine Identity." *The Psychoanalytic Review* 72 (1985): 441–55.

Lucas, Angela. *Women in the Middle Ages: Religion, Marriage, and Letters.* New York: St. Martin's Press, 1983.

Lundberg, Ferdinand, and Marynia Farnham. *Modern Woman: The Lost Sex.* New York: Gosset and Dunlap, 1947.

Luther, Martin. *Lectures on Genesis.* Trans. George V. Schick. In *Luther's Works.* Ed. J. Pelikan. St. Louis: Concordia Publishing House, 1958.

Lyly, John. *Euphues: The Anatomy of Wit.* Birmingham, 1868.

MacCormack, Carol, and Marilyn Strathern. *Nature, Culture, Gender.* Cambridge: Cambridge University Press, 1980.

MacDonald, Michael. "Women and Madness in Tudor and Stuart England." *Social Research* 53 (1986): 261–81.

McDonnell, W. R. "A Study of the Variation and Correlation of the Human Skull, With Special Reference to English Crania." *Biometrika* 3 (1904): 191–244.

McGlone, Jannette. "Sex Differences in Human Brain Asymmetry: A Critical Survey." *Behavioral and Brain Sciences* 8 (1980): 215–63.

MacGuigan, Maryellen. "Is Woman a Question?" *International Philosophical Quarterly* 12 (1973): 485–505.

McLaren, Laura. "The Fallacy of the Superiority of Man." *The Woman's World* 1 (1888–1890): 59.

McLaughlin, Eleanor Commo. "Equality of Souls, Inequality of Sexes: Women in Medieval Theology." In *Women in Western Thought.* Ed. Martha Lee Osborne. New York: Random House, 1979.

MacLean, Ian. *The Renaissance Notion of Woman.* Cambridge: Cambridge University Press, 1980.

McMillan, Carolyn. *Woman, Reason, and Nature.* Princeton: Princeton University Press, 1982.

Macpherson, C. B. *The Political Theory of Possessive Individualism: Hobbes to Locke.* Oxford: Clarendon Press, 1962.

MacRae, G. W. "The Jewish Background of the Gnostic Sophia Myth." *Novum Testamentum* 12.

Maier, Michael. *Michael Maier's Atalanta Fugiens: Sources of an Alchemical Book of Emblems.* Trans. H. M. E. De Jong. Leiden: E. J. Brill, 1969.

Maimonides, Moses. *The Guide of the Perplexed.* Trans. Shiomo Pines. Chicago: University of Chicago Press, 1974.

de Malebranche, Nicolas. *The Search after Truth.* Trans. Thomas M. Lemon and Paul J. Olscamp. Columbus: Ohio State University Press, 1980.

———. "252 Entretiens sur la Métaphysique et sur la Religion." In *Oeuvres Complètes,* vol. 12. Paris: Librairie Philosophique J. Virn, 1965.

Malinowski, Bronislaw. *The Sexual Lives of Savages in Northwest Melanesia.* Cambridge: Harvard University Press, 1932.

Mall, Franklin. "On Several Anatomical Characters of the Human Brain, Said to Vary According to Race and Sex, With Especial Reference to the Weight of the Frontal Lobe." *American Journal of Anatomy* 9 (1909): 1–32.

Marcello Malpighi. *Dissertatio epistolica de formatione pulli in ovo.* Londini: Apud J. Martyn, 1673.

Manouvrier, George. "Conclusions générales sur l'anthropologie des sexes et applications sociales." *Revue de l'Ecole d'Anthropologie* 13 (1903): 405–23.

———. "Sur la grandeur de front et des principales regions du Crane chez l'homme et chez la femme." *Bulletin de l'association française pour l'avancement des sciences* (1882): 623–39.

Marion-Sims, H. "Hystero-epilepsy. Report of Seven Cases Cured by Surgical Treatment." *Transactions of the American Gynecological Society* 18 (1893): 282–98.

Marschand, F. *Uber das Hirnqewicht des Menschen.* 1902.

Marshall, J. H. "Insanity Cured by Castration." *Medical and Surgical Reporter* 13 (1865): 353–64.

Martin, Emily. *The Woman in the Body: A Cultural Analysis of Reproduction.* Boston: Beacon Press, 1987.

Martin, Jane. *Reclaiming a Conversation: The Ideal of the Educated Woman.* New Haven: Yale University Press, 1985.

———. "Sophie and Emile: A Case Study of Sex Bias in the History of Educational Thought." *Harvard Educational Review* 51 (1981): 357–72.

Massa, Niccolo. *Introductory Book of Anatomy.* Trans. L. R. Lind. In *Studies in Pre-Vesalian Anatomy.* Philadelphia: American Philosophical Association, 1975.

Massey, Marilyn Chapin. *Feminine Soul: The Fate of an Ideal.* Boston: Beacon Press, 1985.

Maton, W. P. "A Contribution to the History of Ovariotomy on the Insane." *Transactions of the American Association of Obstetricians and Gynecologists* 2 (1889): 262–65.

Matthews, Gareth B. "Gender and Essence in Aristotle." *Women and Philosophy.* Bundoora: Australian Association of Philosophy, 1986.

Maudsley, Henry. *Body and Mind.* London: MacMillan and Co., 1870.

———. "Illustrations of a Variety of Insanity." *Journal of Mental Science* 14 (1868): 149–62.

———. "Sex in Mind and Education." *Fortnightly Review* 21 (1874): 466–83.

de Maupertuis, Pierre-Louis Moreau. *The Earthly Venus.* Trans. Simone Brangier Boas. New York: Johnson Reprint Corporation, 1966.

May, Herbert, and Bruce Metzger. *The Oxford Annotated Bible With the Apocrypha.* New York: Oxford University Press, 1965.

Meeks, W. "The Image of the Androgyne: Some Uses of a Symbol in Earliest Christianity." *History of Religions* 13 (1974): 165–208.

Meigs, Charles. *Females and their Diseases.* Philadelphia: Lea and Blanchard, 1848.

———. "Lecture on Some of the Distinctive Characteristics of the Female." Delivered before the class of Jefferson Medical College, January 5, 1847.

———. *Woman: Her Diseases and Remedies.* Philadelphia: Lea and Blanchard, 1851.

Mendus, Susan. "Kant: An Honest but Narrow-Minded Bourgeois?" In *Women in Western Political Philosophy: Kant to Nietzsche.* New York: St. Martin's Press, 1987, pp. 21–43.

Merchant, Carolyn. *The Death of Nature: Women, Ecology, and the Scientific Revolution.* San Francisco: Harper and Row, 1980.

Meyer, Arthur William. *Human Generation: Conclusions of Burdach, Dollinger and von Baer.* Stanford: Stanford University Press, 1956.

———. *The Rise of Embryology.* Stanford: Stanford University Press, 1939.

Meyer, Marvin. *The Secret Teachings of Jesus: Four Gnostic Gospels.* New York: Random House, 1984.

Meyers, Diane, and Eva Kittay. *Women and Moral Theory.* Totowa, N.J.: Rowman and Littlefield, 1987.

Midrash Rabbah. Eds. H. Freedman and M. Simon. London: Soncino Press, 1939.

Miegge, Giovanni. *The Virgin Mary: The Roman Catholic Marian Doctrine.* Trans. Waldo Smith. Philadelphia: Westminister Press, 1955.

Mikraot G'dolot. New York: Pardes Publishing, 1951.

Mills, Patricia Jagentowicz. "Hegel and 'The Woman Question': Recognition and Intersubjectivity." In *The Sexism of Social and Political Theory: Women and Reproduction from Plato to Nietzsche.* Eds. Lorenne M. G. Clark and Lynda Lange. Toronto: University of Toronto Press, 1979.

———. "Hegel's *Antigone.*" In *The Owl of Minerva* 17, 2 (1986): 131–52.

———. *Woman, Nature, and Psyche.* New Haven: Yale University Press, 1987.

Mirnefindo. "Tractatus Micreris." *Theatrum Chemicum,* vol. V. Strasbourg, 1613.

Mitchell, S. Weir. *Lectures on Diseases of the Nervous System, Especially in Women.* Philadelphia: Lea Brothers and Co., 1885.

Mohr, James. *Abortion in America: The Origins and Evolution of National Policy, 1800–1900.* New York: Oxford University Press, 1978.

Montefiore, C. G., and H. Loewe. *A Rabbinic Anthology.* New York: Schocken, 1974.

Monter, E. William. "The Pedestal and the Stake." In *Becoming Visible.* Eds. Renate Bridenthal and Claudia Koonz. Boston: Houghton Mifflin, 1977.

————. *Witchcraft in France and Switzerland.* Ithaca: Cornell University Press, 1976.

Montessori, Maria. *Pedagogical Anthropology.* Trans. Frederic Taber Cooper. New York: F. A. Stokes, 1913.

Morsink, Johannes. "Was Aristotle's Biology Sexist?" *Journal of the History of Biology* 12 (1979): 83–112.

Morton, James, trans. *The Nun's Rule.* New York: Cooper Square Publishers, 1966.

Moscucci, Ornella. *The Science of Woman: Gynaecology and Gender in England, 1800–1929.* Cambridge: Cambridge University Press, 1990.

Mullins, Edwin. *The Painted Witch: Female Body: Male Art: How Western Artists Have Viewed the Sexuality of Women.* London: Secker and Warburg, 1985.

Munk, Elie. *The Call of the Torah.* Trans. E. S. Maser. New York: Feldheim, 1980.

Needham, John Turberville. "A Summary of Some Late Observations Upon the Generation, Composition, and Decomposition of Animal and Vegetable Substances." *Philosophical Transactions of the Royal Society of London* 45 (1748): 615–66.

Needham, Joseph. *A History of Embryology.* Cambridge: Cambridge University Press, 1934.

Needham, Rodney. *Right and Left: Essays on Dual Symbolic Classification.* Chicago: University of Chicago Press, 1973.

Nelson, Lynn Hankinson. *Who Knows: From Quine to a Feminist Empiricism.* Philadelphia: Temple University Press, 1990.

Newman, Louise Michele. *Men's Ideas/Women's Realities: Popular Science, 1870–1915.* New York: Pergamon Press, 1985.

Nicholl, Charles. *The Chemical Theatre.* London: Routledge and Kegan Paul, 1980.

Norton, Thomas. *The Ordinall of Alchimy.* In *Theatrum Chemicum Britannicum.* Ed. Elias Ashmole. New York: Johnson Reprint Corporation, 1967.

Nye, Andrea. *Feminist Theory and the Philosophies of Man.* London: Croom Helm, 1988.

O'Brian, Mary. *The Politics of Reproduction.* Boston: Routledge and Kegan Paul, 1981.

O'Brien, Joan. "Nammu, Nami, Eve and Pandora: 'What's In a Name?'" *The Classical Journal* 79 (1983): 35–45.

Ochs, Carol. *Behind the Sex of God.* Boston: Beacon Press, 1977.

O'Faolain, Julia, and Lauro Martines. *Not in God's Image: Women in History from the Greeks to the Victorians.* New York: Harper and Row, 1973.

Okin, Susan Moller. *Justice, Gender and the Family.* New York: Basic Books, 1989.

————. "Philosopher Queens and Private Wives: Plato on Women and the Family." *Philosophy and Public Affairs* 6, 4 (1977): 345–69.

————. "Women and the Making of the Sentimental Family." *Philosophy and Public Affairs* 11, 1 (1981): 65–88.

————. *Women in Western Political Thought.* Princeton: Princeton University Press, 1979.

Oost, Stewart Irvin. "Xenophon's Attitude Toward Women." *The Classical World* 74 (1978).

Oppenheim, A. Leo. *Ancient Mesopotamia: Portrait of a Dead Civilization.* Chicago: University of Chicago Press, 1977.

Origen. *Homilies on Genesis and Exodus.* Trans. Ronald Heine. Washington, D.C.: Catholic University of America Press, 1981.

Orpheus. *Hymns of Orpheus.* Trans. Thomas Taylor. Los Angeles: Philosophical Research Society, 1981.

Osborn, Henry. *Cope: Master Naturalist—Life and Letters.* Princeton: Princeton University Press, 1931.

Osborne, Martha Lee. "Plato's Unchanging View of Women: A Denial that Anatomy Spells Destiny." *Philosophical Forum* 6, 2-3 (1974): 447–52.

Ovid. *Metamorphoses*. Trans. Rolfe Humphries. Bloomington: Indiana University Press, 1955.

The Oxford Annotated Bible with the Apocrypha, Revised Standard Version. Ed. Herbert G. May and Bruce M. Metzger. New York: Oxford University Press, 1965.

Padel, Ruth. "Women: Models for Possession by Greek Daemons." In *Images of Women in Antiquity*. Eds. Averil Cameron and Amelie Kuhrt. Detroit: Wayne State University Press, 1983.

Pagel, Walter. *New Light on William Harvey: William Harvey's Biological Ideas*. Basel: S. Karger, 1976.

———. *Paracelsus: An Introduction to Philosophical Medicine in the Era of the Renaissance*. Basel: S. Karger, 1982.

———. "Paracelsus and the Neoplatonic and Gnostic Tradition." *Ambix* 8 (1960): 125–66.

———. "The Prime Matter of Paracelsus." *Ambix* 9 (1961): 117–35.

———. "The Reaction to Aristotle in Seventeenth Century Biological Thought." In *Science, Medicine, and History*. Ed. E. Ashworth Underwood. London: Oxford University Press, 1953.

———. *The Smiling Spleen: Paracelsianism in Storm and Stress*. Basel: S. Karger, 1984.

Pagel, Walter, and Maryanne Winder. "The Eightness of Adam and Related Gnostic Ideas in the Paracelsian Corpus." *Ambix* 16 (1969): 119–39.

———. "The Higher Elements and Prime Matter in Renaissance Naturalism and in Paracelsus." *Ambix* 21 (1974): 93–127.

Pagels, Elaine. *The Gnostic Gospels*. New York: Random House.

Pallen, M. A. "Some Suggestions with Regard to the Insanities of Females." *American Journal of Obstetrics and Disorders of Women and Children* 10 (1877): 206–217.

Palmer, Paul. *Mary in the Documents of the Church*. Westminister, London: Newman, 1952.

Panofsky, Dora, and Erwin Panofsky. *Pandora's Box: The Changing Aspects of a Mythical Symbol*. New York: Pantheon, 1962.

Paracelsus. *Diseases that Deprive Man of His Reason*. Trans. Henry Sigerist. In *Four Treatises of Paracelsus*. Baltimore: Johns Hopkins University Press, 1941.

———. *Four Treatises of Paracelsus*. Trans. Henry Sigerist. Baltimore: Johns Hopkins University Press, 1941.

———. *The Hermetic and Alchemical Writings of Aureolus Philippus Theophrastus Bombast of Hohenheim, called Paracelsus*. Trans. A. E. Waite. London: James Elliott, 1894.

———. *The Prophecies of Paracelsus: Occult Symbols, and Magic Figures with Esoteric Explanations*. Blauvet: Rudolf Steiner, 1973.

Paré, Ambroise. *The Collected Works of Ambroise Paré*. Trans. Thomas Johnson. New York: Milford House, 1968.

Patai, Raphael. *The Hebrew Goddess*. KTAV Publishing House, 1967.

Pateman, Carole. " 'The Disorder of Women': Women, Love, and the Sense of Justice." *Ethics* 91, 1 (1980): 20–34.

———. *The Problem of Political Obligation: A Critical Analysis of Liberal Theory*. New York: John Wiley and Sons, 1979.

———. *The Sexual Contract*. Stanford: Stanford University Press, 1988.

Pateman, Carole, and Elizabeth Gross, eds. *Feminist Challenges: Social and Political Theory*. Boston: Northeastern University Press, 1987.

Pausanias. *Guide to Greece*. Trans. Peter Levi. Middlesex: Penguin, 1971.

Peacock, Thomas. "Tables of the Weights of the Brain and other Organs of the Human Body." *Monthly Journal of Medical Science* 7 (1847).

Peradotto, John, and J. P. Sullivan, eds. *Women in the Ancient World: The Arethusa Papers*. Albany: State University of New York Press, 1984.

Phillips, John. *Eve: The History of an Idea*. San Francisco: Harper and Row, 1984.

Philo. *Allegorical Interpretation of Genesis.* Trans. F. H. Colson and G. H. Whitaker. London: Loeb Classical Library, 1929.

―――. *On the Account of the World's Creation Given By Moses.* Trans. F. H. Colson and G. H. Whitaker. London: Loeb Classical Library, 1971.

―――. *On the Cherubim, and the Flaming Sword, and Cain the First Man Created Out of Man.* Trans. F. H. Colson and G. H. Whitaker. Cambridge: Harvard University Press, 1968.

―――. *On the Special Laws.* Trans. F. H. Colson. Cambridge: Harvard University Press, 1968.

―――. *On the Virtues.* Trans. F. H. Colson. Cambridge: Harvard University Press, 1939.

―――. *Questions and Answers on Exodus.* Trans. Ralph Marcus. Cambridge: Harvard University Press, 1971.

―――. *Questions and Answers on Genesis.* Trans. Ralph Marcus. Cambridge: Harvard University Press, 1953.

Pierce, Christine. "Equality: Republic IV." *The Monist* 57 (1978): 1–11.

Pindar. *The Odes of Pindar.* Trans. Richard Lattimore. Chicago: University of Chicago Press, 1976.

Pinto, Lucille. "The Folk Practice of Gynaecology and Obstetrics in the Middle Ages." *Bulletin of the History of Medicine* 47 (1973): 513–23.

Plato. *Apology.* Trans. Hugh Tredennick. In *The Collected Dialogues of Plato.* Eds. E. Hamilton and H. Cairns. Princeton: Princeton University Press, 1973.

―――. *Laws.* Trans. A. E. Taylor. In *The Collected Dialogues of Plato.*

―――. *Phaedo.* Trans. Hugh Tredennick. In *The Collected Dialogues of Plato.*

―――. *Republic.* Trans. P. Shorey. In *The Collected Dialogues of Plato.*

―――. *Symposium.* Trans. Michael Joyce. In *The Collected Dialogues of Plato.*

―――. *Timaeus.* Trans. B. Jowett. In *The Collected Dialogues of Plato.*

Pliny. *Selections from the History of the World.* Trans. Paul Turner. Carbondale: Southern Illinois University Press, 1962.

Ploss, Hermann, Max Bartels, and Paul Bartels. *Woman: A Historical Gynaecological and Anthropological Compendium.* London: William Heinemann, 1935.

Pomeroy, Sarah. *Goddesses, Whores, Wives, and Slaves: Women in Classical Antiquity.* New York: Schocken Books, 1975.

―――. *Women in Hellenistic Egypt: From Alexander to Cleopatra.* New York: Schocken Books, 1984.

Pope Pius XII. 1945 Address. In *Woman in the Modern World.* Monks of Solesmes, eds. Boston: Daughters of St. Paul, 1959.

Porter, Roy. "Love, Sex, and Madness in Eighteenth-Century England." *Social Research* 53 (1986): 211–42.

Pouchet, Georges. *The Plurality of the Human Race.* London, 1864.

Preus, Anthony. "Galen's Criticism of Aristotle's Conception Theory." *Journal of the History of Biology* 10 (1977): 65–85.

―――. *Science and Philosophy in Aristotle's Biological Works.* New York: 1975.

―――. "Science and Philosophy in Aristotle's *Generation of Animals.*" *Journal of the History of Biology* 3 (1970): 1–52.

Prichard, James. *Ancient Near Eastern Texts.* Princeton: Princeton University Press, 1950.

―――. *The Ancient Near East: Supplementary Texts and Pictures.* Princeton: Princeton University Press, 1969.

"The Probable Retrogression of Women. *The Saturday Review* July 1, 1871:10–11.

Pucci, Pietro. *Hesiod and the Language of Poetry.* Baltimore: Johns Hopkins University Press, 1977.

Punnett, R. C. "Ovists and Animalculists." *American Naturalist* 62 (1928): 481–507.

Purcell, John. *A Treatise of Vapours, or, Hysterick Fits.* London: Nicholas Cox, 1702.

Pykare, Nina Coombs. "The Sin of Eve and the Christian Conduct Book." *Ohio Journal of Religious Studies* 4 (1976): 34–43.

Radcliff-Umstead, Douglas. *Human Sexuality in the Middle Ages and Renaissance.* Pittsburgh: University of Pittsburgh Publications on the Middle Ages and Renaissance, 1978.

Raming, Ida. *The Exclusion of Women from the Priesthood: Divine Flaw or Sex Discrimination.* Trans. Norman Adams. Metuchen, N.J.: The Scarecrow Press, 1976.

Rappoport, Angelo S. *Myth and Legend of Ancient Israel.* New York: KTAV Publishing House, 1966.

Rashi. *Commentaries on the Pentateuch.* Trans. Chaim Pearl. New York: W. W. Norton and Co., 1970.

Rattansi, P. M. "Paracelsus and the Puritan Revolution." *Ambix* 11 (1963): 24–32.

Ravven, Heidi M. "Has Hegel Anything to Say to Feminists?" *The Owl of Minerva* 19, 2 (1988): 149–68.

Raynalde, Thomas. *The Birth of Mankind: The Woman's Book.* 1565.

Reamy, Thaddeus. "The President's Annual Address." *Transactions of the American Gynecological Society* 11 (1886): 41–59.

Restow, Edward G. "Images and Ideas: Leeuwenhoek's Perception of the Spermatozoa." *Journal of the History of Biology* 16 (1983): 185–224.

Retzius, Anders Adolf. *Cerebra simiarum illustrata. Das Affenhirn in bildlicher Darstellung.* Stockholm, 1906.

Ricci, James. *The Development of Gynaecological Surgery and Instruments.* Philadelphia: Blakiston Co., 1949.

———. *The Genealogy of Gynaecology.* Philadelphia: Blakiston Co., 1950.

Richter, Donald. "The Position of Women in Classical Athens." *The Classical Journal* 67 (1971): 1–8.

Ripley, Sir George. "The Twelve Gates." In *In Pursuit of Gold: Alchemy in Theory and Practice.* London: Neville Spearman, 1976.

Robinson, J. M. *The Nag Hammadi Library in English.* Leiden: E. J. Brill, 1977.

Roe, Shirley. *Matter, Life, and Generation: Eighteenth Century Embryology and the Haller-Wolff Debate.* Cambridge: Cambridge University Press, 1981.

Rogers, Katharine. *The Troublesome Helpmate: A History of Misogyny in Literature.* Seattle: University of Washington Press, 1966.

Rohe, G. H. "The Relation of Pelvic Disease and Psychical Disturbances in Women." *American Journal of Obstetrics and Disorders of Women and Children* 26 (1892): 694–726.

Romanes, George John. *Darwin, After Darwin, and Post-Darwinian Questions.* Chicago: Open Court, 1892.

———. "Mental Differences Between Men and Women." *The Nineteenth Century* 21 (1887): 654–72.

———. *Mental Evolution in Man.* New York: D. Appleton and Co., 1889.

Rordof, W. "Marriage in the New Testament and in the Early Church." *Journal of Ecclesiastical History* 20 (1969): 193–210.

Rose, Hilary. "Beyond Masculinist Realities: A Feminist Epistemology for the Sciences." In *Feminist Approaches to Science.* Ed. Ruth Bleier. New York: Pergamon Press, 1988.

———. "Hand, Brain, and Heart: A Feminist Epistemology for the Social Sciences." *Signs: A Journal of Women in Culture and Society* 9, 1 (1983): 73–90.

Rosenberg, Rosalind. "In Search of Women's Nature." *Feminist Studies* 3 (1975): 141–54.

Rothman, Sheila M. *Woman's Proper Place: A History of Changing Ideals and Practices, 1870 to Present.* New York: Basic Books, 1978.

Rousseau, Jean Jacques. *Discourse on the Origin of Inequality.* In *The Social Contract and Discourses.* G. D. H. Cole. London, 1973.

————. *Discourse on Political Economy.* Trans. Judith R. Masters. In *On the Social Contract and Discourses.* New York: St. Martin's Press, 1978.

————. *Emile, or, On Education.* Trans. Allan Bloom. New York: Basic Books, 1979.

————. *The First and Second Discourses.* Trans. Roger D. Masters and Judith R. Masters. New York: St. Martin's Press, 1964.

————. "Letter to D'Alembert." Trans. Allan Bloom. In *Politics and the Arts.* Ithaca: Cornell University Press, 1960.

————. *On the Social Contract.* Trans. Judith Masters. New York: St. Martin's Press, 1978.

Rowland, Beryl. *Medieval Woman's Guide to Health: The First English Gynecological Handbook.* Kent, Ohio: Kent State University Press, 1981.

Rubin. *Testament of Rubin.* In *Testaments of the Twelve Patriarchs.* Trans. M. DeJonge. In *The Apocryphal Old Testament.* Ed. H. F. D. Sparks. Oxford: Clarendon Press, 1984.

Ruddick, Sara. *Maternal Thinking: Toward a Politics of Peace.* Boston: Beacon Press, 1989.

Ruether, Rosemary. *New Woman, New Earth.* New York: Seabury Press, 1978.

————. *Religion and Sexism: Images of Woman in the Jewish and Christian Literature.* New York: Simon and Schuster, 1974.

————. *Women-Church: The Theology and Practice of Feminist Liturgical Communities.* New York: Harper and Row, 1986.

Ruether, Rosemary, and Eleanor A. McLaughlin, eds. *Women of Spirit: Female Leadership in the Jewish and Christian Traditions.* New York: Simon and Schuster, 1979.

Rumsey, Jean P. "The Development of Character in Kantian Moral Theory." *Journal of the History of Philosophy* XXVII, 2 (1989): 247–65.

Ruse, Michael. *Sociobiology: Sense or Nonsense?* Dordrecht: D. Reidel, 1979.

Russ, Joanna. *The Female Man.* New York: Bantam Books, 1975.

Russell, Hope Robbins. "Medical Manuscripts in Middle English." *Speculum* 45 (1970): 393–415.

Russell, Letty. *Feminist Interpretation of the Bible.* Philadelphia: Westminister Press, 1985.

Russett, Cynthia Eagle. *Sexual Science: The Victorian Construction of Womanhood.* Cambridge: Harvard University Press, 1989.

Ryan, Mary. *Women in Public: From Banners to Ballots, 1825–1880.* Baltimore: Johns Hopkins University Press, 1990.

de Sade, Comte Donatien. *Juliette.* Trans. Austryn Wainhouse. New York: Grove Press, 1968.

Saxonhouse, Arlene. "The Philosopher and the Female in the Political Thought of Plato." *Political Theory* 4, 2 (1976): 195–212.

————. *Women in the History of Political Thought: Ancient Greece to Machiavelli.* Westport, Conn.: Praeger, 1985.

Sayers, Janet. *Biological Politics: Feminist and Anti-Feminist Perspectives.* New York: Tavistock, 1982.

Schaaffhausen, Hermann. "On the Primitive Form of the Human Skull." *Anthropological Review* 6 (1868): 412–31.

Schiebinger, Londa. *The Mind Has No Sex? Women in the Origins of Modern Science.* Cambridge: Harvard University Press, 1989.

Scholem, Gershom. "Lilith." *Encyclopedia Judaica,* vol. 11. New York: Macmillan, 1971.

Schopenhauer, Arthur. "On Women." In *Selected Essays of Schopenhauer.* Ed. Ernest Bax. London: G. Bell and Sons, 1926.

Schott, Robin May. *Cognition and Eros: A Critique of the Kantian Paradigm.* Boston: Beacon Press, 1988.

Schulenberg, J. "Sexism and the Celestial Gynaeceum." *Journal of Medieval History* 4 (1978): 117–33.

Schwartz, Joel. *The Sexual Politics of Jean-Jacques Rousseau.* Chicago: University of Chicago Press, 1984.

Scott, Reginald. *Discoverie of Witchcraft.* Arundel, England: Centaur Press, 1964 (1584).

Scull, Andrew, and Diane Favreau. "The Clitoridectomy Craze." *Social Research* 53 (1986): 243–60.

Scully, Diane, and Pauline Bart. "A Funny Thing Happened on the Way to the Orifice: Women in Gynecological Textbooks." *American Journal of Sociology* 78 (1972): 1045–1050.

Seltman, Charles. *Women in Antiquity.* London: Thames and Hudson, 1956.

Shakespeare, William. *King Lear.* In *Complete Works.* Ed. William Aldis Wright. Garden City: Doubleday and Co., 1936.

Shanley, Mary Lyndon, and Carole Pateman, eds. *Feminist Interpretations and Political Theory.* University Park: Pennsylvania State University Press, 1991.

Shaw, James R. "Scientific Empiricism in the Middle Ages: Albertus Magnus on Sexual Anatomy and Physiology." *Clio Medica* 10 (1975): 53–64.

Shklar, Judith N. *Freedom and Independence: A Study of the Political Ideas of Hegel's Phenomenology of Mind.* Cambridge: Cambridge University Press, 1976.

Short, R. V. "Sex Determination and Differentiation." In *Embryonic and Fetal Development.* Eds. C. R. Austin and R. V. Short. London: Cambridge University Press, 1972.

Shorter, Edward. *A History of Women's Bodies.* New York: Basic Books, 1982.

_____. "Paralysis and Hysteria." *Journal of Social History* 19 (1986): 549–82.

Showalter, Elaine. *The Female Malady: Women, Madness and English Culture, 1830–1980.* New York: Pantheon, 1985.

_____. "Victorian Women and Insanity." *Victorian Studies* 23 (1980): 157–81.

Siebert, Rudolf J. *Hegel's Concept of Marriage and Family: The Origin of Subjective Freedom.* Washington, D.C.: University Press of America, 1979.

Simon, B. *Mind and Madness in Ancient Greece: The Classical Roots of Modern Psychiatry.* Ithaca: Cornell University Press, 1978.

Sims, J. Marion. "Remarks on Battey's Operation." *British Medical Journal* 2 (1877): 793–94, 840–42, 881–82, 916–18.

Singer, Charles. *The Evolution of Anatomy.* London: Kegan Paul, 1925.

Slater, Philip. *The Glory of Hera: Greek Mythology and the Greek Family.* Boston: Beacon Press, 1968.

Sleeth Mosedale, Susan. "Science Corrupted: Victorian Biologists Consider the Women Question." *Journal of the History of Biology* 11 (1977): 1–55.

Smith, A. Lapthorn. "What Civilization is Doing for the Human Female." *Transactions of the Southern Surgical and Gynecological Association* 2 (1890).

Smith, Hilda. "Gynecology and Ideology in Seventeenth-Century England." In *Liberating Women's History: Theoretical and Critical Essays.* Ed. Berenice Carroll. Urbana: University of Illinois Press, 1976.

Smith, Janet Farrell. "Plato, Irony, and Equality." *Women's Studies International Forum* 6, 6 (1983): 597–607.

Smith, Nicholas. "Aristotle's Theory of Natural Slavery." *Phoenix* 37 (1983): 109–122.

Smith-Rosenberg, Carroll. *Disorderly Conduct: Visions of Gender in Victorian America.* New York: Alfred A. Knopf, 1985.

_____. "The Hysterical Woman: Sex Roles and Role Conflict in Nineteenth Century America." *Social Research* 39 (1972): 652–78.

_____. "Puberty to Menopause: The Cycle of Femininity in Nineteenth Century America." *Feminist Studies* 1 (1973): 58–72.

Smith-Rosenberg, Carroll, and Charles Rosenberg. "The Female Animal: Medical and Biological Views of Women and her Role in Nineteenth Century America." *Journal of American History* 60 (1973): 332–56.

Soranus of Ephesus. *Gynecology.* Trans. O. Temkin. Baltimore: Johns Hopkins University Press, 1956.

Sparshott, F. "Aristotle on Women." *Philosophical Inquiry* VII, 3–4 (1985): 177–200.

Spatz, L. *Aristophanes.* Boston: Twayne Publications, 1978.

Speert, Harold. *Iconographia Gyniatrica: A Pictorial History of Gynecology and Obstetrics.* Philadelphia: F. A. Davis, 1973.

Spelman, Elizabeth. "Aristotle and the Politicization of the Soul." In *Discovering Reality.* Eds. Sandra Harding and Merrill Hintikka. Dordrecht: D. Reidel, 1983.

———. *Inessential Woman: Problems of Exclusion in Feminist Thought.* Boston: Beacon Press, 1988.

———. "Woman as Body: Ancient and Contemporary Views." *Feminist Studies* 8 (1982): 109–31.

Spencer, Herbert. *Education: Intellectual, Moral, and Physical.* Akron: Werner Co., 1860.

———. *Principles of Biology.* New York: D. Appleton, 1897.

———. *The Principles of Ethics.* New York: D. Appleton and Co., 1897.

———. *Principles of Sociology.* New York: D. Appleton and Co., 1904.

———. "Psychology of the Sexes." *Popular Science Monthly* 4 (1873): 30–38.

———. *The Study of Sociology.* New York: D. Appleton and Co., 1884.

Spitzka, E. A. "A Study of the Brain of the Late Major J. W. Powell." *American Anthropologist* 5 (1903): 585–643.

Sprenger, Jacob, and Heinrich Kramer. *Malleus Maleficarum.* Trans. Rev. Montague Summers. New York: Benjamin Blom, 1970.

Squadrito, Kathy. "Locke on the Equality of the Sexes." *Journal of Social Philosophy* 10 (1979): 6–11.

Stahl, Georg Ernst. *Theoria Medica Vera, Physiologiam et Pathologiam.* Halle, 1708.

Stanton, William. *The Leopard's Spots: Scientific Attitudes Toward Race in America, 1815–1857.* Chicago: University of Chicago Press, 1960.

Stead, G. C. "The Valentian Myth of Sophia." *Journal of Theological Studies* 20 (1969): 75–104.

Stepan, Nancy. *The Idea of Race in Science: Great Britain, 1800–1960.* Hamden, Conn.: Archon Books, 1982.

Stern, Karl. *The Flight from Women.* New York: Paragon House, 1985.

Stocking, George. *Race, Culture and Evolution: Essays in the History of Anthropology.* New York: Free Press, 1968.

Stoltzius, Daniel. *Pleasure Garden of Chemistry.* Chicago: Aries Press, 1937.

Stone, Merlin. *When God Was a Woman.* New York: Harcourt, Brace, Jovanovich, 1976.

Storer, Horatio Robinson. *The Causation, Course, and Treatment of Reflex Insanity in Women.* 1871. Reprint, New York: Arno Press, 1972.

———. *Criminal Abortion.* Boston, 1868.

Suleiman, Susan Rubin, ed. *The Female Body in Western Culture.* Cambridge: Harvard University Press, 1986.

Sutherland, Alexander. "Woman's Brain." *Nineteenth Century* 47 (1900): 802–810.

Swammerdam, J. *Miraculum Naturae.* 1672.

Swidler, Leonard. *Women in Judaism: The Status of Women in Formative Judaism.* Metuchen, N.J.: The Scarecrow Press, 1976.

Sydenham, Thomas. *The Compleat Method of Curing Almost All Diseases.* In *The Whole Works.* Trans. John Pechey. London: Richard Wellington, 1697.

Talbot, Charles. *Medicine in Medieval England.* London: Oldbourne, 1967.

Tate, George. *Treatise on Hysteria.* Philadelphia: E. L. Carey and A. Hart, 1831.

Taylor, J. Lionel. *The Nature of Woman.* A. C. Fifield, 1912.

Temkin, Oswei. "The Elusiveness of Paracelsus." *Bulletin of the History of Medicine* 26 (1952): 201–217.

———. *Soranus' Gynecology.* Baltimore: Johns Hopkins University Press, 1956.

Tertullian. *Adversus Marcionem.* Trans. Ernest Evans. Oxford: Oxford University Press, 1972.

———. *Apology.* Trans T. R. Glover. Cambridge: Harvard University Press, 1953.

———. *The Treatise Against Hermogenes.* Trans. J. H. Waszink. Westminister, M.D.: Newman Press, 1956.

———. *Treatises on Marriage and Remarriage.* Trans. W. P. Le Saint. *The Ante Nicene Fathers.* Westminster, MD: Newman Press, 1951.

Thompson, Janna. "Women and the High Priests of Reason." *Radical Philosophy* 34 (1983): 10–14.

Thorndike, Lynn. "Further Consideration of the *Experimenta, Speculum astronomiae,* and *De secretis mulierum* Ascribed to Albertus Magnus." *Speculum* 30 (1955): 413–43.

"Thoughts and Facts Contributing to the History of Man." *Anthropological Review* 2, 4 (1864): 173–90.

Tiedemann, Friedrich. *A Systematic Treatise of Comparative Physiology.* London, 1834.

Tobach, E., and B. Rosoff, eds. *Genes and Gender I.* New York: Gordian, 1978.

Tosefta. Trans. Jacob Neusner. New York: Ktav Publishing House, 1979.

Trible, Phyllis. "Depatriarchalizing in Biblical Interpretation." *Journal of the American Academy of Religion* 41 (1973): 30-48.

———. *Texts of Terror.* Philadelphia: Fortress Press, 1984.

Trismosin, Solomon. *Splendor Solis.* 1582. Reprint, London: Kegan Paul, 1920.

Trotula of Salerno. *Diseases of Women.* Trans. Elizabeth Mason-Hohl. 1087. Reprint, Ward Ritchie Press, 1940.

Tuana, Nancy. "Aristotle and the Politics of Reproduction." In *Critical Feminist Essays on the History of Western Philosophy.* Ed. Bat-Ami Bar On. Albany: State University of New York Press, 1993.

———, ed. *Feminism and Science.* Bloomington: Indiana University Press, 1989.

———. *Woman and the History of Philosophy.* New York: Paragon House, 1992.

Tuana, Nancy, and William Cowling. "Plato and Feminism." *American Philosophical Association Newsletter on Feminism and Philosophy* 90, 1 (1990): 110–115.

Tyndale, William. *The New Testament,* 1526. Reprint, London: D. Paradine Developments, 1976.

Tyrone, Curtis. "Certain Aspects of Gynecologic Practice in the Late Nineteenth Century." *American Journal of Surgery* 84 (1952): 95–106.

Van Dyke, F. W. "High Education a Cause of Physical Decay in Women." *Medical Record* 67 (1905): 296–98.

Van Herik, Judith. *Freud on Femininity and Faith.* Berkeley: University of California Press, 1982.

Vaughan, Thomas. *The Works of Thomas Vaughan, Mystic and Alchemist.* Ed. Arthur Waite. New Hyde Park, N.Y.: University Books, 1968.

Vawter, Bruce. *On Genesis.* New York: Doubleday, 1977.

Veith, Ilza. *Hysteria: The History of a Disease.* Chicago: University of Chicago Press, 1965.

Vesalius, Andreas. *The Epitome of Andreas Vesalius.* Trans. L. R. Lind. Cambridge: Massachusetts Institute of Technology Press, 1949.

———. *Illustrations from the Works of Andreas Vesalius of Brussels.* Trans. J. B. Saunders and C. O'Malley. Cleveland: World Publishing Co., 1950.

Vicinus, Martha. *Independent Women: Work and Community for Single Women, 1850–1920.* Chicago: University of Chicago Press, 1985.

———. *Suffer and Be Still: Women in the Victorian Age.* Bloomington: Indiana University Press, 1972.

———. *A Widening Sphere: Changing Roles of Victorian Women.* Bloomington: Indiana University Press, 1977.

Vierordt, Hermann. *Anatomische, physiologische und physikalische: Daten and Tabellen.* Jena, 1906.

Vlastos, Gregory. "Was Plato a Feminist?" *Times Literary Supplement* 7 (1989): 725–31.

Waite, Arthur Edward. *The Hermetic Museum Restored and Enlarged.* London: James El-
    liott and Co., 1893.
———. *The Secret Tradition in Alchemy: Its Development and Records.* 1926. Reprint,
    New York: Samuel Weiser, 1969.
Walcott, Peter. "Herodotus on Rape." *Aresthusa* 11 (1978): 137–47.
Walker, Alexander. *Women Physiologically Considered as to Mind, Morals, Marriage, Mat-
    rimonial Slavery, Infidelity and Divorce.* Birmingham: Edward Baker, 1898.
Walker, Sayer. *Observations on the Constitution of Women.* London: W. Phillips, 1803.
van de Warker, E. "The Fetish of the Ovary." *American Journal of Obstetric Disorders of
    Women and Children* 54 (1906): 366–73.
Warner, Lucien. *A Popular Treatise on the Functions and Diseases of Woman.* Courtland,
    N.Y.: Lucien Warner, 1873.
Webster, Charles. *Biology, Medicine, and Society, 1840–1940.* Cambridge: Cambridge Uni-
    versity Press, 1981.
Weininger, Otto. *Sex and Character.* 1906. Reprint, New York: G. P. Putnam's Sons, 1975.
Weisheipl, James. *Albertus Magnus and the Sciences.* Toronto: Pontificial Institute for Me-
    diaeval Studies, 1980.
Weismann, August. *Die Bedeutung der sexuellen Fortpflanzung fur die Selektions-theorie.*
    1886.
———. *Essays Upon Heredity.* 1889.
———. *The Evolution Theory.* Trans. J. Arthur Thomson and Margaret R. Thomson.
    London: Edward Arnold, 1904.
———. *Continuity of the Germ-Plasm.* London, 1893.
———. *Studies in the Theory of Descent.* Trans. Meldola. London, 1880–1882.
Weiss, Penny A. "Rousseau, Antifeminism, and Woman's Nature." *Political Theory* 15, 1
    (1987): 81–98.
Weiss, Penny, and Anne Harper. "Rousseau's Political Defense of the Sex-Roled Family."
    Hypatia: A Journal of Feminist Philosophy 5, 3 (1990): 90–109.
Wells, T. S. "Castration in Mental and Nervous Diseases." *American Journal of the Med-
    ical Sciences* 184 (1886): 455–71.
Wender, Dorothea. "Plato: Misogynist, Paedophile, and Feminist." *Aresthusa* 6 (1973):
    75–90.
Wesler, V. G. "Made for Man's Delight: Rousseau as Anti-feminist." *American Historical
    Review* 81 (1976): 266–91.
West, Robert. *Reginald Scot and Renaissance Writings on Witchcraft.* Boston: Twayne
    Publishers, 1984.
Whytt, Robert. *Observations on the Nature, Causes and Cure of those Disorders which have
    been Commonly Called Nervous, Hypochondriac or Hysteric.* Edinburgh: T. Beckel,
    1767.
Wilkie, J. S. "Preformation and Epigenesis: A New Historical Treatment." *History of Sci-
    ence* 6 (1967): 138–50.
Williams, George Huntston. "Religious Residues and Presuppositions in the American
    Debate on Abortion." *Theological Studies* 31, 10 (1970): 10–75.
Wilson, Andrew. *Medical Researches.* London: S. Hooper, 1776.
Wilson, Edward Osborne. *Sociobiology: The New Synthesis.* Cambridge: Belknap Press,
    1975.
Wiltbank, John. *Introductory Lecture To the Course of Midwifery.* Philadelphia: Edward
    Grattan, 1854.
Wood, Charles. "The Doctor's Dilemma: Sin, Salvation, and the Menstrual Cycle in Me-
    dieval Thought." *Speculum* 56 (1981): 710–27.
Wright, Sir Almroth E. *The Unexpurgated Case Against Woman Suffrage.* London: Con-
    stable, 1913.
Wright, F. A. *Feminism in Greek Literature from Homer to Aristotle.* 1923. Reprint, Port
    Washington: Kennikat Press, 1969.

Xenophon. *Oeconomicus.* Trans. C. Lord. Ithaca: Cornell University Press, 1970.

Yates, Francis. *Giordano Bruno and the Hermetic Tradition.* Chicago: University of Chicago Press, 1979.

Zeitlin, Froma. "Cultic Models of the Female Rites of Dionysus and Demeter." *Aresthusa* 15 (1982): 129–58.

———. "The Dynamics of Misogyny: Myth and Mythmaking in the Oresteia." *Aresthusa* 11 (1978): 149–84.

Zohar, The Book of Splendor: Basic Readings from the Kabbalah. Trans. Gershom Scholem. New York: Schocken, 1966.

Zola, Émile. *Nana.* London: Penguin, 1972.

Index

Abortion, 24–25
Achillini, Alessandro, 138
Aeschylus, 122
Albertus Magnus, 137
Alchemy: Genesis creation myth and, 14–15, 17; metaphysics and view of woman as inferior, 25–28, 31, 34; embryology and primacy of male generative powers, 141–48; women as alchemists, 175n.48, 176–77n.40; image of creation compared to *Enuma Elis*, 185n.24
Allan, James McGrigor, 39–40, 74, 164
Allen, Christine, 174n.14
Ames, Azel, 164
Anglici, Ricardi, 136–37
Apocryphon of John, 127–28, 187–88n.82
Aquinas, Thomas: association of woman with sensation and passions, 11–12; man as microcosm of universe, 15; reconciliation of Aristotelian biology with Christian theology, 22, 24, 25; primacy of male generative powers, 136; on conjugal authority, 159
Aretaeus, 94–95
Aristotle: theme of woman as misbegotten man in Western intellectual tradition, ix; systematic scientific explanation of woman's imperfection, 18–21; influence on science from Galen to Paré, 21–22, 24–25; influence on alchemy, 25, 27, 34; compared to Spencer on reproduction and energy, 47; theoretical biases and empirical proofs, 48, 50; Geddes's theory compared to, 49; biology and woman's soul, 55–56; brain size and intellectual capacity, 68, 186n.44; human nature and moral character of women, 80; classical medical theory and sexual intercourse, 94; primacy of male generative powers, 130–33; influence on embryology, 152, 191n.3; conjugal authority as theme of, 155–56; women as threat to social order, 166; on humanity of slaves, 176n.8; female infanticide and, 176n.10
Aristotle's Masterpiece, 138
Arnold, Thomas, 97
Astruc, Jean, 152
Augustine, 11–12, 58–59, 158–59
Aulus Cornelius Celsus, 95
Avicenna, 139

Bacon, Francis, 64
Bal, Mieke, 9, 10, 185n.3
Bassuk, Ellen, 184n.50
Battey, Robert, 105
Bell, William Blair, 106
Benedetti, Alessandro, 138

Bible: birth reversals and Christian tradition, 125–26; women and system of ritual purity, 186n.26. *See also* Genesis; Romans
Birth reversals: in classical mythology, 121–22; in Christian tradition, 125–29
Blakeman, J., 73
Blandford, G. Fielding, 101
Bliss, W. W., 105
Body: Descartes's conception of rationality and, 61–62
Boerhaave, Herman, 140–41, 151
Boyd, Robert, 70
Boylan, Michael, 20, 170–71
Broca, Paul, 69–70, 71, 72–73
Brown, Isaac Baker, 104–105
Brunner, Emil, 171
Buchner, Ludwig, 73
Buckley, Jorunn Jacobsen, 187n.80
Burrows, George Man, 101

Calvin, John, 14, 175n.41
Campbell, Harry, 177n.74
Canon law, 56
Carlson, Bruce, 170
Carter, Robert Brudenell, 103
Cato, 157
Children: paternity and political theory, 162–63; scientists and philosophers on role of women, 165
Christianity: Genesis creation myth and, 10–12; images of the soul, 56–60; birth reversals and, 125–29; embryology and, 136; conjugal authority and, 157–59
Civilization: sex role differentiation and, 39–41
Clark, Lorenne M. G., 190n.37
Clarke, Edward, 76–78
Class: Plato's philosophy of natural differences, 54–55; Descartes's rational man and, 64; consideration of women as group, 173n.11; nonsexist model of rationality and, 180n.58
Cleland, John, 44, 46
Clitoridectomy, 104–105, 184n.61
Conjugal authority: as central theme of classical philosophy and biology, 155–57; early Christian tradition and, 157–59; impact of Genesis creation myth on Western philosophy, 160–63
Conway, Jill, 178n.88
Cooke, John, 151
Cope, Edward Drinker, 42–44, 67
Craniology: sex role differentiation and brain size of women, 39–40, 68–74; problem of evidence, 44, 46; racial prejudices and, 180–81n.87

Creation myths: place of humans in hierarchy as focus of Western, 3; Plato's *Timaeus* as, 6–7; images of women compared to nineteenth-century evolutionary theory, 50; creativity and gender, 111–18, 121–22; birth reversals in Christian tradition, 125–29. *See also Enuma Elis;* Genesis; *Theogony*

Creativity: and gender in creation myths, 111–18, 121–22; relationship of generative powers to artistic, literary, or scientific, 185n.2

Critical empiricism, 20

Curtis, E., 104

Darwin, Charles, 34, 36–39, 66–67

Darwin, Erasmus, 151

Davis, Joseph Barnard, 70, 71

Decretum (Gratian), 56

Delauney, Gaetan, 40

Descartes, René, 60–64, 179–80n.54, 180n.58

The Descent of Man (Darwin), 38–39

Developmental arrest, woman's, 43, 67

Difference. *See* Gender differences; Sex differences

Doell, Ruth, ix

Domesticity, 164

Dunn, Robert, 73

Ecker, Alexander, 44, 46

Education, women's: scientific views of sex differences and, 74–78

Ego: women and development of, 88–92

Elizabeth of Bohemia, Princess, 63

Elshtain, Jean Bethke, 175n.39

Embryology: classical views on primacy of male generative powers, 130–34; early medical science and male generative primacy, 135–41; alchemy and male generative primacy, 141–48; preformation doctrine and, 148–52; persistence of belief in passivity of female role, 169–71, 191n.6. *See also* Reproduction

Emotion: Plato's *Timaeus* as creation myth, 6–7; Descartes's conception of rationality, 61–62. *See also* Passions

Energy: woman and reproduction, 46–50, 75

Enuma Elis, 113, 115–18, 185n.24. *See also* Creation myths

Ephrem, Saint, 126

Euripedes, 155

Eve: compared to Pandora, 12; women and morality, 79; myth of as justification of conjugal authority, 157–59. *See also* Genesis

Evolutionary theory: sexual differentiation and, 34, 36–39; recapitulation theory, 41–44, 46; reproduction and energy, 46–50; scientific images of woman's morality, 86–87

Family: relegation of women to private realm of, 166–67. *See also* Children; Conjugal authority

Fear of woman, 65–66, 155

Femininity: Freud on woman's moral development and, 92; nonsexist model of rationality and, 180n.58

Feminism: absence metaphor and Levin's attack on, 170; concepts of difference and, 172, 191n.11. *See also* Women's rights movement

Filmer, Robert, 160, 190n.29

Freud, Sigmund: influence of Galen's anatomy on, 25; on inferiority of woman's moral development, 88–92; on exclusion of women from public realm, 166–67

Galen: influence of Aristotelian tradition on, 21–22, 25; hysteria and female sexual organs, 95; on primacy of male generative powers, 133–34; anatomy of female reproductive system, 138; influence on Western views of human generation, 152, 191n.3

Garden, George, 151

Gardner, Augustus, 103–104

Geddes, Patrick: Aristotelian biology and heat, 24; germ-plasm theory and, 47, 48–49, 67–68

Gender: and creativity in creation myths, 111–18; models of rationality and, 180n.58

Gender differences: Plato's philosophy concerning nature of the soul, 53–55; development of new concept of, 191n.11. *See also* Sex differences

Genesis: accounts of creation of humankind, 7–17; creativity and gender in, 111–13, 117–18, 125–26, 185n.3, 185n.7, 185n.25; compared to *Enuma Elis,* 116; justification for sexual division of labor, 158. *See also* Creation myths

Germ-plasm theory, 47–49, 67–68

Giles of Rome, 137

Gnosticism, 126–29

Good, J. M., 151–52

Goodell, William, 106

The Gospel of Thomas, 57

Gottwald, Norman, 185n.7

Gould, Stephen Jay, 180–81n.87

Government: Christian tradition on conjugal authority, 158; opposition of nineteenth-century scientists to women's rights, 165; view of women as threat to society, 166–67. *See also* Politics

Gratian: Aristotelian worldview and abortion in canonical law, 24; Christian images of woman's soul, 56–57, 65; justification of conjugal authority, 159

Gratiolet, Louis Pierre, 72, 73

Greek mythology. *See* Creation myths; *Theogony*

Gregory of Nyssa, Saint, 136

Guainerius, Anthonius, 96

Haeckel, Ernst, 41

Hall, G. Stanley, 41

Hamm, Louis Dominicus, 149

Nancy Tuana is Professor of the History of Ideas at the University of Texas at Dallas. She has published in the area of feminist philosophy of science and on the subject of woman in philosophy. Her publications include *Woman and the History of Philosophy, Feminism and Science,* and *Re-Reading the Canon: Feminist Interpretations of Plato.* She is the founding editor of the *APA Newsletter on Feminism and Philosophy.*